MW00958456

BABY IN A BOX

By LeRoy and Jane Ramsey

With donut joy,
LeRoy & Jane

John 14:18

PRESS

The story is true; however some of the names and locations mentioned in this book have been changed for security reasons.

This is the story of Mei Mei, [Kali Jane Bonife]. It was written through the viewpoint of Jane Ramsey, with LeRoy Ramsey doing most of the writing.

This Book is dedicated to

Kali Jane Bonife

(One Chosen by God)

Contents

Acknowledgements

Kali Jane Bonife –

>Child of our Heart. There is no story without her. Her story continues. She is a blessing to many people.

John and Lynn Bonife –

>Thanks for letting us continue to be a part of Kali's life.

Wanda Miller -

>Labor of Love. She worked so hard in editing this book to bring it up to proper standards.

Dr. Mel Miller -

>Thanks for letting us borrow Wanda for awhile.

David and Marianne –

>For living this story with us.

Shelly Schaller –

> Voted teammate of the century by all of our family.

Chinese Friends –

> We never stood alone as so many of our Chinese brothers and sisters in the Lord stood with us.

Foreign Friends –

> Thanks to those across the ocean who held the ropes for us and those in Nanchang who were our hands and feet.

Now we have come to the last year of our second decade in China. It seems like it was just a short time ago that we stood on the Great Wall for the first time and marveled at this ancient land. There are so many stories to tell but this one is the one everyone kept telling us to write a book about. So here's the story that needed to be told.

2004

Prelude

It is still dark as she slips quietly from the bed. Her husband remains motionless. The dawn is coming within a few hours, and she has only the time before daylight to accomplish her task. It has been a very quiet night, but there have been only a few moments of sleep. She was tired enough to sleep, for she had not slept well the night before. However, her mind – her thoughts, her conscience, the knowledge of the deed to be done this day – would not allow her more than an hour or two at the most.

She rises silently, looking at her husband – knowing from his breathing that he is not asleep. Yet, he does not stir; he is just there, saying nothing, indicating nothing, as his back remains toward her. He has lain in that position throughout the night as she tossed and turned.

She does not spend much time looking at her husband's back, because when she looks at him, she can only despise him. He could have stopped all this; he could have said "no," but he was unwilling to do so. He allows her to do this thing, to let her bear the brunt of the shame of it all – possibly to have her caught and imprisoned.

And there, sleeping soundly, between her husband and the covers from which she has just risen, is their baby, a child that brought joy to the whole family when she first announced that a baby was within her. Even now, she can remember how her husband smiled when she told him that he would soon be a father. His parents seemed to almost sigh with relief when they learned of the impending birth of their grandchild. As the birth approached, she tried to ignore the discomfort that comes with being so pregnant that there is no chair comfortable enough, no bathroom close enough, no clothes that fit properly; instead, she bore it all as a good wife and mother-to-be should. As her belly rounded, the more her husband smiled, and the more his parents planned for the upcoming event.

And then, when she refocused after the shearing pain of childbirth, she saw that the smiles were not so wide on her husband's face; and the grandparents did not seem to be smiling at all. Gradually, over the weeks and months, the nonsmiles soon turned to scowls, and those scowls led to this moment on this day – even before the dawning of this day. Xiao Shu is now forced into taking steps that she abhors, detests – that make her flesh crawl with the thought of it all.

All this is coursing through her brain, as it has been for weeks now, while she dresses against the coolness of the autumn day. Her baby makes some of those restless baby sounds. Xiao Shu scoops her into her arms, holds her only child close, kisses her, and smells the sweetness of a 6-month-old child of innocence. She whispers pet names that only she uses when it is just she and her baby alone; Ying Ying cuddles into the softness of her mother's cotton coat, feeling safe, knowing the security of her mother's heartbeat, totally unaware of the abrupt change that is about to occur in her very young life.

She hurriedly dresses Ying Ying against the brisk fall morning, covering her in two layers before putting on her padded cotton coat. Xiao Shu then prepares another bottle of milk to be given to Ying Ying later. She does this all quickly, keeping thoughts from her mind as much as she can, going through the motions, but checking to make sure she does everything that has to be done, at the same time working quietly and only by the light of a candle.

Several times she passes by the curtain that partitions her husband's parents' room from the rest of the house. She never once glances that direction – she wills herself not to think about them. In the past few months they have rapidly become nonpersons to her. If she has to think of them as people, she will plot to harm them. If they do not exist in her mind, then she does not have to be concerned with nonentities.

Ying Ying waits patiently after she is dressed, only partially awake as she nurses on a half-empty bottle.

After finishing the preparations, Xiao Shu puts Ying Ying in a small box with some straw scattered in the bottom. Ying Ying thinks it is all a game and is content with her bottle and the comfort of being near her mother, even though she is being carried in a box. Xiao Shu walks out of the front door without looking back, without thinking of her husband, with a mind closed off from everything that is taking place.

She quickly, stealthily descends the five flights of stairs from their apartment to the ground floor and slips into the early morning air. It is still dark, but just above the apartment buildings that surround the work unit where they live, she can see a slight dimming of the stars as a paleness begins to spread around the sky. She hurries, since she knows she must in order to keep her appointment.

Carrying Ying Ying in the box makes the journey more difficult, and she is going more slowly than anticipated. But Ying Ying remains passive, so she manages to slip quietly through the streets on her way toward the large square downtown. She hopes that Ying Ying will go back into a deep sleep so that everything can be done without disturbance. Of course, there are almost no policemen around at such an hour, but an unhealthy amount of noise might bring one quickly enough – too quickly.

As Xiao Shu hurries along, she begins to doubt that she can make the square before dawn. If she is unable to reach the square in time, what can she do? Already some of the morning people are beginning to enter the streets – to be the first to their morning exercise sessions.

Ying Ying is at peace – she is warm, she has her bottle, and her mother is nearby – thus she has ultimate security.

Xiao Shu quickens her pace, but the outlines of the trees on the street are easily distinguishable now; the street lights are fading, and more people are entering the street. She realizes she has miscalculated the time needed to walk from their apartment to the square; she will never make her goal now.

Can she return home without accomplishing the task? No, it will not be allowed. She is already on the verge of being an outcast; failing in this task will assure her of being shunned by all.

Her eyes dart from the sky, to the street lights, to the people (growing more numerous by the minute), to the area where she is walking. For a few minutes she is alone. She stops, sets the cardboard box against the wall, looks once more at her only child, who has been lulled back to sleep, turns and walks away.

Xiao shu has just thrown away her baby.

Chapter I

Return to the "Motherland"

Our fifth year in China.

Another year – another Chinese apartment – more dealings with officials at our school who sometimes liked us and sometimes detested us, just because we were foreigners. One more cheese-less, butter-less, car-less, many-other-comforts-less year in the People's Republic of China.

As we entered China in August 1991, Communism was dying a quick death in the USSR and all points west, with the exception of Cuba. Cuba and China – the Big C's in Communism – were hanging tough in a changing world, with the Chinese leaders proclaiming, "We will succeed with China's brand of socialism; we know how to do it right."

The Chinese people had fought their battle – Tiananmen Square in downtown Beijing in the spring of 1989 – and died in the streets. Now, they watched in disbelief with freedom pangs dying in their hearts as the Russian people said "no more Communism" and stood the test.

In 1991 the eyes of the world were on Eastern Europe and the Soviet Union. Great and wonderful events were happening there. So much freedom, so fast, that many people were unable to digest it and threw it back at their new leaders later on. But what of China?

In 1985, when we first entered China, we had seen the

seeds of freedom begin to sprout throughout the land. In 1987-89 we saw the small freedom flowers seemingly about to burst into bloom, until June 4, 1989, when those beginning blossoms were crushed under the tanks of the People's Liberation Army. When we returned in 1990, we saw the repressive regime of the Communist Party in full control again, and we felt them squeezing the very life out of the few seeds of freedom that remained.

As much of the world reveled in freedom [America] or groped for freedom [Russia] or stumbled down a path to democracy [Latin American countries], the Chinese remembered June 1989 and wondered 'Why?'

Because that "Why?" remained unanswered, the Chinese people heaved a collective, wistful sigh and moved back into the shadows. Many proclaimed themselves "a people with no hope."

Jesus said: I AM the resurrection and the life.
> He who believes in Me,
> though he may die,
> he shall live. {John 11:25}

We personally knew the blessed hope of Jesus Christ. We carried that hope with us each time we went to China.

That hope took on a whole new dimension in our lives in Nanchang, Jiangxi Province, as the morning of October 26, 1991, dawned bright and clear – as Xiao Shu stumbled back into her sixth floor apartment. On the street her baby began to feel uncomfortable as the cold from the concrete sidewalk pierced through the straw in the bottom of the box and crept into her.

It was Saturday.

We were peacefully sleeping, comfortably settled into our new apartment, content with our new medical college students, who, after 7 weeks of instruction, were fairly at ease with their blue-eyed, big-nosed teachers from America.

Our world began turning upside down when the phone rang that morning at 6:30. Our phone does not normally ring at 6:30 in the morning in China or America. Our first thoughts were that it might be someone from America. Friends had never quite calculated the time difference, so they would call us at their convenience— and we were indeed usually home when they called because they would jangle us from a peaceful night's sleep.

In the spring of 1989, when China was all over the West's TV screens, we received a call shortly after midnight. The caller was relaxed in his nice, air-conditioned office in the middle of the afternoon in the middle of America. We were sleeping. His first statement was, "I just wanted to see if you were still alive." We were, but it did get some thoughts started charging around our heads. We knew very little of what was taking place around us, since the Chinese TV stations showed us the latest pig progress reports and thrilled viewers with scenes of the wonderful wheat fields. Farm reports had always been a staple of Chinese telecasts. We were asking ourselves, "Are we supposed to be alive?"

We have had pleasure calls at 2 in the morning, 4 in the morning. We have always appreciated them, but we were never sure what we said after we hung up – and sometimes we asked ourselves, "Now, who was that we just talked to?"

LeRoy answered the call that Saturday morning.

It was from Tom (his English name), a Chinese friend who knew we were interested in helping American friends adopt a baby. He was calling from outside the Friendship Store, China's upscale department store of the time.

"I've found a baby in a box! Do you want to come look at it and see if you want it?"

That was a shocking question at 6:30 in the morning.

We had never done such a thing and had never considered taking a baby off the street. Yet, there was the question thrust upon us, a decision to be made immediately. Did we want to take an abandoned Chinese baby into our home?

He described the location of the baby and said, "Come down here and see what you think. I've told the others to leave her, that a foreigner is coming to look at her."

That made things even worse. Chinese thrilled at anything a foreigner did. They laughed uproariously at our bike wrecks. They snickered at our attempts to speak Chinese, pointed at us as we passed by and laughed for no discernible reason. We would find ourselves checking our clothing to see what we had put on backwards.

By then I was crawling out of bed, wanting to know who was calling so early. LeRoy told him we would come look.

LeRoy and I both knew we had to pray right then, but there was little time to pray, since something could happen to the baby. So, we prayed a simple prayer for God's guidance, then I headed out on my bicycle while LeRoy remained at home to pray more.

But we actually made the decision when I walked out the front door, got on my bicycle, and headed toward the child. What was I going to do once I got there? Inspect it like a chunk of meat? Decide it did not measure up? Put it back down and walk away? I did not think it was possible to do such a thing. We were dealing with a precious creation of the Most High God. He would not reject her, how could we?

LeRoy prayed at home. I prayed and rode, but before I got to the location where Tom said the baby would be found – on the opposite side of the street— I saw a crowd gathered.

It was not unusual to see a crowd gathered on the sidewalks of China. They would gather for anything. Any little diversion was viewed as good entertainment. And there were always people around to watch monkeys doing tricks, fortunetellers, dentists, barbers, and all types of salesmen, or a good fight between any two people— all would bring onlookers. A good yelling, shoving, swinging fight would draw the best crowd of all. However, it was unusual for crowds to gather so early for entertainment on a downtown street.

I felt drawn to that crowd on the opposite side of the wide boulevard from where I was riding, hundreds of yards from where the baby was supposed to be. I crossed the street and peered past the shoulders of the Chinese; there was a baby in a box – crying. An old woman was bent over trying to get the baby to take some of her bottle. She wanted none of it. She just continued to cry and reach out to the old woman, who refused to pick her up. The others, mainly older women returning from *Tai Qi* exercises, just watched. Some had turned away to go home. But they suddenly spotted the foreign woman [me] coming toward the crowd, and they turned back to see what the foreigner would do.

I looked around, but Tom was not in sight. I continued walking my bike toward the crowd, wondering what to do now: "What if this is another baby? What if Tom is waiting at the appointed spot with the baby he found?" It was a possibility, since babies are discarded daily in China.

The crowd was becoming increasingly interested in me as I locked my bike and started walking toward them. They made way, and I was able to clearly see the baby and the old woman, who was not yet aware of my presence. She looked up, saw me, and began backing away, all the while indicating that I was to take the baby.

I stopped about five yards away from the baby and in my best elementary Chinese asked, "Mama, baba, zai nar?" They either did not understand, which I doubted, or did not care to answer the question, which seemed more likely.

I tried again, "Where's the mother and father?"
No response, only dozens of hands ushering me towards the baby, wanting me to take her [at least I assumed it was a

girl, since about 90% of those abandoned are girls].

The baby was sitting in a box, holding the sides of the box, reaching out to anyone who might pick her up and hold her. The tears had flowed so long that they had left tracks down her now dirtied face. I was drawn to her, not really caring if it was the right baby, not caring what those in the crowd would think, not caring what the authorities would do. I could not resist the ache in her heart.

I reached out to her, and she reached up to me. As I encircled her in my arms, she grasped my coat with both her hands and pulled herself tightly against me. She clung to me desperately, as if I was her last hope for life itself. And, according to the statistics that we have seen concerning babies abandoned in China, this little baby had ascertained the situation correctly.

Chapter II

Throw-Away Babies

B aby girls have been thrown out with the garbage in China for generations. It is not an original idea with Communists. As unconcerned with individual lives as Communists are, it was not their idea first.

Grab most any book that deals with Chinese people and you will read about children disposed of on garbage heaps. It is their history. Read Pearl Buck's <u>The Good Earth,</u> and hear the wife bemoaning the fact that she has erred terribly by bearing another poor, miserable slave (a girl) to her master. Read about the life of medical missionary Dr. Nelson Bell (Billy Graham's father-in-law) and discover again that baby girls are considered garbage, unworthy of the effort to raise them. His story is found in <u>Foreign Devil in China</u>. No, Communists did not force this idea upon the Chinese. They have lived with this curse for hundreds, perhaps thousands, of years.

But by the time we entered China there was a difference. That difference had to do with population control.

China has the largest population of any country in the world. Over one billion Chinese presently populate a country that is little larger than the continental U.S. The majority of these people are packed into an area along China's eastern seaboard— an area that compares to the eastern U.S. from the Mississippi River to the Atlantic Ocean. That is also where the majority of their farmland is; only 15% of China is arable.

China has almost always been teeming with people. The population took a large jump in the 1960s, when the Great Helmsman, Mao Zedong, told the people to produce more people. The more children a woman had, the more she was honored. Mao's idea was that China would control the world by simply outproducing the rest of the world. There was some creditability to this notion, since he had been able pour thousands of troops into North Korea during the Korean War and saw the South Korean and American forces fall back from the massive onslaught. The Chinese did not have air power, they did not have tank power; but they had waves and waves of Chinese soldiers. They kept coming— no matter how many died, there were always more coming over the top of the embankments. They never stopped. It is estimated that Mao sacrificed 900,000 Chinese young men to help sustain Communism in North Korea.

So, couples produced more children, and the Great Helmsman smiled. Of course, there were some problems attached to feeding so many people, and there were times when the problems became so bad that famine swept the land, and people starved.

A few years after Mao's death in 1976, Deng Xiao Ping gained control and he set about changing things. In 1979 he introduced the one-child policy. Each couple could have one child and only one child. There were a few rare exceptions to this policy, but a couple having more than one child, faced punishment. The Chinese people have never liked this practice, but what could be done when such a powerful person said that it would be so? The majority obeyed; some found a way around it, some faced the stiff punishment. But most sought to have the perfect child. The perfect child was a healthy baby boy.

Birth control was almost nonexistent as most Westerners

practice it, so it was not unusual for women to become pregnant more than once. What then? Usually the women got voluntary abortions. Many others were forced to have abortions. Some babies were destroyed in the womb, at 8 and 9 months, with the mothers pleading for their babies.

Mei Ling, a Chinese English teacher at Yantai University in Northeast China, was just one example. She was 23 and had been teaching at the university for only a few years. It was a good position for one so young. She was happy, her parents were happy, and she became even happier when another young English teacher began to pay more and more attention to her. Their romance was unusual for most Chinese in that they initiated the contact themselves; and they began to make plans for their marriage. They thought they were being secretive, but it was too apparent on their faces in the teachers' meetings.

There was one giant problem with their plan – Mei Ling was too young to be married. Their work unit did not have housing for any more couples and had exceeded their limit of births dictated to them from Beijing. The age for marriage on their work unit was 25. Mei Ling would have to wait two years.

But they were in love, and exceptions had been made, and they had a good relationship with the Communist cadre of the Foreign Language Department. And Mei Ling's father was a very good friend of the Communist Party leader of the university. They believed it could be done.

They asked, they pressed, they bided their time and within 8 months they were married and living in one room of the fifth floor of the Post Graduate Building. But, at least they were together, and it was a very beautiful time for them. It did not matter to Mei Ling that she was on a floor populated with all males, and she had to go to the third floor to have her cold shower or just to go the bathroom. They were warm and enjoying each other's presence.

The evidence of that loving relationship began to show itself in a few short months when Mei Ling discovered she was pregnant. At first, there was the urging of joy, that burst forth in her soul at the discovery. But any joy was quickly squelched with the realization of what this meant. She was not yet 24, married before the proper age, and now pregnant. According to the regulations of the work unit, a woman must be 27 years of age before she can give birth. A problem.

But they had faced one problem and seen the victory. They could face this problem. They called her father, and he asked the officials to ignore her age again. That was not to be the case, however, because it proved to be the wrong time at the wrong work unit. The university had just received notification that they were not being strict enough concerning the birth control policy. They were to strictly enforce the policy or face unnamed consequences. Even her father was unable to effect the change. The policy was firm. She had to get rid of her baby.

Mei Ling shared her predicament with an American teacher, who prayed with her and told her that she would continue to pray for her. It so happened that the day Mei Ling boarded the bus for the clinic in order to abort her baby, that same Christian teacher was also on the bus. She encouraged Mei Ling to save her baby – to wait on God. Mei Ling had no relationship with God. She knew almost nothing of God. Her god was the government, and the government said to destroy the baby. She saw no alternative. Even as our American friend pleaded with her to not do this thing, Mei Ling saw no hope and that day destroyed the life within her that the love of her and her husband had produced.

And what if she became pregnant again in a few months? The abortion clinic would still be just a short bus ride away, and she would be forced to destroy another child. That process would continue until she became 27— when the government approved of her carrying a baby to term.

Yes, China does still destroy her children. And it continued to be mostly baby girls who disappear from homes. But now, thanks to modern technology, even more girls are being destroyed more often in the womb. An article in Hong Kong's South China Morning Post newspaper of July 22, 1993 delivered an interesting insight into this practice.

"Last year, we had only one girl born in the village— everybody else had boys," Y. H. Chen said in a tone of awe, as the others nodded agreement. He explained that for a bribe of US$35 to US$50, a doctor would tell whether a woman was pregnant with a boy or a girl.

"Then if it's a girl, you get an abortion," he said.

This interview was held in one of China's many country villages where modern medicine is still just a dream, with one big exception— the ultrasound scanner. The article continues:

In the China of the 1990s, the modern machine that is having the most far-reaching effect on society is probably not the personal computer, the fax, or even the car. It is the ultrasound scanner.

Partly because of ultrasound scans to check the sex of foetuses, followed by abortions of females, the sex ratio of newborn children in China last year reached 118.5 boys for every 100 girls. That statistic, based on an official survey of 385,000 people conducted last September and October, is a preliminary one, but it so shocked the authorities that they ordered that it be kept secret.

Normally, women of all races give birth to about 105 or 106 boys for every 100 girls. China's ratio last year was about 13 points off this international norm, meaning that more than 12 percent of all female foetuses were aborted or otherwise unaccounted for.

Because China's population is so huge – 1.17 billion– that adds up to more than 1.7 million missing girls each year.

In five of China's 30 provinces, the sex ratio is already more than 120 boys for every 100 girls.

Doctors are officially banned from telling parents the gender of a foetus, but peasants say a gift of a carton of cigarettes will usually open the doctor's mouth.

"One family here in the village has five girls," said Y.C. Chen, a peasant in a hamlet of a few hundred people in the southern part of coastal Fujian Province. "They were desperate for a son, and so they kept on having another child in hopes that it would be a son."

"But now you don't need to do that," Chen added proudly. "Now technology is changing things."

It is such a contrast as you see the Chinese' great love for children. And, thankfully, the attitudes toward girls are slowly changing in the cities. In the countryside change arrives on a donkey cart and is often forced out of town! The peasants care little for what Beijing or Communist leaders in their area have to say. There is a Chinese adage that holds true today:

> I plow my ground and eat,
> I dig my well and drink;
> for king or emperor,
> what use have I?

Mei Ling is an example of what happens to millions of Chinese women every day. She went to the clinic on her own accord, knowing no other choice. Other women, pregnant too early or bearing a second child, refuse to go to the clinic for an abortion in the early months of their pregnancies and face the consequences of a forced abortion in the third trimester.

There were others, like Xiao Shu, who had their babies, according to the law, and then were forced to give them away by their relatives or through other social pressures. Xiao Shu's story is a fictionalized account of why the baby I found was abandoned on the streets of our city. We have often wondered, "How could a mother do this?" But it may not have been her mother who abandoned her. Her mother may have never known what happened to her child as a grandparent whisked it away. Or perhaps the mother was dead. We could only guess and wonder why. But Xiao Shu is not alone. Children are discarded by the millions in the People's Republic of China.

We have friends, American English teachers in Xian, who desired to adopt a Chinese baby. They went to the orphanage in their city in northwest China, looking for a boy.

The officials were unable to find one in the entire orphanage; but the couple looked around a bit more closely and asked about a very frail child who was in a corner by itself. It was approximately two months old, but looked more like a newborn. They realized by its condition that the baby had been put there to die. It was a boy with a harelip and cleft pallet. No one had ever adopted a child from the orphanage before, so the officials were unaware of how it was or was not to be done. They simply saw it as an opportunity to rid themselves of one child to a nice foreign couple. They let them take the baby home that day— they thought better of it later on when other government officials became involved. That child had apparently been discarded simply because of the harelip and cleft pallet. Even in China, where medical care is not always the best, repairing a harelip and cleft pallet is considered relatively simple. Later, the American couple had the surgery done. That little boy now eats as if there were no tomorrow and is a two-year-old trying to take control of the family— like a good two-year-old.

Another American friend told the story of a crowd gathered outside a hospital in a central China city. She was curious herself, so she joined the crowd. They were all staring at a newborn, wrapped in a blanket, lying on the sidewalk next to a busy street, crying. No one would touch it. They just looked at it. The foreigner was urged to pick it up. She did so and marched into the hospital with the baby. They refused it. They kept sending her down different corridors to different people. All refused to take the child. There was no communication problem; the foreigner spoke fluent Chinese. There was simply a refusal on everyone's part to assume responsibility for the child. The foreigner made such a scene that a physician finally agreed to take the child, supposedly to the nursery.

"I don't actually know where they went with that child,"

she said. "I went back the next day because I realized I had probably condemned that child by my actions. If I could find it, I had determined that I would take it and try to get it out of the country."

She never found it.

She has related that story to many Chinese. More than a few hear it with tears forming in their eyes. They do care for their children. Such a story saddened them. They were embarrassed that a foreigner had witnessed such a thing in their country. Yes, nationalistic pride was part of it; but they were also saddened that it happens at all. They realized that it might one day happen to one of their children, and they are unable to explain it to a foreigner. They do not know how to explain it to themselves. It is a pain within that has not disappeared from their country and they do not know how to make it vanish.

Many long for more children and believe that if they were able to have more this problem of discarding baby girls, would be solved; but they are not positive of that. But they still desire more children. A mother with twin boys is greatly honored in her family. That father smiles broadly. Twins are allowed. A woman told us that the government could do nothing about multiple births.

Enjoy an early morning jog and take careful notice of areas such as bus stations, post offices, train stations, hospitals and busy intersections. One day out of the week you will probably come upon a baby that has been discarded. They leave them in the early morning hours in such places with the hope that they will be taken to the orphanage and cared for. Most of the parents have no idea just how bad the orphanages are. They remain one of the blights on China.

No orphanage can be considered a good place, because children need the love and affection of someone who cares specifically for them. Even in the United States, where the majority of social workers sincerely try to help children, most in orphanages still miss that individual love that they so desperately need.

In most areas of China, the majority of children in orphanages are essentially prisoners. By far, the majority are only passing through on their way to death. The baby I found was not an isolated case in our city. She was most likely one of two or three babies thrown away in that city of 1.5 million people that day.

According to the statistics given to us by the Nanchang orphanage director herself, they accepted 852 live babies in 1991. Through an arrangement with a Canadian agency, people from Quebec Province adopted 59 babies that year. By March 1992, 187 more babies had been abandoned to the orphanage. That made a total of 1,039 babies passing through the orphanage from January 1991 to March 1992. Take away the 59 adopted by the Canadians, and there were 980 babies that should have been in the care of the orphanage by that time. We counted somewhere over 50 babies when we were there in March. It was a strain for the personnel to keep up with even that many. Where did the other 930 babies go? During that time no Chinese families adopted babies from the orphanage. It was rarely, if ever, done anywhere in China. Those 930 babies died, we have no doubt. Most died within a few weeks of their arrival.

Some babies arrived dead; others were so close to death that very little, if anything, was done for them. An orphanage worker told us that they determined the state of the baby's health upon arrival and decided then if they were healthy enough to try saving. If they were deemed unacceptable, they were put on half rations and allowed to slowly starve to death. Some were given enough rations to survive, but only a few made it.

What would have been our baby's fate if I had not arrived on the scene? Most likely she would have remained in that box most of the day. If no one had taken her by evening, if she was still alive by that time, she would have been taken to the orphanage. And, of course, there would be no reason for a Chinese person to take her. If someone threw her away, why would someone else want to take on an extra burden of a child that was not a relative? She might or she might not have survived in the orphanage.

Chapter III

What Do We Do
With This Baby?

When you go to China, you go in order to involve yourself in the lives of the people. You never know what depth of involvement that may mean. There are many people within the Chinese borders who have no direction in their lives. All they know to do is marchstep according to the Communist Party's plan; they know that this is not a fulfilling life, so you encounter many people with various emotional pain.

During our first five years in China, living in three different cities, we became involved with many people. Some were only surface relationships; other friendships went to the depth of knowing their pain and feeling their suffering. We faced the death of an aged parent with one Chinese friend, rejoiced at marriages, almost marched with the 1989 protesters, and did join them one time to remember the students who died at Tiananmen Square in Beijing. We cried when we said goodbye, only to greet those same weeping friends a year later. Yes, China and her people will play havoc with your emotions; but we had never experienced such an emotional roller-coaster ride as the one that started when that filthy, urine-soaked child grasped my coat and would not let go.

As she pulled herself to me bodily, she was in fact

pulling herself into our lives until we found ourselves clutching her physically, mentally, and emotionally. We clung to her, believing that the God who loves her even more than we, would not let her go. Throughout the bad news, as we heard the nurse say, "She can't use her legs" after a spinal tap, and on into the night of despair when we faced a crossroads of faith in our lives, we remained determined to not give her up to a system that had proven its callousness.

We would not release our grasp upon her.

I had picked her up from her cardboard box that day on the street, carrying her close to me. That began my trek home and our journey as a family into the valley of the shadow that required total trust and led to a more complete faith as we were given the option to plumb our faith and find out just how deep it went.

The Scriptures we had mouthed for so long and the verses we had sung for years now had the opportunity to come to the forefront of our lives or be shunted to the side in our frustration. The choice was ours— God's way or our way.

The Chinese cheered as I began to walk back toward my bicycle with the baby. Several of them followed to see what I would really do. I felt like a pied piper leading the way to some undetermined point. I marched; they followed, saying indistinguishable things about the foreigner. They celebrated me for a brief time. I did not feel very deserving of their acclaim. Tom was still nowhere in sight. Would I have two babies at home when he tired of waiting for me and simply scooped up another baby himself and was now waiting for me at our apartment?

However, I was soon relieved of that fear as he suddenly appeared beside me, wondering where I had been. Thankfully, we had both found the same baby. We simply misunderstood his directions.

He walked with me, guiding my bike home as I held our

new treasure. A few of the ladies continued to follow us, all smiles at the reality that I was most likely heading to my home. I was unsure if I should smile, cry, or run for cover. In the months to come, I did a great deal of all three.

My initial thinking was to find a policeman and ask him what I should do. I knew that there would be one at the next intersection. There were always policemen (at least one) at every intersection. First intersection – no policeman. Second intersection – no policeman. I mentioned this to Tom, but he just ignored my comments. I found it very unusual that there were no policemen around anywhere; at least none that I could see.

I felt better as we stepped through the gate on our campus. The old women let us go in peace. The campus of Jiangxi Medical College did not always seem serene to me, but on this day a welcome peacefulness greeted me as we walked down the tree-lined streets. All the trees are sycamores, planted in the past 10 years to replace all the trees the people used for heating years ago. They had reached the point that they shaded most of the roadway— a roadway that saw 20 times more bicycles than cars.

I looked for people looking at me as we turned the corner that would lead past the pond, past the administration building, where the *wai ban* (a loose term foreigners use for anyone involved in their Foreign Affair's Office, but usually the director) has an office, past the teacher's cafeteria, and on to our home. The sun was shining brighter now, and many people were busily heading toward their workstations, but they seemingly paid little attention to us. Saturday was just another workday for the Chinese.

As we neared our home, I wondered if LeRoy would think I had made the right decision. "Is this what he really wants? And what of our kids? What will they think about this intrusion of a baby into our relatively peaceful home?" I had all kinds of questions buzzing through my head as I walked up the stairs to our second-story apartment.

I smiled at LeRoy as I entered our apartment, and I think he smiled, or perhaps it was at least the hint of a smile. The baby had now fallen into a peaceful sleep and had released her grasp on me. David and Marianne were all around me, trying to get a good look at her. I lay her on our bed, after spreading a small blanket down so our sheets would not become totally filthy. She continued to sleep. We all gazed at her and visually checked her over. She looked good, only dirty. We took a couple of steps back into our living/dining room to discuss what to do next.

I briefly looked at each person in the room as we all stopped a moment to gather our wits. LeRoy still looked a little quizzical. Tom was confident that we all had done the right thing. David, our 15-year-old son, was happy to be involved in anything this important. Marianne, our 11-year-old daughter, could not stop looking at the baby. Shelly, our teammate and good friend who lived above us, was doubting our wisdom, but she was ready to go the distance with us.

A rather unique group of conspirators. That was what we looked like, and that was what I felt like. I knew that this simply could not be correct action, according to Chinese law; yet I felt very good and very confident about it. I in no way doubted that we had done the right thing. I was unsure what kind of baby I had brought home, but I was very sure it was what God wanted and that what we had done was right at this point. What of the days ahead? Those were our discussions.

For a few moments we all relaxed and looked at each other with goofy smiles, thinking, "this is stupid, but it is certainly invigorating." Of course, no one actually said that. Instead I said, "We need to notify the foreign affairs office right away."

We had encountered so many difficulties with the *wai ban* that we were unsure that would be the best plan. (Actually *wai ban* means foreign office. Every university campus has one. We are in the care of those in that office. They are responsible for us while we are in China.)

"They've caused us many problems; how can they help?" LeRoy questioned.

"We really have no choice," I reasoned. "They are in charge of us, and if we go over their heads or around them, it'll only mean more trouble. I think that the sooner we tell them, the better."

Nods of agreement went around.

"Now, what do we tell them?"

The truth seemed the logical answer, but how much of the truth? That did not seem to be the correct discussion for moral folks who came as representatives of the Truth. Yet, we also realized our responsibility to the Chinese, specifically Tom, and that we had no right to jeopardize any Chinese at any time. Our thinking in these matters had always followed one line: "If we get in trouble, the worst they can do is to send us back to the land of burgers and fries and pizza. But if our Chinese friends get in trouble, there is the possibility of a long prison term, or the officials can simply make the rest of their lives miserable." So we have always had to judge how our actions would affect our Chinese friends. That was all going through our minds, and it was also making its way through Tom's mind.

"I think it's best if you don't mention me," he finally said. "It could mean more legal problems for the baby and could possibly be trouble for me. We're not sure about the law."

We agreed. We always agreed when a Chinese told us they did not want to be mentioned or their presence acknowledged. They know the repercussions better than we do.

"If we leave you out," LeRoy said, "then the truth is that Jane was riding her bike this morning, saw a crowd, went to investigate, found this baby and brought her home. I don't think it's necessary to ever mention your name."

It was agreed.

Since it was Saturday, we were scheduled to be across town, at the foreigners' worship meeting, a one-hour bike ride away. Shelly, David and LeRoy got on their bikes and headed out while the baby still slept. She had not stirred, had not even made a sound, despite our many peeks at her. She was exhausted.

Marianne and I remained behind. Tom decided it was best for him to be out of our apartment, so he left before the rest. After everything quieted down, I looked again at the small bundle of precious that had just been deposited into our lives. She looked healthy; she looked cute, despite the layers of dirt and the smell. She looked like a baby that any mother would love to hold.

Before Tom left, he called a pediatrician friend of ours, who said she could be free in a few hours and come to our home. I also called the *wai ban*, explaining the situation as briefly as possible over the phone. She said they would come just as soon as they could, but that they were about to go into a meeting.

They did not seem surprised by my announcement. The Chinese always seemed to know everything about their foreign teachers, and I was sure the early morning arrival of a baby had attracted enough attention that they had already been informed. The meeting was probably to discuss what to do with the new problem that their crazy foreigners had created.

Just one small example of their knowledge of our actions: We had left fairly early one morning to visit friends on another campus, a 30-minute bike ride away. When we returned in the early afternoon, we happened to encounter our interpreter when we entered our campus.

"Did you have a nice visit over at Shi Da?" she asked.

We smiled and replied politely, "Yes, it was a good time with our friends," wondering how she knew so quickly. But it was probably a simple matter. The foreign teachers at the other campus are watched, so the watchers undoubtedly saw us and called our *wai ban* to say, "Your foreigners are over here visiting our foreigners." It was really quite simple, but it was also a simple example of how they keep watch over us.

Many thoughts went through my mind as I watched the baby sleeping in my bedroom. "Why do we have her, and what are we going to do with her now? What will the Chinese authorities tell us? Will they come and take her away today?"

I did not know the answers to any of my questions, but I retained a quiet confidence that this was all from God. I had peace, and that is usually a very good sign of God's presence.

As I pondered all these things in my heart, the baby began to stir. Her bottle was still about half full. I had cleaned it, and it was ready for her. She gradually opened her eyes, looking all around, seeking something familiar. I gently picked her up and held her— dirt-streaked face, urine smell and all. She did not grasp me this time. Instead she pushed away to look into my face. It was possibly the first foreign face she had ever seen. She never even looked at me when I picked her up on the street. This time she took a very good look. I prepared myself for a scream of terror. It had happened more than once. Some Chinese babies react in total fear when a foreign face comes near them. They have never seen such a face before. Chinese all have similar features. This is not to say that they all look alike— they have many distinguishing characteristics; but they do have the same basic features and coloring. My face looks very Anglo-Saxon (round eyes, high nose). I certainly do not look Chinese. She knew this, and duly noted it, but only looked.

I almost burst out laughing as I watched her looking at me. But I restrained myself, because I knew that to do so would upset her. She seemed unconcerned that a total stranger— a very strange stranger, was holding her. She looked around some more, but there was nothing she wanted to see in our apartment. It was very similar to most Chinese apartments, except that it looked cleaner and neater because of the recent halfpaint job. Also we had a Western (as in sit-down— no squatting) toilet. I said our apartment was half painted because that was the way Chinese painted walls. Sometimes they would leave them all whitewashed, which meant your clothes got whitewashed any time you brushed too close to the wall. But we were blessed with a lime-green color lower half to our walls. The upper half retained its whitewash. Our place looked better simply because of the fresh paint job, and we did not have our extended family living with us as most Chinese do. The apartment merely appeared good because it was not wall-to-wall people. Chinese do not own much, but when there are two or three families living in a three-room apartment, it becomes quite crowded and cannot look very neat.

After the baby completed her visual tour of our apartment, I gave her the bottle. She reached greedily for it. As she slurped down the milk, I tried to get her clothes off so that I could clean her up before she finished the bottle. Working quickly I managed to complete the task. She still found me interesting, but was relatively unconcerned about me. Marianne was trying to keep the baby entertained while I got her into something clean.

Late morning, Angel arrived to inspect the baby. She was our pediatrician friend, a young Chinese Christian who attended a weekly Bible study in our apartment.

She almost always smiled, even when she was not beating on her boyfriend. She was currently unable to beat on her boyfriend because he was studying in another city. I think she only gave him playful love pats, but sometimes I wondered. She showed her white teeth as she took the baby from me.

"Ni hao, xiao pengyou," she said to the baby as she

took her from my arms. The baby went willingly to Angel, probably very happy to see someone who looked *normal*. Angel examined her while I related the story. Angel laughed throughout the story. I was not sure it was all that amusing, but she seemed to think it was. As she laughed, the baby seemed to relax even more. Further, the more Chinese she heard from Angel, the more the child responded positively. But she still looked around from time to time, perhaps hoping to see her mother approaching or trying to find someone or something that looked familiar. She would not find it.

Marianne and I played with the baby while Angel examined her.

"Um.. um.. ..oh" she said as she ran her stethoscope over the baby and then did the necessary finger thumping on her body.

"Hmm," she finally concluded as she rubbed her chin and looked at me. I chose to say nothing, having no idea what it meant when a Chinese doctor said, "umm, oh," and "hmm," during an examination. I soon found out that it is universal doctor talk for "don't bother me now while I'm trying to find your kidneys; I know they're in there somewhere."

"She seems healthy to me," she pronounced, "except that she seems to have a cold in her chest, in those tubes— what are those tubes called?"

"I think you mean bronchial," I responded from my Mother's Medical Encyclopedia knowledge. She agreed and told me the name in Chinese, which I promptly forgot. I have to be ready for a Chinese lesson if I absorb anything, so I did not absorb that.

"What's her name?" Angel asked.

"Her name? I have no idea. She's just *Baby* so far."

Angel laughed out loud again, looked for her boyfriend to hit, and then suggested we have some name for her. I told her we would think about it. She left, because she had to return to the children's hospital to complete her rounds.

I felt much better after her visit. She had pronounced our little flower healthy and had found it all to be a very funny experience. If she thought it was so funny, surely the Chinese authorities on our campus would at least think it was all right. The people on the street thought I was wonderful. Angel thought we were a little crazy, but that it was all very good. The baby was healthy. So, what could the *wai ban* folks think? Surely they would be positive also.

I was about to find out, because Zhou Li, our interpreter, and her boss, Ms. Yue, were approaching the apartment. Moreover, they were not alone. I become concerned when I saw two men, dressed in Public Security Bureau uniforms, walking with them. Maybe they did not think this was such a good idea after all.

I greeted them holding the baby. Only Zhou Li and Ms. Yue were at the door. I looked into the stairwell, but no one else was there. They reached out to the baby immediately, and she was happy to go to some more people who looked *normal* and knew how to speak *correctly*. I was sure she had no idea what was coming out of my mouth when I opened it. I always tried to speak very calmly to the baby. She was still acting as if she were in a nether world and, if she gave it time, everything would eventually right itself and she would find herself in her own home.

After a brief discussion that was very cordial and a long time spent playing with the baby, Zhou Li and Ms. Yue gave me their opinion on our situation. I was still wondering about the PSB officials, so I tried to casually drop it into the conversation.

"I thought the security people came with you," I said, not so casually.

They Looked astonished, as if they had no idea what I was talking about. I went to look out the window, and they were gone— at least I could not see them. They never mentioned anything about PSB people, and I was unable to understand what it all meant.

We continued our conversation, and I advised them that we had friends who wanted to adopt this baby and that we would do everything we could to help them adopt her. Could they help us help them?

Smiles all around as, the *wai ban* told me, "No problem. This should only take about two weeks."

That *was not* a prophecy from God.

Two weeks stretched into months— months when we wondered if God could actually still be on His throne and if He was truly watching over His own.

But within six weeks came a crisis that not only almost destroyed our plans, but also saw us staring into the face of death.

Chapter IV

Walking God's Path

Chinese Airspace. August, 1985

The 747 adjusted its flight pattern to come in straight over Shanghai, one of the few air corridors where it was permissible to enter the People's Republic of China. The cabin of the plane was populated mostly with Chinese. There were a few Americans and perhaps a few others of varied nationalities. Most were sleeping, but some, like us, were straining to get their first look at the mysterious land of China.

Our first indication that we were arriving in this great land was the darkening of the Pacific Ocean where the Yangtze River empties into it on the northern edge of Shanghai. Then, rather abruptly, we saw the coast, and we were over the city itself in the next few minutes. Then only a few minutes more, and we were on the western edge of Shanghai, passing over the airport and banking north, flying on to Beijing.

It had all happened so fast that nothing had time to register. We were looking down on China from 30,000 feet as the sun was setting on the Middle Kingdom. The shadows deepened as we flew on toward the capital. As I gazed down on the darkness settling upon the land, I began to reflect on what first led us to the multitude of unknowns that any

Westerner would face upon entering this land of over one billion people, who live their lives predicated on 5,000 years of history. I also looked forward to the upcoming months with some trepidation; in many ways this was an unchanging, yet ever-changing, multitude.

This was a country that had seen many conquerors, a country that was so very untrusting of the foreigner, yet reaching out to many foreign ways while also trying to block other foreign ideas.

I was now staring intently out the window, noticing what appeared to be campfires below. In fact, they looked convincingly like campfires, but I could not comprehend why there would be so many campfires burning across the landscape. I knew that China was still pretty backward, yet I had no idea how much so. However, I was soon to learn that those 'campfires' were lights of towns and small cities; they just did not shine as brightly as in America since there were fewer lights in each town.

As we flew on into the night, with Beijing awaiting us, I wondered to myself, "How did we come to this? What are we doing here? What have we gotten into?"

We were taking our family into a potentially hostile situation in a country where we would be almost totally dependent on Communist leaders to take care of us. Like most Americans, we could think of little worthwhile that any Communist had ever accomplished, especially in a humanitarian way. It was not a comforting thought. Our children were not sure what they were involved in— they only trusted us. We were not sure where our steps would lead— we could only trust God. Trust is a precious commodity. Our children knew only a little of what they were leaving behind— so far, it was an adventure and had been fun, a wonderful vacation. But soon would come the day-to-day living in Communist China and that might not be so much fun.

We did not know the language, much less the customs,

or even how to get from one place to another. We were like little children who had to be led from place to place simply in order to exist. We could not find the restrooms. We would have to have a Chinese person point them out to us. By the time we used our first public restroom in China, we knew for certain that we were in a hostile environment. Our senses were assaulted by the public facility.

There was one consolation in the fact that we were also unable to effectively use the 'tableware' – chopsticks: therefore very little food made it to our mouths. We were also still unsure about the water. So simple subtraction kept us out of the restrooms. The less we ate and drank, the fewer times we had to visit the toilet.

But, we reminded ourselves, if God was able to put us in this situation, He was also quite capable of taking care of us in it. Our task would be to trust Him and listen to the Holy Spirit. He was the Guide within us. 'Trust and Obey' became a clarion call for our spirits.

*****

In the early 1980s we had felt very clearly that God was calling us to something different. We had always been involved in secular work and never felt any inclination to join the 'clergy' in America. We had also never felt any leading to go overseas. In reality, we had only recently awakened spiritually, but God had been preparing us for His service in China many years before we ever even thought about China.

Actually God did not reveal China as our destination until 7 months before we stepped onto the Asian continent.

We were knocking on the door of the 30s age bracket when God knocked a little harder on our yuppie exterior. We were yuppies before there was such a title. We were contentedly going about the American pursuit of making money to buy a newer car to buy a bigger house to try to impress our neighbors, who were busily doing the same thing. Furthermore we were succeeding.

Then, one fall Sunday morning, it happened. We were calmly sitting in a Sunday school class, showing our best spiritual side, when God struck. We had no suspicions, but He really "got us". We were not unhappy; we were not broke, we were not deeply in debt; we had no strange addictions; we were, in fact, living the American dream. We had a new three-bedroom house with a two-car garage, and we had two almost-new cars parked in that garage. We were living in a good neighborhood in one of the fastest growing suburbs of the Dallas/Fort Worth area. We were perfectly content in the American dream environment that we had created in Arlington, Texas. Perhaps all of this was the reason we were totally surprised when God suddenly "zapped" us.

It was an extremely subtle attack. We were merely sitting in the Sunday school class of about 200 people at First United Methodist Church. Most people would not consider that a likely place for God to lay claim to one; but He certainly did. We were dressed in our Sunday best, pretending to be spiritual, when it suddenly occurred to us that something was missing.

A few men in the Sunday school class were testifying about God's goodness, about His great and wonderful provisions for them in their times of need. They gave specific examples that could have only been from God. It was their testimonies that began to nudge us from our spiritual complacency. We soon found ourselves in a small group that was studying the Bible and praying together. Every week we met together, and from that beginning, we finally began to grow in our spirits, even though we had both been reared in the church and had attended church most of our lives. We had both "accepted Jesus as our Savior" during childhood. We had been living out what could be called "Sunday Christianity", instead of being real followers of the King of Kings.

We were nurtured and led along gently by God through that study group. The couple that induced us to involve ourselves was Joe and Sharon Hall. They took us under their wing and became our spiritual mentors. Ever since, they have continued to assist us in many ways.

We began to realize that God was open for business on weekdays and Saturday as well as on Sunday. We were also very happy to discover that God was not "cooped up" in a church. I guess we thought He was there anxiously awaiting our arrival on Sunday mornings and smiling like some benevolent old aunt when we finally arrived. Perhaps we thought God gave us another mark in the "good" column when we showed up at church. It was so very much fun and such a great adventure to discover that God is real and personal and nearby every minute of every day.

God began to "grow us up" in His very loving, very kind way until He finally had prepared us for His service in China.

After eight years of nurturing through the work of many dedicated teachers, both of us felt very clearly that God was preparing us for a totally new experience of some sort, but we did not know what. As the months went by, LeRoy began to believe that God was going to involve us in Africa in some way. I, too, believed God was going to be using us overseas. LeRoy felt so inclined toward Africa that he wrote a couple of people in ministry in Nigeria, just to see if we should be going in that direction. We never heard from them. Still, we knew God was going to do something "different" in our lives, and we believed that it meant going overseas. That was a year before we picked up any information about China, and 18 months prior to our actually going to China. He led; we followed and became more excited as it looked more and more as though God would send us to China. Our families somehow missed the excitement. They explained that there is "a great need for witnesses right here in America", the usual objection to overseas witness.

We now realize if all the believers would be witnesses in the U.S., we could most likely claim this as a really Christian nation; instead it is only the shadow of a Christian nation.

We first heard about service in China in January 1985, and in August of the same year we were walking on the Great Wall, preparing to take up residence in the Middle Kingdom. It is amazing how fast things can fall into place when God is shifting the gears.

Some have said we went to China as 'bootleg missionaries,' spreading the Gospel while accepting assignments as English teachers. The Beijing bigwigs have accused the American English teachers of being "sheep in wolves' clothing" – a unique turn to Scripture, indeed.

Yes, we went to China as teachers. Yes, we do share the Good News of Jesus Christ whenever the opportunity avails itself. As we understand the Bible, we are supposed to communicate the Word no matter where we live, regardless of our occupation. We were Christian professionals, merely doing the job we were asked to do.

But we also diligently worked to be the best teachers that we could be. That was the work assignment we had accepted, and it was our desire to do our very best. Thankfully, we had the help of the Holy Spirit in doing so.

*****

After landing in Beijing, we sorted through luggage, readjusted our bodies to being on the other side of the world, enjoyed the sights, sounds, and smells of Beijing, then flew on to our assignment in Wuhan. Wuhan, a central China city with a population of 5 1/2 million, greeted us warmly. In fact, it was a little too warm. As we stepped off the airplane onto the tarmac we walked into a new kind of liquid sunshine. It must have been liquid sunshine because our clothes were quickly wet from perspiration.

We crammed our family into an extremely small apartment with closet-size kitchen and bathroom. In the bathroom, LeRoy could stretch his arms out lengthwise and touch the walls. He could bend his elbows pointing them toward the nearer walls, and his elbows would touch each side. We were cramped. Then, we had food problems. We could eat at the teacher's dining hall for all our meals, but they served strange and unusual food. Not only did our children find it to be strange and unusual, but so did we. We also found out that we could not afford to keep staying in China, if we continued to pay the prices at the dining hall.

"We'll go broke if we keep eating there," we told our *waiban*. After they "picked themselves up from the floor," where they fell after laughing so hard at our American joke, we were almost able to continue the conversation. However, we had great difficulty convincing them that all Americans do not carry around pockets full of money.

When we quit eating at the dining hall, they at least began to think that we might be serious. Meanwhile, we wrote to our family and friends in America. "Help! Send food." The cry was heard, and **four months** later, care packages arrived. It took that long by sea. It was usually too expensive to ship boxes by air. In those intervening four months we had to learn how to operate on our own, and I learned to cook over an open flame, fueled by a gas tank. Only once did I get my eyebrows and eyelashes scorched.

It was also an opportunity to learn how the system worked and what the Chinese faced daily in the way of control of their lives. We needed rice and flour in order to cook. Those are basics, especially the rice, in a Chinese diet. At that time everyone had to go to a government distribution point to buy staples. I went there, lined up with the Chinese and asked to purchase the items.

I soon discovered another problem of existence in China in those days, especially for a foreigner: you must have ration coupons in order to purchase rice and flour. I had no ration coupons; therefore I was unable to buy the needed staples. My logical question was, "how do I get coupons?"

Their logical answer was, "You can't; foreigners aren't allowed to have them."

"Then how do I buy rice and flour?"

"You don't."

It all seemed very logical to them. However, it made no sense to me. I went to one of the Chinese English teachers who had befriended us, and I almost literally cried on her shoulder as I told the whole story.

She went into her bedroom, rummaged around for a while, and returned with a handful of coupons and gave them to me. I protested. She insisted and said, "I have plenty more. We hoarded them during the Cultural Revolution, and now we have more than enough."

Sure enough the dates on the coupons were for 1967. She had kept them almost 20 years. She assured me that they were still valid.

I went to try them. The officials at the distribution point looked at me suspiciously, doubled the price of rice and flour, took my coupons and money, and gave me the food.

That was the way it went from then on. My friend gave me the coupons; I stood in line with the Chinese (but paid double the price) and got my flour and rice.

Chinese friends helped us to find cooking utensils and more food to cook. I also eventually learned to cook some semblance of American food. One major difference between Chinese and American cooking is the lack of variety in Chinese meals. It was almost always a bowl of rice with vegetables scattered over the top. That was the daily fare. A banquet was something totally different.

If you want to visualize a picture of cooking in China then, think about cooking at a primitive campout every meal, and you will be rather close to the truth.

We also had to find the food before we could cook it. There was no such thing as a supermarket. However, there was a market. Thankfully, it was directly across the street from our university. We crossed the street and looked at the offerings up close and personal, for they were scattered on the ground, but they were at least nicely divided into different sections. Eggs (chicken and duck— 1,000-year-old or fresh) were in one area, meat hanging on a hook (all pork) in another, bread (baked inside a barrel that had been coated with clay) at another, and so on.

I discovered vegetables that have yet to be discovered in America. They reminded me more of plants that landscape American yards, but they tasted remarkably good. With the help of Chinese friends we were able to somehow put it all together so that we did not starve. We lost a lot of weight the first few months, but by the end of October, it all leveled off. I still came out of China after our first year weighing less than I had weighed since high school. Remarkably, and as a testimony to God's provision, our children did not lose weight. They continued to grow just as they would have grown if they had remained in America.

We also learned how to teach in a Chinese classroom. We adapted to having a *monitor* always in the classroom, a monitor put there to meet our every need, of course, and later to report all our 'interesting' words.

We found many differences between the Chinese classroom and the American classroom, but our students, looking at a foreign teacher for the first time, eventually adapted to our ways. We, looking into a classroom of totally Chinese faces for the first time, also eventually adjusted. They gave a little; we gave a little. It worked. We found we liked some of the Chinese ways, and they liked some of the American ways.

We also made some great and wonderful discoveries along the way that helped make our lives a little easier. *Swan nai*, something that we had disdained even before trying, because it translated "sour milk," turned out to be a very good-tasting yogurt, which filled in our total lack of regular milk. It also rescued me from a rumbling stomach at night. For weeks my stomach would begin its complaining around bedtime, and at times I would double up with the pain from it. This continued for some time, with changes in my Chinese diet making little difference. I was the only one in the family experiencing it. I could find no relief until I tried the yogurt at night. It brought a complete change to my digestive system and then I slept peacefully.

Our children also found the yogurt appealing, a fact which was a relief to us since they needed something to supplement the vitamins and minerals they were missing.

Of course our whole first year was one giant learning experience for our whole family. We grew spiritually as we had to lean on God and trust Him.

We leaned and learned, and China became a part of us as we struggled to become a part of it. We were changed, and with that change came the yearning to return to China at the end of summer vacation; so we returned for another year.

And we kept on returning to Communist China, learning more, adapting more, sharing more, until a phone call in August 1991 eventually reshaped our focus in the land of Confucius.

We were enjoying a fairly restful summer in America when an American friend, a former teacher in China, called us with an unusual request.

"Will you find out what you can about adopting a Chinese baby?"

"Are you wanting to adopt?" was our question.

"John and I are seriously considering it. Find out what

you can from the orphanage in your city and let me know what you find out. We're wanting to know if it's feasible to adopt directly from an orphanage, or do we need to go through an organization there?"

We did not know the answer to that question, but we told her that we would check on it. One of the first things I did after we resettled in our Chinese apartment was to go with a Chinese friend on the 45-minute bike ride to the orphanage. It was not a pleasant sight, but we did get the needed information. I did not stay long because I did not want to get too close to the suffering I saw there, the hopelessness that I saw in the blank stares of the children. It was difficult to ascertain if there was actually life behind those blank, brown eyes.

Only later would I be forced to confront all of that and know the deep pain of seeing the full truth.

I notified my friend of the procedures necessary to begin adopting a baby from the orphanage; then I tried to forget about the place and concentrated my attention on existing in China and being about the purposes for which God had put us there. Six weeks later, God twisted our lives in such a way that our faith was truly tested and tried.

Chapter V

Fighting For Life

"How's she doing?"

"No better – she's looking worse."

"Did you anoint her with oil?"

"Yes, we've anointed her with oil. We prayed for her. I don't see any change. I'm getting worried."

It was 10:10 a.m. Monday, December 2. The baby had been a part of our lives for almost 6 weeks now. We had adapted to having her around. We had more than adapted; we had grown accustomed to her being part of our lives, part of our family, and even a part of the greater family of foreign believers in our city. And we had named her. We called her Mei Mei. The Chinese found this amusing.

Mei Mei is not a name. It is similar to a nickname. It means 'little sister'. Thousands of Chinese girls are called Mei Mei, but none are named Mei Mei. Still, we liked it, and that was her name.

She had started being fussy and running a low-grade fever late Sunday afternoon. She had slept in bed with me that night. Actually, we had slept very little. We were convinced she was teething; she already had four beautiful pearly whites and she kept rubbing her gums. After guiding our own kids through all the baby things you would think we would be able to do better, but we had never faced anything like this before. We did not know what was going on, and we had no idea what to do.

LeRoy returned from class mid-morning. We then prayed for her again. Our family gathered around her to claim God's great healing promises for her.

"She's not moving her eyes," David noticed.

"Mei Mei, look here," LeRoy ordered. Her eyes remained fixed, staring blankly toward the upward right. There was nothing there to see.

This new development quickly alarmed us. "We've got to get her to a doctor," I responded with fear rising in my voice. I began to wrap her in a blanket. The blank stare continued even as the children tried to get her attention – there was no response. This was the most frightening thing we had ever faced with any child – ever. We continued praying as I prepared to head out into the December mid-morning, looking for a doctor.

LeRoy jumped on his bike and rode toward the clinic, located at the front gate on our campus. We had a pediatrician friend, officially retired, who worked there part-time.

It was a ten-minute walk. As I was halfway there, LeRoy came back; telling me that Dr. Xu was there. I walked as fast as I could, holding the baby without stumbling over the debris that you find littering most sidewalks and streets in China. My heart sank even more as I noticed a white foam forming at Mei Mei's lips, and she continued the trance-like stare into nothing. My prayers had not ceased since I left the building.

I could not believe God had placed this child in our lives to enjoy her presence a short six weeks only to watch her die. I refused to accept it. It could not be God's will for her. It could not be God's will for us.

Still there was no response from Mei Mei. She now felt almost rigid in my arms. I could not imagine such a thing happening, and yet I was living it at that very moment. I quickened my pace even more, as best I could. LeRoy had returned to the clinic to tell Dr. Xu that I was coming with Mei Mei; he described her condition to Dr. Xu.

Mei Mei now seemed to be having difficulty breathing. My heart ached with what could be, but I hurried on, praying, trusting, believing that God would keep her alive.

I walked into the clinic, which was filled with patients. Dr. Xu was at a table in the back, looking at a 5-year-old child who was surrounded by family and friends. When Dr. Xu saw me, she quickly moved them aside and took Mei Mei in her arms. I knew she could tell from my expression that it was serious and not just something that a foreigner thought was serious.

We began to see God's hand in all this as Dr. Xu quickly examined Mei Mei, saw that she was having convulsions, and got an anticonvulsant that she quickly administered.

Looking back, we know that God had prepared the way before any of this had ever happened.

Dr. Xu had been a neighbor of ours, and she continued to be a friend that we saw occasionally. She had spent a year in America, visiting her daughter and family, when her only grandchild was born. Her English was fairly good. She understood us and was able to relate information to us.

She was also one of the top pediatricians in that province. It is true that she was working only part-time, but she was at work precisely when we needed her.

LeRoy went outside to look for one of our students or someone who would be able to help us if we needed to go to the hospital. He found the interpreter from the *waiban* riding out the gate with her friend.

"Zhou Li, we need your help; Mei Mei is sick," LeRoy called to her.

She slowed just enough to say, "I can't help you now; I have to go with my friend. She needs my help."

"But Mei Mei is very sick," LeRoy pleaded. By then

Zhou Li was already heading down the street with her friend.

"I'll be back in a little bit, and I'll help you then," she called over her shoulder. So much for help from the *waiban*.

LeRoy returned to the clinic, anxious because he had been unable to find anyone to help. Dr. Xu had finished administering the medicine. She examined Mei Mei.

"Her soft spot – it is pulsating," she said. "We must hurry to hospital." She told us to go to the garage where the college kept all its vehicles. It was just a five-minute walk around the corner.

We arrived, and there was no one there who could speak English. In our limited Chinese we could not make much progress. We pointed to the baby, told them *laiduzha*, which is the only word we could muster. It means 'diarrhea'. We tried to emphasize the great importance of taking the baby to the hospital. They were more interested in their Chinese chess game than they were in foreigners who did not know their language.

Chinese drivers were notorious for operating on their own time schedule. They could do that because a Chinese driver was powerful. A university president did not have his own car to drive. He had to use one of the campus drivers to drive him in one of the university's cars. If the driver was upset with the president, he may decide that the car is being repaired or that some other errand is more important; then the university president had to take the public bus. The drivers had such powers.

And, no, you could not fire them. The system is called 'the iron rice bowl,' because you can not 'break their rice bowl' – their means of obtaining money to buy food.

A Chinese driver may or may not take an interest in the foreigners on campus and be helpful to them. These drivers obviously did not find us very interesting.

We were hitting a high frustration level, since Mei Mei was not moving at all now, and her eyes were closed. We did not know what her condition really was, only that the doctor had told us to take her quickly to the hospital; and we were making no progress in doing so. All our motions and physical pleadings and bad Chinese were accomplishing nothing.

"Let's just walk," I finally said disgustedly. "We'll get there quicker that way than trying to do this." It was probably a 30- to 35-minute walk to the hospital, and we might encounter the same situation there – no English speaker plus our limited Chinese could mean no help. Surely someone would visually see our problem and help us, we reasoned. "It's better than standing here," we both agreed.

We had started to walk out of the garage area when Dr. Xu turned the corner. Dr. Xu was barely more than five feet tall and weighed only about 100 pounds. She walked into the driver's office, into the midst of the chess game, said about two abrupt words in Chinese, and the driver whose car was nearest the gate almost ran to his car and opened the door for me. LeRoy and Dr. Xu also jumped in and we hurried toward the hospital.

We had no idea what she had said or done, but she certainly produced action. We realized that she must have had some type of influence with the drivers, or they would have never jumped when she spoke.

We arrived at the pediatric wing of the hospital in only a few minutes. Dr. Xu walked in giving orders as if she ran the place. The nurses there reacted as if she did. Within a very short time, doctors and nurses surrounded Mei Mei as Dr. Xu directed the whole process and explained the problem.

Mei Mei was still not responding to anything. She just lay on the emergency room table. It seemed as if everything happened in one motion as Mei Mei was suddenly receiving oxygen through a tube in her nose, receiving glucose through a vein in her scalp, and having a needle jabbed abruptly into her spine. However, the team was unable to properly tap into her spine.

It was obviously an emergency situation to them, and they were in appropriate action. I was relieved to see them working so diligently, but apprehensive, because it obviously meant that Mei Mei was seriously ill and dangerously close to death.

Prayers continued through my mind and over my lips. LeRoy had gone off with someone to discuss payment. I was alone with the doctors surrounding Mei Mei, watching them work, wincing each time they injected the needle; wondering and doubting and reaching for my faith in the All-Loving God that I know.

During all the turmoil of saving this child's life, a man walked into the emergency room with a ladder and a fluorescent light with a cigarette dangling from his lips. He saw everything that was transpiring, but ignored it and began the process of doing his job – changing the light, directly over Mei Mei, which was burned out. I had noticed that the doctors had turned her toward the light from the window when they tried the second and third spinal tap. During all the piercing and poking Mei Mei, remained motionless with one exception, her legs jerked whenever they tried to insert the needle into her spine. The doctors and nurses continued to work on her, while the man with the light and ladder tried to position his ladder so that he could reach the light hanging from the ceiling directly over Mei Mei.

It was almost beyond my imagination to imagine this scene, but after five years in China under the socialist system, I had found 'expect the unexpected' to be a good motto.

Finally someone remembered that they had oxygen flowing and that there now was a man present with a cigarette in his mouth. One of the doctors was able to quickly usher the man out the door, to my great relief. The worker did not seem to understand why they wanted him out.

I fully understood. Cigarettes and oxygen can be lethal. What I <u>did not</u> understand is why the doctor then escorted the workman back in – minus the cigarette – and encouraged him to go ahead with his work of changing the light directly over Mei Mei.

While the doctors and nurses worked, this man continued his job of changing the light. One of the nurses persuaded me to help her hold a bed cover over Mei Mei in case the workman dropped anything while changing the light.

It turned out that this was all another one of those wonders of the socialist system. Here is a man who changes lights. He has the proper equipment to do such things. He is an important cog in the workings of the hospital. Apparently they had been trying to get him there to change that bulb for weeks. They were certainly not going to let him get away now.

They finally gave up on the spinal tap, and the crowd around Mei Mei began to disappear until only she and I remained in the room. She looked so small, so innocent, so sick, with tubes and needles protruding from her. Mei Mei still had not moved, but before Dr. Xu left, she assured me that they had stabilized her and that we would just have to wait and see what happened next. They guessed that she might have encephalitis, but said they were not sure. After the blood samples were diagnosed, they would have a better idea.

So much trauma for such a small child! If she lived, how much of this would she remember? What damage had been done to her by this disease? What damage would all this do on the emotions through her growing years? So many thoughts cascaded through my mind as I looked at her and gave thanks for the good news and wondered what the later news would be.

LeRoy eventually returned. I gave him the report.

"I had to assure them we would bring 300 yuan [\$57] later today as a deposit for her treatment," he related.

"They told me what they were doing and probably going

to do. They said I could have some of the money back if it didn't cost that much."

The medicine to stop the convulsions was imported from Japan and was quite costly. Usually a trip to the doctor or for medicine was only $5 to $10, at the most.

After we updated each other, we again recognized how seriously ill Mei Mei was. LeRoy and I both had grim expressions. LeRoy looked more closely at Mei Mei and smiled slightly as he bent over her. She was the type of child that often brought a smile.

As the day wore on, and she remained motionless, and LeRoy and I waited helplessly by her side, we remembered the many smiles she had brought during her brief stay in our apartment.

Chapter VI

New Sleeping Arrangements

As our baby lay seriously ill in the hospital emergency room, I found myself wondering how our family had managed to survive with this child up to this point.

Our Chinese baby amused the Chinese. They were especially amused at the name we had given her – Mei Mei. The *Little Sister* that had entered our lives had taken over the household.

Oh, she was a joy to behold all right and she could flash a smile that would turn everyone's face into 'happy'. However, we had faced so many sleepless nights with her, that LeRoy and I finally resorted to sleeping in different rooms just so we could get some sleep every other night. We moved David out of his room one night and Marianne out of her room the next. That meant that they were sleeping in the same room with Mei Mei every other night, meaning that they were also losing sleep.

Mei Mei was not a heavy sleeper. In fact Mei Mei could be used as a synonym for 'light sleeper.' If you happened to move in the bed at the wrong time of night, she would be instantly awake, and once she was awake, she went back to bed only if you followed all her prescribed procedures. We never knew exactly what those procedures were, because they changed from night to night. I think she was just entertaining herself by watching us sleepwalk from place to place, doing her nocturnal bidding. In reality, it probably had a lot to do with her still not adjusting to the loss of everything familiar.

As she was adjusting to her losses, we were scrambling to find ways to provide for this child. It was fine to sit around and discuss her future and formulate all the "why's and wherefore's," but this child had needs that had to be met, and some of them were very immediate. Her only clothes were filthy. "What does she eat? Where will she sleep? What are we going to do about diapers?" These were all serious questions, needing immediate answers.

The last one was the big question. They did not sell diapers in China, except in stores designed for foreigners, in places overrun with *weiguoren* (foreigners), places like Beijing or Guangzhou.

We lived in a provincial capital, but did not have an abundance of foreigners there; thus there was a distinctive lack of foreign products available. Rolled toilet paper was considered a special find. Toilet paper without bamboo slivers was an especially fortunate find. The foreign community was diverse, an equal mix of Americans, French, and Yugoslavs (before Yugoslavia became involved in their strange version of Russian Roulette). The Americans were in Nanchang to teach English, the French were working on a bridge project and the Yugoslavs were involved with an airplane factory.

We also had a smattering of Brits and Germans, with a couple of Danes thrown in for good measure. We rarely ran across the foreign business community, so we communicated and commiserated and laughed uproariously with the American teachers. Each Saturday we gathered specifically with the other foreign Christians at the apartment of one of the members to encourage, exhort, and build one another up for the next week. It was a time cherished by us all. We sang songs of praise, studied the Scriptures and prayed. We prayed for our students and Chinese friends, for our friends and relatives in America, and we prayed for ourselves. We also discussed the latest finds in this city of over 1½ million people— that semi-soft toilet paper, strawberry jam, sliced bread, a good bicycle for only 330 yuan— with exclamations of delight over any other such 'exotic' finds.

And, like any good American church group, we ate. Sometimes we would all go to a nearby restaurant. Yes, it was a Chinese restaurant. There was no other kind of restaurant available in Nanchang. Often we would have potluck in the home where we were meeting.

After Mei Mei entered our lives, many 'good finds' were located for her, but diapers continued to be a problem.

Chinese babies do not wear diapers; neither washable nor disposable touches their tiny posteriors. Only the four winds, and whatever they sit on, caress their bottoms. They wear split pants, allowing their rear ends to breathe and allowing them to squat anytime, anywhere, to take care of business. (Be careful the next time you're on the Great Wall.) Very young babies have a cloth inserted, but after a few months their bottoms are fully exposed to the elements. Parents spend hours squatting out on the sidewalk with their prodigies balanced on their knees with the baby positioned appropriately, waiting. As they wait, the parent whistles softly from time to time. That is the signal. Pavlov would be proud. The sooner the baby learns the signal, the better. One whistle and out comes the urine once the child is properly trained. It works, but it feels a little strange to be riding down the street with baby bottoms pointing toward you. I felt like a moving target at times.

At night, after the final whistle, the baby gets a cloth applied and then is put down on a pad to sleep, to be awakened during the night and whistled into action again.

By the time they are walking, they know to squat when

they hear the whistle, and are eventually able to squat without prompting.

So, no diapers.

"Can you whistle?" I asked LeRoy that first day. He did not find it to be a very amusing question.

"I can whistle, but I can't squat on my heels like a Chinese and hold that baby out there with her bottom exposed to the world."

Since we did not want to try the Chinese method, but there were no diapers, we improvised— LeRoy's T-shirts became diapers, and we cut up plastic bags as 'rubber pants.' The system worked remarkably well, but LeRoy only had a small supply of T-shirts and he liked to wear them too.

One problem somewhat solved— for the time being.

As more foreigners learned about the newest member of our family they quickly arrived at our apartment, and almost as quickly, were dispatched on their mission, seeking provisions for the baby.

As days went by Chinese friends also heard, and they began to arrive, but much more slowly, since they were concerned what the 'official' word would be concerning a foreigner taking a Chinese baby off the street. As the Chinese arrived, we pumped them for information concerning the care and feeding of a Chinese baby. We knew some things were different about Chinese babies, but we did not know how many things. Do you feed them rice four times a day? How do they sleep best? (This truly was a difference, we found out later). Do they develop more slowly? How old is she, really? We had doctors and others tell us that she was 6 months old; some said 8 months; according to the note found with her in the box, she was a 18 months; a Chinese baby is considered aged one at birth. We could only guess, since no one seemed to have an informed opinion. She did have 4 teeth and could stand when holding on to something.

Thankfully, on that first day, a foreign veteran to the city arrived with her nurse friend. Her friend spoke no English, but our friend Pat King was fairly good in Chinese. Pat had brought the nurse to examine Mei Mei, so for the second time within a few hours, Mei Mei received a full physical. Again, she appeared healthy. The nurse did not tell us anything we did not already know, but it was good to talk to her and have her with us.

China had baby formula, imported from America (pretty expensive) and Germany (not so expensive), and they had powdered milk. Our Chinese friends were able to recommend a formula that did the job.

All in all, Mei Mei had had a most eventful first day in our home, having been poked and prodded by a doctor and a nurse, examined by the *waiban* and a vice-chairman of the medical college, and admired by many, both Chinese and foreign.

The two officials from our school offered the possibility that Mei Mei had been abandoned because she could not speak; we were to hear this theory more for the simple reason that most Chinese did not want to admit she had been abandoned because she was a girl. The Chinese kept saying one phrase about her: "She is so lucky. This baby will go to America; she is very lucky." That is how they surmised the situation.

It had been a bewildering day for her. She had been mostly dumbstruck, showing very little emotion. When she was awake, her eyes wandered from face to face, never seeming to focus on a foreign face, yet spending more time on the faces of her countrymen; ever searching, never sure of her place, yet peaceful. Her only cries were when she wanted her bottle, which she clung to most of the time, and when she needed changing. Diaper-changing was a totally new experience for her, and she was not pleased about it. She wailed during those times and squirmed to get free from our grasp. One of the problems with the diaper-changing was our slowness of hand. Our children were raised on disposable diapers. This folding of T-shirts to fit, jabbing pins in without sticking her or our fumbling fingers became a great feat; and getting the plastic-bag pants on her was all a chore not to be done swiftly. During the day, her only display of emotion came at these times, with one exception.

After Pat's friend finished examining her, Pat and the nurse conversed in Chinese. It was the first time that day that a complete conversation has been conducted in Chinese. Pat continued to talk to Mei Mei in Chinese as she picked her up and played with her. It was then that the mere hint of a smile showed on her lips. But it was quickly gone, and that was all we saw that first day.

Finally, she had a bath, took another long nap, enjoyed her bottles of milk (she refused water or any other liquid) ate just a little food from our meals, and then we prepared her for bed.

She was definitely tired. We put her on our bed with pillows piled around her, gave her the bottle, and quietly retreated to the next room where we all talked in whispered tones. Mei Mei fell asleep with her bottle close by, still over half full.

All the others had left. It was only our family and our teammate, Shelly. We reviewed the marvels of the day and wondered what would happen in the days to come. We finally concluded that we would have no way of knowing anything of the future. We spent time in prayer to put it all in God's hands; then Shelly headed upstairs to spend some time alone.

After we prepared for bed, we gathered in Marianne's room to have our family time; it was a fairly regular gathering to read and pray. At the time, we were reading Charles Colson's Loving God. As our prayers went around, Mei Mei was lifted up over and over again, mainly for her protection and for God's guidance in what we should do with this young life entrusted to us. At university campuses throughout the city the foreign believers were lifting up similar requests. Also, in the small rooms of our Chinese Christian friends, prayers for this baby were being brought before the throne of God. This was only the beginning of a group of pray-ers that would soon spread to various parts of the world.

We closed out our day confident that we had made the right decisions and had notified the right people. We had put the situation into God's hands, and we were waiting for Him to move. We later found out we did not have a full understanding of what it means to 'wait on God.'

"Is she still asleep?"

"Yes, I think so."

"Good, let's get into bed— this has been a very long day, and my emotions are stretched to the breaking point."

When we had move in, we had taken two 3/4 beds, put them together, put a blanket across the space and created a king-size bed. It worked fairly well as long as the beds did not slide apart during the night. That meant you had to sleep easy. However, with Mei Mei now sleeping with us, the extra space was appreciated.

"Now, be quiet," I reminded LeRoy as we eased into bed. "It has been a long time since we've had babies around, and sometimes you get too loud, you know."

"I'm not the one who snores," he said jokingly. At least I think he was joking.

We were feeling very happy and content with ourselves as we settled in for a well-deserved rest. Our minds busily replayed the day and the wonder of the tomorrows, but gradually sleep began its welcomed encroachment on our brains.

"Um, uh, um."

Baby sounds emanated from Mei Mei as she moved around, but her eyes were still closed. She continued to rustle about and stretch. LeRoy and I both were leaning on our elbows watching her. A baby just awakening is almost always a beautiful sight. But she had only been asleep for about an hour, and we were just falling asleep. Still, we watched and sleepily enjoyed the sight.

"Whaa!" was Mei Mei's comment that moved us to action.

I put the bottle in her mouth. She sucked on it a little, but did not want it. She spit it out and ..."Whaaa." She was not happy about something. I tried the bottle again. Instant rejection that time. I finally got up and walked her and sang to her and was reminded of many nights with my own children when they were up for no reason and I was longing for sleep. However, then I had the comfort of a rocking chair. I had learned to sleep in a rocking chair holding a baby. A rocking chair was a luxury we did not have in China. I had never seen a rocking chair in China. Sometimes I wondered how they ever managed to raise children to maturity with no diapers and no rocking chair. A rocking chair was a sign of security to me.

Finally, she eased back into sleep. I crawled into bed, holding her, relaxed for a few minutes with Mei Mei sleeping on top of me, and then gradually eased her to the bed beside me. She slept. We slept.

"Whaa!" erupted in our ears again. We both sat upright in bed, looking for the attacker. "Uh, um, waaa!" Mei Mei explained again. I tried the bottle. She went for it greedily this time.

"What time is it?" I asked drowsily. LeRoy fumbled for the clock, knocking a book and flashlight off the night table before finding the clock.

"It's 12: 30." She had slept for about two hours. This time, she was satisfied with the bottle. As she drank, she breathed through her nose with noises like a 250-pound man snoring. Still, we managed to ease back into sleep— almost. The bottle was less than half full, and she wanted more.

I lifted Mei Mei over to LeRoy. He tried to quiet her as he lay in bed, while I took the few steps to our small kitchen. I heard Mei Mei cranking up the volume and LeRoy doing some type of singing/moaning that did not seem to comfort anyone. He finally got up to walk her, and that made her a little happier.

Meanwhile, I was muttering to myself while it suddenly dawned upon me that we were not properly prepared for this. In America, it would be easy enough; we would simply put some formula in a bottle and mix in water until we had the correct temperature, give the bottle to the baby, and all return to a blissful sleep. In China, all our water must be boiled; after boiling, we keep in thermos bottles to keep it hot. Chinese prefer hot drinks even when it is a hundred and two under the sycamores. They know, through years of study and knowledge accumulated from herbal medicine doctors, that cold liquid colliding with a warm thorax, esophagus, and stomach lining would produce catastrophic conditions within the body. It would be something like a blue Texas norther colliding with a moist warm front that had been sucking moisture out of the Gulf of Mexico for a week. We, being from the southern portion of the U.S. of A., naturally enjoy a tall, cool, ice-laden drink of tea. That would have been a great shock to the Chinese body. We never got to present such a drink to them because Chinese ice tea (green tea) just did not sound right, and ice cubes were difficult to come by. Many of our colleagues still did not own a refrigerator.

So, the water that I had with which to prepare Mei Mei's

bottle was hot. Earlier, we had prepared bottles of formula in advance, but had none ready for now. After mixing the formula, I put it in the small refrigerator and waited.

And we waited; but Mei Mei did not want to wait. She was not thrilled with LeRoy's rendition of <u>Jesus Loves the Little Children</u>, especially since it was coming out as a moan/groan song. He tried another tactic, explaining the situation to her calmly.

"Now, Mei Mei," he began patiently, "there are some things that are out of our control, and this is one of them. You must learn to be patient and wait until the bottle is ready. Now, we must admit that it was our mistake, and hopefully we won't make such a mistake again. You also must learn to be forgiving when people make mistakes. So, now you should practice patience and forgiveness. I don't think you're listening closely, Mei Mei. You need to practice patience, <u>now</u>," and he emphasized the 'now' so that she would get the point.

She did. She kicked those little vocal cords into a high-pitched wail. It was amazing. Dogs started howling out on the street. Thankfully, she could not keep it up at that rate for long, and she eased back into the regular irritating cry. Patience— it is something we must learn, for sure.

I was willing the formula to hurry and cool while LeRoy was having his bonding time with Mei Mei. That must be what it was, because he insisted that he could handle it— even after the dog-calling screech. While he was persisting, so was Mei Mei. He had tried most of the tricks that had worked with our own children, but our sure-fire methods were not available to us in the middle of the night in the middle of the People's Republic of China, so we had to resort to others.

When David was a baby he was a fan of fast rocking. We would hold him in a rocking chair and kick the thing into high gear. I guess he would become dizzy from the fluid sloshing around in his brain or something and finally surrender to sleep. Then we would gradually slow the rocker. He would always let us know if he was not ready to slow down.

With Marianne, it was looking at the stars. She did not like fast rocking, but a walk under the stars would usually bring a calming influence.

If all else failed, a ride in the car would almost always produce the desired results. If that failed, we knew something was seriously wrong. I am sure our neighbors wondered where we were going when we slipped out to the car half-dressed in the middle of the night to take a tour of the town. It was a good time to go out, except you tended to be followed by police cars. The car ride never failed us in inducing sleep.

However, in China— no car, no rocking chair, and, tonight, no starry, starry night. The latter was not unusual in the wet part of China where we lived, just south of the Yangtze River. Clouds were blocking the stars.

Mei Mei was crying, our neighbors were wondering what we foreigners were doing to this poor child, and the dogs were howling, as the bottle slowly, slowly cooled in the refrigerator. I had tested it on my wrist at least five times by now.

We were wondering if the woman downstairs would soon be knocking on our door to rescue this poor Chinese baby. Some still harbored in their minds those stories told about the missionary doctors who were in China years ago. The anti-Christian folks liked to spread rumors that the foreign doctors would take the Chinese children into the hospital to cut them up and use their body parts for potions. If a child went into the hospital and didn't come out, they had all the proof they needed.

Finally, Mei Mei was distracted enough so that she calmed down, and the bottle was ready. She attacked it like a shark going for the kill. We put her back in bed.

"Whaddaya think?"

"I think it's after one in the morning and we should be asleep, but is she going to sleep now?"

We cautiously got in bed again. Mei Mei did not even notice us as she worked on the bottle. After a few healthy slurps on the bottle, she dozed off. We breathed carefully, feeling captives in our own bed, not knowing if we would set her off again by just turning over. But, this time she was asleep, and before long, so were we.

In the next few weeks we developed a sleep pattern that was not to be envied by anyone, but we also both began to really enjoy holding her close, singing her to sleep. We were enjoying falling in love with her. The same was true for David, Marianne, Shelly, and all those who spent time with our baby.

As she molded herself into our family, completely wrapping us up with each of her winsome smiles, we were preparing to give her up. We realized with each passing day that a corner of our hearts would go with her.

Marianne verbalized it in "She's so cute."

David pointed out, "She's the smartest baby in the whole world."

Those were daily utterances from our children. We agreed completely as we groggily passed through each day.

Shelly stopped in a minimum of twice a day to play with Mei Mei. Before Mei Mei, she inquired about our health and well being when she dropped by. Now, she came in the door of our apartment with only the obligatory knock (no waiting — she acted more Chinese every day) and, as she headed for Mei Mei, asked, "How's our baby?"

There she sat— one-foot-nine— eyes that shine; brown on white— a twinkling delight.

When she smiled her face was white teeth, no eyes, and

dimples invaded the fat of her cheekbones. She had a year-round tan. Shelly constantly coveted Mei Mei's brown tummy. We were amazed at her small bottom (typically Chinese). The purple spot on her bottom that marked her as Asian was gradually fading.

She soon became our joy. The baby in the box quickly became the baby in our hearts.

We were a family doing a Chinese shuffle. We abruptly went from a four-person American family making our way in China, with little concern for Chinese orphans, to being controlled by a seven-month-old Chinese baby. On the day I picked her up from the box, she grasped me and we were now returning the grasp. We all clung together as we marked a new pathway for us all.

We were suddenly parents of a baby again— a Chinese baby, in China. Somehow, some way, we had to find the route to get her out of China and into a home where she would be loved. It sounded simple enough. There was a couple that wanted to adopt a Chinese baby girl. We had a Chinese baby girl who needed a home. We make the connection, and everyone lives happily ever after.

If we could keep governments out of it, the above would probably come to pass. But there were four different governments seemingly just waiting to foil God's plan. The governments of the United States and the People's Republic of China were the two biggest stumbling blocks. We were offered several opportunities to quit, but each time, after the tears dried, we brushed ourselves off, leaned a little heavier on God, and plodded on through the bureaucratic mire.

After the evening meal, as a quietness began to settle over our small apartment, I retreated to our bedroom. I prepared her for the night, praying all the while for a full eight hours of sleep, but my pessimistic mind was mumbling, "she'll be awake in two hours." I was developing a bad attitude about sleep— or lack of sleep.

I clicked off the bedroom light and shut the door. I sat in the straight-backed chair at LeRoy's desk. There was just enough room for the chair between the desk and the wardrobe. The battle began as I tried to convince Mei Mei that it was bedtime. She forced herself off my shoulder to remind me that she is Chinese, we are in China, and that she is in control; this part of the battle I enjoyed, because she would usually give in quickly and I would hold her with her head resting on my shoulder as I sang to her. I missed that rocking chair, but I rocked back and forth in the straight-backed chair until she slept in my arms. Then I rested and enjoyed the pleasures of motherhood all over again, and I was most thankful God had placed this child in our lives.

God graciously sent me a Scripture in December, just in time to keep me sane. I claimed it for her and reminded her of it every day.

"Darling, God told you, I will not leave you an orphan. That means that you will never be left without a family. God has prepared a family for you. He has a home for you, and He will take care of you. And we love you. It is safe here with us. We love you. I love you."

Almost every time I told her that, tears would come to my eyes, but I was so grateful that God gave me that verse, because I desperately clung to it in the coming months.

"I will not leave you an orphan" became my battle cry— during the day, at night. I constantly brought this verse before God and reminded Him of what He promised to Mei Mei. It became my lifeline. It was my hope – "I will not leave you an orphan."

Often, after she fell asleep, I would lay her back on my knees and just enjoy the beauty of God's special creation. Such special times. Such times of joy and peace. I gave thanks again that God chose to trust us with this little life.

And then the time came when we were in an unheated hospital room, looking at that "corner of our hearts" as she was filled with needles and tubes and she would not wake up.

*And the Word became flesh
and dwelt among us.*

Chapter VII   John 1:14

Faith Reaching

"What do we do now?"

"Wait."

"We're not very good at waiting," I reminded LeRoy.

"And pray," he added.

We were still alone with Mei Mei in what passed for an ICU on the pediatric wing of Hospital No. 1 in Nanchang, Jiangxi Province of the People's Republic of China.

We held hands and began to pray together. As I heard LeRoy's petition to God, the tears began to trickle down my cheeks for the first time that day.

"Lord, we're sorry if we've messed up and haven't properly provided for this sweet baby you gave to us. You know it's our desire to take good care of her. You know how much we love her already – she has become our child.

"And now, Lord Jesus, we believe and expect for You to touch her and heal her with Your perfect healing. We do claim it and proclaim it in the precious name of Jesus."

"Amen," I sniffed.

A nurse walked in on the 'amens' to check our baby. She folded back the Chinese comforter that swallowed Mei Mei but did ward off the cold. There was no heat in this hospital in December. Very few people in this city of approximately 1.5 million have any heat in their homes or public buildings.

Mei Mei showed no signs of movement. The nurse picked up her tiny legs and allowed them to drop back to the bed. She did it again. We could not imagine what she was doing.

"Her legs have no feeling," she announced in her best English. "They may not work."

We only looked at her and nodded. What is there to say? She checked the IV and oxygen, then covered Mei Mei again and left us alone with her.

Her diagnosis dropped us a little lower into the depths as our emotions reeled.

"What is she talking about?" I responded when she left. "How do they expect her to have any feeling anywhere when she's totally out. They're crazy. When they jabbed her with that huge needle while trying to do the spinal tap, she didn't flinch. Do they expect her to jump off the bed and walk away just because they dropped her legs? I don't believe this! She's not old enough to walk anyway."

My ranting and raving continued for a bit. LeRoy patiently agreed with me, but said very little. I could not tell if he believed what the nurse said. His words sounded positive, but I was not sure what he was really thinking.

As the minutes ticked by, we realized that what was going to be done had been done. We started making arrangements for me to have a more comfortable place to stay so that I could spend the night. LeRoy had tried to call the children and Shelly from the hospital, but never could get the phones to connect. He finally started home, hoping to avoid people we knew, since he did not want to talk right then about everything that was happening. But he did want David and Marianne and Shelly to know something as soon as possible knowing that we had left them under traumatic circumstances. We were still unsure of the outcome, but Mei Mei was receiving care, and they reported her as having been stabilized, so we believed that we had some good news to share and wanted our children to know right away.

LeRoy wound his way through the marketplace, which was fairly calm, because it was *xue xi* time. Chinese believe in setting aside two hours in the afternoon to take a nap. We had found it to be a very good time to get things done, as we usually were not interrupted during the two hours after lunch.

David and Marianne were on the balcony looking toward the direction from which we would most likely return. When they saw LeRoy walking alone, they were unsure what to think. They dreaded the news they might hear, but called out, "Daddy, what happened?"

LeRoy was so involved in thought that he had not seen them there. He offered a wan smile and shouted, "She's doing a lot better. She's in the hospital. I'll tell you about it in the apartment."

Shelly heard LeRoy and met him at the landing on the second floor of our five-floor apartment building. She lived on the third floor of the same apartment complex. The whole story was then replayed for them. They had spent many anxious periods in prayer while we were gone. They had only a few questions and comments about it all; they could only think of coming to see me and Mei Mei as soon as possible.

"You must wait," LeRoy told them, "because she is in intensive care, and the fewer disturbances, the better. As soon as we feel like it's okay, we'll get you up there."

"I'm going to get something to eat and take some up there for your mother." Shelly had already prepared lunch for them. She helped LeRoy prepare a snack, and in a short time he was on his bike, heading back to the hospital.

"How's she doing?"

"The same," I replied, trying to keep a calm facial

expression without belying my fears and the worrisome thoughts that had crisscrossed my brain during the time LeRoy was gone.

"Some of our students have been by." I told him the ones who had come by. "Dr. Wang, the head of the pediatric department, has also been here. She checked Mei Mei and seemed satisfied, even though she didn't tell me much of anything."

"I guess there wasn't much to say."

"She did say that they were unable to get any fluid when they kept on jabbing her with the needle – trying to do a spinal tap. She said the reason they couldn't get any fluid was because there was no fluid in her spine."

We pondered that for awhile, knowing that you have to have fluid in your spine to be alive. It was just another one of those things they told us that made absolutely no sense. We decided to just let it pass. We had no other option.

After awhile I said, "Well, I feel a little better knowing that Dr. Wang knows we're here. I saw her talking to some of the nurses after she left us.

"She did tell me that Mei Mei would get excellent care at minimal cost. She said, 'you are our foreign teachers and are caring for this baby, so she'll get the best care.' She even explained why they couldn't transfer her over to the wing that is used for foreigners and high party officials. And she told me that they'll charge us the Chinese price because she is a Chinese baby."

"It sounds like we're getting the best of both worlds in this one. We have such wonderful *guanxi* – sometimes."

One thing about this 'classless society,' everything is based on class, and if you are a foreigner, you are usually fair game for them to extract as much real money as they can from you. So, this was a great blessing that they were making this exception for us. The head of the department and some of the nurses had been in our English classes at Jiangxi Medical

College. That made the difference. That is *guanxi.*

We had grown to accept and tolerate the usual attitude towards foreigners, within limits, of course.

We used to think that this accepted approach towards foreigners was for foreign businessmen and tourists – that since we were foreign experts, and had come to China to help the people, people would not "run the prices up the flagpole" just to see how high we would salute.

LeRoy had had some dental work done (with great trepidation) at a Chinese Air Force hospital one year. He was taken there because that was where the best dentist in the city worked, and a foreigner must have the best. We did not object, because many times, "the best" just begins to come up to the level that is expected in America.

He was a good dentist, and he did a good job. LeRoy had a root canal job and a partial new tooth done, so that he had a "partial Chinese tooth." Ever since then, he has been telling Chinese that he is part Chinese. They have never been overly impressed, but they usually get the joke and think it is partly funny. This good dentist was also kind when it came time to pay the bill. He said he would charge LeRoy only five times the Chinese price; that normally he would charge a foreigner ten times the normal amount. He told us all of this so we would realize what a wonderful fellow he was and would think highly of him. We did so and were thankful to leave the place paying the stated price. It was still far below what it would have cost us in the U.S. The cost was 130 yuan (approximately $25), including three trips to the dentist.

We do know of foreigners who have paid 10 times the Chinese price for purchases. An American businessman or tourist would proclaim this a great price, but for a foreign teacher trying to make the *renmenbi* (People's money) last, we were not impressed. However, we try not to argue about it with the wrong people. An unhappy dentist could ruin your mouth. It was best for LeRoy to pay up, smile as he walked into the dentist's office, keep his mouth wide open, and try to continue to smile when he walked out.

We were thankful for small blessings at the hospital as we continued to watch, pray, and wait for some movement from Mei Mei. The doctors and nurses told us very little except to say, "She's doing much better."

We waited, we paced the floor, and we watched the Chinese watching us through the little windows in the ICU doors. Chinese find all foreigners very interesting. Many had never seen a foreigner before. The Chinese patients and families who were wandering the halls were not sure what was happening with these foreigners in the hospital with a Chinese baby, but it surely kept their minds off their problems for awhile.

The long day continued, and still Mei Mei lay perfectly still. The only movement was when a nurse would come in to check on her and they would move her. Still no response from her as the winter sun slowly faded into the night.

If we had never been to a Chinese hospital before, we would have been more than a little concerned about the diseases that seemed to visibly crawl up out of the spittoons stationed every 10 to 15 feet along the corridors. We most likely would have cringed every time we heard someone "harking up another luggie", as we used to say. There was no other way to properly describe it – "expelling phlegm" just does not present the proper picture. Getting the unwanted mucus from deep in the lungs early every morning is a very popular Chinese sport. It is seemingly played by Chinese of all ages and all positions. We had to learn to be very careful when we went out in the mornings. LeRoy was riding his bicycle one day when a fellow brought up the phlegmish mixture end expressed it (special delivery) towards LeRoy. He did not do it on purpose; he just did not see LeRoy. The projectile missed only by inches.

We could see the telltale signs of the coagulated phlegm as we walked in stairways or along corridors at universities and, yes, hospitals. Most places, including department stores, had spittoons. Most people would miss, or prefer walls and floors to the spittoons. The signs of shots gone awry were all over the place, but we learned to ignore them. They were still there, but after a while, we just did not care anymore.

Americans passion for cleanliness has not been exported to the majority of the world's people. Inside America's institutions the hall floors shine. I am always amazed when I look into any American school building and see the sparkle from the floor – amazing! Not so with Chinese floors. Many of their floors are made of the same material as those American floors – good, solid granite; but any shine that had been there went away a long time ago. They have an interesting way of cleaning floors that tends to take away the shine rather quickly. They take a mop that has picked up layer upon layer of dirt through the years and sling the mop over the floors. It picks up some dust and lays it back down in the form of mud. And the floors are then pronounced clean.

It was probably not nearly as bad as we assumed. We came from the spic-and-span USA, where there was always a fear that germs might creep up after us from a variety of seats, drinking glasses, mud or anything we could imagine. The Chinese never have had such a problem. Admittedly, they could stand to sanitize more, but Americans usually go two steps beyond clean.

As the night shift began arriving by bicycle to begin their work, we realized that we needed some sort of plan. We were not sure what we could and could not do. We were unsure of the rules and regulations. It is typical for Chinese family members to stay with the one hospitalized. They usually provided the food for them and took care of other needs. But we were unsure if they would allow us foreigners to stay.

Mei Mei had remained motionless, unchanging through-out the afternoon. The only variation had been around 2 p.m., when her fever escalated suddenly. That brought more doctors and nurses scurrying around. But they had her stabilized again rather quickly. After that, she continued to lie in her bundle of covers, looking so frail, so helpless.

I went home for dinner while LeRoy remained with Mei Mei. It was good to just be back at our apartment for a while. Shelly had prepared dinner for us. I was only gone from the hospital about 90 minutes. I returned to the hospital prepared to spend the night.

"Well?" I asked of LeRoy when I returned. It was a hope based on nothing, since I could see she still lay there – no movement, not even a flutter of an eyelid. This uncertainty was beginning to torment us as we were told nothing and just continued to wait and pray.

"They've been in to check on her, but they aren't telling me anything. I haven't been asking, because I didn't like what they had to say last time."

"Why don't you go on home," I suggested to LeRoy. He agreed that he would, after helping me get settled. They had provided a small room just down the hall. It was unique that I could get a room, since almost everyone was in a ward with a minimum of 8 to 12 people. The crowding was exacerbated by all the family members who remained through-out a good portion of the day, with some staying into the night. Mei Mei was the only patient in what we were calling an ICU/emergency room. There was just one type of bed in there, which was really an examination table. However, it was located directly across from the nurses' station. That was the best part.

LeRoy helped find covers for me. I had enough covers to ward off the cold. I was not expecting to sleep very much anyway.

LeRoy checked on Mei Mei on his way out, then rode

home in the dark. He helped settle David and Marianne into bed, let Shelly know that he was going back to the hospital, and returned around 10:15 p.m.

"Well?" he questioned upon his return.

Same question; same answer. "No change."

I went to bed in the room provided. LeRoy said that he was going to stay a little longer and then go home.

"Wake me before you go," I told him. He replied, "Okay," but it sounded more like "You need sleep too, so I won't wake you."

Thus, I was a little surprised to be awakened by him later. I had fallen into a deep sleep, being so exhausted from the events of the day.

He was excited or agitated or something! He was shaking my shoulder rather vigorously. I awoke quickly; my first thought was that something had happened.

I was right. Something had happened. Something very good. When my eyes focused better, I knew it was good news because LeRoy was smiling. He does not usually smile that much when he is still awake around midnight.

He told me that he had returned to check on Mei Mei again before going home for the night. She was still motionless. Still swamped by her covers. Still looking so very fragile. She still had an oxygen tube in her nose and an IV needle protruding from her scalp. No one was in there at the time, so he decided to sit and read the Bible he had brought with him.

As he opened his Bible and read, He believed that God was speaking to him about Mei Mei from Isaiah 42 and 43.

I, the Lord have called you in righteousness, and will hold your hand. I will keep you and give you as a covenant to the people, as a light to the Gentiles, to open the blind eyes, to bring out prisoners from the prisons, those

who sit in darkness from the prison house.
– Isaiah 42:6-7

. . . Fear not, for I have redeemed you, I have called you by your name. You are mine. When you pass through the waters I will be with you and through the rivers, they shall not overflow you when you walk through the fire, you shall not be burned nor shall the flame scorch you for I AM the Lord your God, the Holy One of Israel. Isaiah 43:1-3

As he was reading, a nurse came in. She just glanced at Mei Mei at first; then she looked more closely. She waved her hand over Mei Mei's face. That was when she got LeRoy's attention. He stood up to see what was happening. What he saw almost made him jump with excitement. Mei Mei's eyes were open.

The nurse left the room without saying anything.

LeRoy looked directly into Mei Mei's eyes. He was not sure, but she seemed to be looking at him – focusing on him— something she had been unable to do before.

Within a short time the nurse returned with a warm bottle of milk. She slowly passed it in front of Mei Mei's face. In just a few moments Mei Mei reached up for it. The nurse moved it from side to side. Mei Mei followed it with her eyes and with her hands.

She gave Mei Mei the bottle, and she sucked on it greedily just as she always had. The nurse smiled.

That was when LeRoy came to awaken me.

It was the first time Mei Mei had responded to anything in over 12 hours. We were smiling and saying "thank you, Jesus" prayers, so very excited to see her out of the coma.

She was still hooked up to all the tubes, so we could not hold her, but we held the bottle, stroked her head, and generally had a good time of rejoicing at that hospital after midnight.

After enjoying her bottle for awhile Mei Mei went into a normal sleep. After more giving of thanks, LeRoy rode his bike home. He had a good time of praising God on the silent streets of Nanchang on his way home after one in the morning.

After the nurse came again and gave another smile as if to say, "This is very good," and Mei Mei was sleeping, I went back down the hall to my little room and slept.

We both slept with much lighter hearts even though we did not know what long-term damage there might be. We were so greatly encouraged to see what God had already done in such a short time!

I awoke before six in the morning and went immediately to Mei Mei. There was a nurse with her. They had changed her IV drip and shifted her around some. I did not know what else they might have done with her. However, I was encouraged again when I saw the nurse smile.

LeRoy appeared at the hospital about 6:30.

He did not even have to ask "Well?" this time. He could see by my smile that I was still rejoicing.

The progress continued so quickly that Mei Mei was out of the hospital and off all medication in less than three days.

We had arrived at the hospital with her in a coma on a Monday morning. It was only Wednesday afternoon when she was back in our home. I had spent most of that time at the hospital with her. We had a great time of rejoicing to all be home together again.

On Friday we scrounged a tree from a nearby nursery and decorated it for Christmas. It was Friday, December 6. Mei Mei, being the youngest, was lifted to the top of the tree to crown it with an angel. Marianne did not seem to be bothered at all that Mei Mei had usurped her position as Crowner of the Christmas Tree.

God had sustained us and seen us through one crisis in the life of a very small Chinese girl. It was just the beginning.

*Suffer the little children
to come to me.*
Jesus

Chapter VIII

My First Glimpse into a Chinese Orphanage

Heartache upon heartache was ahead of us, but all we saw at the time were multiple reasons for rejoicing. Mei Mei was home with us celebrating her first Christmas, and she was healthy. There was no sign that she had ever been sick.

We were still unsure of what had happened. Either the translation was faulty or the doctors just never did know for sure. They finally told us that she had encephalitis. We accepted their diagnosis, but really did not care any longer; we simply enjoyed having Mei Mei home and healthy.

The rest of our December would have to be declared uneventful compared to our hospital experience. But, as always in the People's Republic of China, there was much going on all around us. Some we were aware of, and in other cases, we were totally oblivious to what was transpiring. Some of it was visible— but not to our eyes— at the time, and some were battles taking place in the Heavenlies.

We had arrived at this point through a most circuitous route. We had never intended to be involved with a baby. We had had no dealings with orphans prior to this time. Our first three years in China had brought us in contact with many people – singles and families -but we had known nothing of orphans in China. We had never been to an orphanage. We had three children of our own. At that time Chad was 21, David was 15, and Marianne was 11. LeRoy and I were past the age of looking for any more children.

That all changed abruptly with a phone call from Portland, Oregon in the summer of 1991. We were making our way back to China via the "visiting family and friends route." We were in Albuquerque, visiting the couple who had helped train us for China in 1985 – Jack and Carol Nuzum.

Lynn Bonife had tracked us down there and wanted to ask a favor of us.

We could not say "no" to someone who had helped us so many times. She had served as our personnel officer one year in China. That meant that she would arrive in China from Hong Kong bearing goodies such as chocolate, almost-current newspapers and American magazines. We thought of her as some kind of short, female Santa Claus when she appeared each semester of the 1987-88 school year.

Her favor: "Will you see what you can find out about our adopting a Chinese baby?"

"Okay, Lynn, no big deal. We can do that for you."

It was a simple request, and I was willing to see what I could do.

If we had known what it would eventually involve, I am not sure we would have said "yes."

Within a month of our arrival in Nanchang I was asking around about the local orphanage. It was our second year at the medical college in Nanchang, so it was fairly easy for us to settle in. I also knew people who could help me in this endeavor.

One of the interesting aspects about this great adventure, and an example of how one should be careful lest he miss some great plans that God has, is the fact that I voted to not return to Nanchang for the school year of 1991-92. I was outvoted.

One of the temporal aspects of our life in China was that we were given only a one-year contract as a "foreign expert" at the colleges and universities. It is renewable, but we, or our sponsoring organization, and the university must come to an agreement.

Jiangxi Medical College was requesting that our team return. Shelly had already been there for 18 months. We had served one year. The decision was ours. We prayed. Shelly prayed. We prayed some together, and we prayed separately. Nanchang is not a beautiful city. Jiangxi Province is known as one of the poorest in China. Deng Xiao Ping once passed through, called the city leaders together, and told them they had better make improvements in Nanchang "or else".

They did seem to get the point, because the mid- to late-'90s did see some improvements in Nanchang.

But in the early 1990s the few improvements in Nanchang were not exactly shining forth. There was too much dirt and garbage and pollution. You could not see improvements through all that. Nanchang held no particular appeal to me. Daily living there was difficult. I was responsible to provide meals of substance to my family, and it was a task that I did not enjoy. On many days, I had to walk past the woman selling snakes to get to the open market where I bought my eggs, vegetables, and fruit. The snake woman would hold the snakes by the tail. She liked to point them toward me and yell at me whenever she saw me coming. The Chinese bystanders enjoyed the joke. I did not laugh. The snakes were alive, and some were poisonous.

I was ready to depart Nanchang after one year. Most of our American friends were leaving, most to return to the U.S. They had "served their time" in the middle of Communist China and were ready to move on. I agreed with them.

LeRoy was leaning toward returning to Nanchang for a second year. I suggested we let David and Marianne express their opinion, then decide. I was pretty sure I had their vote locked in going my way.

About that time Shelly announced to us that she believed God was leading her to return for another year in Nanchang. That seemed to turn the tide. Our children viewed Shelly as a big sister – one that they liked. It ended up that I was the only one voting to leave Nanchang.

So September 1991 found us back in Nanchang for our second year and found me on my bike heading toward the Nanchang orphanage – a 45-minute ride away.

Tom, who a few months later would open the door to our involvement with Mei Mei, was my escort and translator at the orphanage.

He readily agreed to help me facilitate my friends' adopting a Chinese baby. Tom had been reared in an orphanage. Both his parents were killed during the Cultural Revolution, a ten-year (1966-76) nightmare in Chinese history. He and his sister were elementary age and stayed in the orphanage until they finished school. He did not have a good opinion of orphanages in China. Most children who end up there are infants, and well over 90% die within the first year.

As we cycled along, dodging potholes and water thrown out into the street from nearby shops, Tom filled me in on Chinese orphanages. It was not very encouraging. The closer we came, the more I wished I was elsewhere. I had never had a desire to visit an orphanage. I had difficulty just reading newspapers about tragedies to children without having nightmares. My mind had always been sensitive to horrors done to children.

My plan was to visit the orphanage, get the information for Lynn, and return home. In and out. Speak with one official in an office, then get back on our bikes and return home. I did not want to spend time around the orphanage. Quickly in and quickly out seemed like the best plan to me. In addition, the orphanage was on the wrong side of town. It was not a good place for a foreigner to be seen. Even with Tom escorting me, I entered that area of town with trepidation. It took us almost an hour to bike there.

When we biked up to the orphanage gates, the guard looked intently at us. I am sure the only foreigners he had seen had arrived by car or van. The past spring, we had met some French-speaking Canadians at one of the tourist hotels and discovered that they were adopting baby girls from the Nanchang orphanage.

Tom asked for directions to the office, and we went on to the main building. The man that met us was not the director, but he tried his best to give us the information we needed. He offered us tea, and cigarettes to Tom. Tom did not smoke, which is a rarity among Chinese men, but the offering of a cigarette is very culturally polite. Tom told him that a friend of mine in the U.S. was interested in adopting a baby. The man said he knew only that the orphanage had arranged adoptions for Canadians, but he would find out for us. We thanked him and started to leave.

"Would you like to see the children?" Tom asked.

"No," was my abrupt, final response.

"Why not?" Tom wanted to know. According to his reasoning, you did not go to an orphanage and not see the children.

It was difficult for me to explain to Tom why I refused. I knew I would never be able to put the faces of the children out of my mind. Little did I know that not many months from then, I would be on the inside staring into the little, pitiful faces I had tried to avoid.

"I just don't think it would be a good idea now," I finally managed to offer as an excuse.

He shrugged and got on his bike. I was already on my bike and ready to ride out of the gate.

Besides the information Tom and I received from the orphanage, Pat King had gathered a list of documents required for the government paperwork. Pat had lived and taught in Nanchang for several years and had friends in the Public Security Bureau (PSB). This was the days before e-mail, so I wrote out all the information and mailed it to John and Lynn in Portland, Oregon.

When I sealed that envelope, put the stamps on it, and shoved it into the proper slot at the Nanchang post office, I felt as though I had accomplished the task for our friends. I had done what they had asked. I was finished with orphanages and orphans in China.

Later, at our weekly Bible study in our home, Tom and I shared about going to the orphanage to get the information. Our group included English teachers, a dentist, and a pediatrician. They were all Chinese except for our team. All of them said our friend should not get a baby from an orphanage.

"Get one off the streets," the dentist suggested.

Such a thought horrified me. I could not imagine such a thing. But while that thought was tumbling around in my mind, another in the group agreed:

"Yes, that's right. If you get one off the street, they're fresher. Most of those in the orphanage are dying or have picked up some kind of disease."

"It would be much better for your friends if you got a baby off the streets."

They all agreed. And these were intelligent, professional people. They also knew that it would not be difficult to find a baby abandoned on the streets of Nanchang.

Months later as I stared into the faces of the babies in the orphanage, I fully understood what they meant. When no one responded to a baby's cry, the baby eventually just lay still and stared at the ceiling. They learned very quickly that no one would answer their call, and they were wasting their energy crying. They became very weak and listless. They were giving up.

The group members said we should go look at hospitals, train stations, and bus stations, since those were common places where infants were abandoned. I told them I was not about to go out on the streets looking for a child. All I had agreed to do was get the information for Lynn.

Lynn was a friend of ours who had also lived and worked in China. When she returned to the U.S., she returned to her high school teaching position and married John Bonife. During our first year in Nanchang, we received a letter from Lynn telling us of the birth of their first child, Kristin Diane, in December. Kristin was a Down Syndrome baby and had to undergo open-heart surgery before she was 4 months old. John and Lynn wanted to have more children, but after genetic counseling, the doctors recommended that they adopt. When Lynn contacted me in the summer of 1991, I told her that most likely the only children available would be a girl. She said that was fine and that they would appreciate any information I could find for them.

I was only looking for information but God used His ways to bring Mei Mei into our lives.

After Mei Mei had been in our home for several weeks, we met a businessman at one of the local hotels. He saw us with Mei Mei in the restaurant and asked about her. He was not surprised when we told him her story. He said he walked every morning for exercise and almost always passed a box or basket with an abandoned infant! Evidently finding infants on the streets was not difficult.

We had not asked to enter into this task of sheltering a "throwaway baby." It was not our plan to help this discarded child be adopted. But it had become very obvious to us that God had plans for her, and He was asking us to be obedient to Him. He wanted us to play a part in His plans for this child – His special creation. We could not even begin to imagine what great plans the God of the universe must have for Mei Mei, but He certainly was the One in charge of rescuing her.

We were just functioning – taking baby steps from day-to-day in the hope that we were being obedient to God.

At times, it was especially difficult to discern exactly what we were supposed to be doing toward Mei Mei's being adopted. Normally we took timid little steps, but at one point we went with massive, bold steps.

Walking That Fine Line

W e have discovered over the years that there is a fine line between **faith** and **foolishness**. Perhaps we could think of the "foolishness" more as presuming upon God's goodness.

At times we are not sure if it is demanding of God what we think He should want; or was it us truly seeking His will, then taking the steps of faith? There have been times when we wanted something so very much; and it seemed right, it seemed spiritual, and most would say it was "right," but it did not happen.

After weeks of inactivity on the part of the authorities in Nanchang, and with the Chinese New Year break quickly approaching, we decided to take a "step of faith."

University semesters in China are divided according to the Chinese New Year holiday. We had had a most enjoyable Christmas, the one when Mei Mei crowned the Christmas tree.

As the time approached for the semester break, we were unsure what we should do. Under normal conditions, we would have headed south, to find some solar solace in Guangzhou prior to attending a conference in Hong Kong. We thought about what we could do "legally" with Mei Mei in regard to all this. Actually there was nothing "legal" about any of this, as it was illegal for us to have a "throw-away" Chinese baby in our home in the first place. We had not been informed of this fact yet, though.

But there was nothing "illegal" about all of this, because Mei Mei remained a nonentity. She had no papers – no type of identification at all – therefore she did not exist, according to the Chinese legal system.

After seeking God, we decided to head south, once the semester was complete in early January. We did not ask anyone, we did not seek anyone's advice, we just got our train tickets and headed south. It is cold in Nanchang in the winter, because there is little or no heat indoors. We often taught students who were bundled up and rocking back and forth in their seats, trying to stay warm.

It was warm in Guangzhou. Our favorite place to stay there was the youth hostel. It was across the street from a Five-Star hotel, which was very expensive. But we could afford to eat their hamburgers at the hotel – they were good hamburgers – while staying in the cheap, but clean, youth hostel.

We settled in. Mei Mei loved it. She was able to get out of her layers and was really enjoying her first trip to southern China.

On the trip south ideas had been stirring in my mind.

The authorities in Nanchang are doing nothing," I reasoned. "Every time we try to accomplish anything with them, it's like hitting a blank wall. They are doing nothing, and we are going nowhere. We have made absolutely no progress with the paper-movers. They are moving no paper.

"What if we go to the authorities in Guangzhou and see if they can do something?" I thought. It made sense to me. I decided to approach LeRoy with my new tactic.

"What if we go to the authorities in Guangzhou and see if they can do something?" I sort of blurted it out to see how it hit him.

His quick affirmative response led me to believe that he

had been thinking along the same lines.

"What do we tell them?" was his only question.

We tried to come up with some type of plausible scenario that made enough sense to them so that they would do *something*.

It still came down to telling the truth and letting God sort it out.

We found the appropriate authorities. There was a good English-speaker available. That was a good sign. We explained everything to them.

Their response: "We can't do anything with this baby. She's not from this province. You'll have to take care of everything in Jiangxi Province."

"Well, at least they gave us a verdict right away – no hemming and hawing around with them," LeRoy said, as we exited the government building.

Another bright idea gone by the wayside.

Meanwhile, another problem was looming. We were due to take a ship to Hong Kong in a few days. We had tickets for the overnight boat. However, Mei Mei had no passport, no legal papers of any kind. The school had given us a letter in Chinese with the official school "chop" on it explaining that we were not trying to abduct a Chinese baby. The letter explained that we needed to go to Hong Kong for a conference and wanted to take Mei Mei with us.

It was a "punchless" paper, but it was all we had, especially since the Guangzhou authorities told us to go away.

We began pondering the possibilities. Would the paper from our school make any difference? We doubted it. What were our options? We had to go through Chinese immigration in Guangzhou, and then we would have to go through Hong Kong immigration.

Mei Mei had no identification.

A family council was called.

"First things first; we'll pray," LeRoy announced in our small room in the youth hostel.

We prayed for God's guidance.

"Now, as you know, we tried to get something going with Mei Mei here in Guangzhou. They quickly shut that door."

"God shuts a door, He opens a window," Marianne quickly threw in some of her theology.

"Yes," I replied, trying to sound spiritual. "Well, it certainly looks like any door that might have opened in Guangzhou has been firmly shut. We don't know of any other door to try here."

"We have to take her to Hong Kong with us," David quickly interjected. "There's nothing else we can do."

"Yeah, that's right" Marianne quickly affirmed.

During all this time Mei Mei was enjoying the absence of her heavy clothing, crawling around in her diapers and her own baby-sized T-shirt for a change. We never let her crawl on the floor because they are rarely clean. She was crawling around on us, the beds, anywhere we would let her. She was happy. Usually, if she was happy, we were happy. But a decision had to be made soon, and LeRoy and I were beginning to feel the heaviness of having a question needing an answer, while not knowing the answer.

David and Marianne were at peace with their decision. "We have to take her to Hong Kong." There was no doubt in their minds. LeRoy and I knew that it was not possible without the intervention of God; and yet, what else could we do?

Mei Mei continued to gurgle and burble and enjoy herself – crawling around from one family member to the other.

Even after we spent time in prayer, David and Marianne were still convinced that it was a "go" for crossing over to Hong Kong.

As adults, LeRoy and I had to make the decision. As

adults, we were supposed to be spiritually mature, able to discern the will of God. However, we also believe that God speaks through children and often uses children for His purposes. Even when our children were very young we would ask them to pray for us when we were sick. We believed in the uncluttered faith of a child. We had seen God answer their healing prayers for us.

So, on something this important, we certainly did not want to dismiss what they had to offer simply because of their youth.

"What are our options?" I asked.

LeRoy said we did not really have any options. "We came south looking for a way to make something happen, to get something moving. Nothing is moving here.

"What are we going to do, turn around and go back to Nanchang?" he asked. "Nothing is happening there either."

No one wanted to do that. The bright lights of Hong Kong were just a short ride away. Awaiting us were burgers and fries and pizzas and hot showers any time you wanted.

We were all pointed toward Hong Kong. Mei Mei was definitely included in the "we."

"God has blinded the eyes of officials before. He doesn't change. What He has done before, He can do again," LeRoy reasoned. It sounded as though he were trying to convince himself that abducting a Chinese baby and smuggling her into Hong Kong was the Christian thing to do. I was with him. David and Marianne were way out in front of us on this one. We really did not know what else to do.

As we awaited our fate at the immigration checkpoint, we tried to put the swiftly approaching time out of our mind and enjoy our time in Guangzhou. Mei Mei was certainly enjoying herself.

A few days before our embarking for Hong Kong the couple who had adopted the baby boy from Xian appeared at the youth hostel.

We had many stories to share. It was encouraging for us to hear their story and see the progress that had been made toward adopting this child. They were going to Hong Kong with him. Of course, they had official papers for him. He was a documented child.

There was no record of Mei Mei anywhere. And China is a country that closely documents each of its citizens. Mei Mei did not exist, according to the government of the People's Republic of China. Mei Mei was a non-person, a nonentity. But there she was crawling all around us demanding our attention, as any baby does. All four of us made sure she received plenty of that attention. She certainly was not feeling abandoned at this time. She was loved. Yet, to the government of the People's Republic of China, there was no such person.

The day dawned when we were expecting to see God do the miracle of the shutting of eyes. It was a cooler day; a cold front had passed through overnight. We were ticketed to board a ship for Hong Kong at nine that night.

A lot of praying took place that day, and there were still doubts about what we were to try to do. To the world, it would all seem a very foolish idea; but we were trusting and believing in the God who made the world.

We were packed early. LeRoy walked out the door about mid-afternoon. He said that he was just going for a walk. That was his way of saying that the pressure was too much right now.

I spent most of my time playing with Mei Mei. David and Marianne were across the street at the hotel playing one of the favorite family games – watching tourists and trying to guess their nationality. Many tourists stayed at the Five-Star hotel.

It was almost dark when LeRoy returned to our room. He seemed ready to go, as if some "official decision" had been made. He told me that he had been at the hotel too. He had been to the floor that opens outside where they had outdoor activities for their guests.

No one was there, so he said he stayed there and prayed for clear guidance as he watched the sun settling over the Pearl River.

"I can't say I got any clear leading from God," he reported, "but I definitely believe that we should take steps forward – knowing that God will direct our steps. We can't accomplish anything just sitting and waiting. There comes a time to go forward. Now is that time."

He was not going to get any argument from me or our children. We were anxious to get going and see what God would do.

Faith or foolishness? We were stumbling all over that fine line at this moment.

We took a taxi to the dock. We all crammed into one taxi, with our luggage crammed in with us.

We made one concession to the possibility that Mei Mei might not be allowed on the ship; we reserved our room at the hostel for one more night.

We had debated about hiding Mei Mei under a blanket and carrying her onto the ship as luggage. We knew we would have to drug her to do that. She would not quietly submit to having herself wrapped in a blanket and carried around like a suitcase. She had freely expressed her opinion on such matters in previous months. We certainly did not expect her to become baggage now.

We decided to approach the immigration official boldly and let God be in charge. We, of course, continued to plead with Him to "blind seeing eyes" for this moment.

We got our luggage out of the taxi, put Mei Mei in her little stroller and boldly went toward the building housing the immigration checkpoint for the ship docked just a few steps beyond.

It was evening at this point. The ship was set to sail at

9 p.m. We tried to time it so that we would not be too early, yet we did not want to be very late.

We strode boldly into the brightly-lit building and lost a little of our faith. We decided to sit down until the crowd thinned.

"So many bright lights," I thought. Usually Chinese places are not so well lit.

"Why so many bright lights here tonight?"

I was praying quietly as we approached the immigration booth. David and Marianne went first. The official smiled at them as he looked at their passports.

"Going to Hong Kong?" he asked in English. They nodded their heads and replied quietly, "Yes."

"That's good," he replied as he stamped their passports and waved them through. I could not tell if anyone else was praying or what anyone else was thinking as LeRoy and I approached the counter – with Mei Mei in the stroller. I could feel my heart beating. I was not actually frightened. I am unable to describe my feelings at that time. It was show time – time for God to do His stuff.

Mei Mei was in the stroller, below the officer's counter. Maybe he would just fail to notice her at all. Maybe he would think I was pushing some baggage instead of a Chinese baby. Maybe. However, I doubted that he could miss that I was a Western woman and that in that stroller was an obviously Chinese baby.

Well, he would have to be more observant than some people are, of course. I was holding Mei Mei in an elevator in a Nanchang hotel one day when a Westerner got on. We smiled at each other and said "Hello." He commented something about *my* cute baby. I gratefully acknowledged his compliment. He was looking right at us and made the comment, "All babies look alike."

I did well to make it until he left the elevator before I burst out laughing.

The immigration official was making small talk with LeRoy. They almost always induce you to say something. I suppose it is part of the check. I only heard meaningless words being spoken. I was looking down and praying.

He waved LeRoy through. He stayed there, and the official did not dismiss him.

I gave him my passport. He asked me a question. I answered. He stamped my passport, but did not wave me through.

"May I have the baby's passport please?"

I wanted to say, "What baby?" but I could see that his eyes were open, and he was leaning over the counter to look at Mei Mei. He made no mention of her being Chinese. He just requested her passport.

"We don't have a passport for her just yet," I quickly answered. Lying has never been part of my makeup. I would always get caught.

LeRoy stepped up and began to explain a little further. I thought that he was not making much sense.

I interrupted him. "We have this paper from the school where we are foreign experts," I offered.

"We are going to Hong Kong for a conference for just 10 days, then we'll be returning to China," LeRoy added. "We are working with the government in Nanchang to get all the official papers but we don't have them yet. That paper from our school explains everything."

The officer looked closely at the paper. It looked very official. He read it carefully, then said, "Wait here."

We waited.

He was gone far longer than we thought he should be. Hope began to build within that we would make it through on the flimsy strength of the paper from our school.

David and Marianne were in another waiting room just on the other side of immigration, but we could still see them. They were watching intently. Mei Mei was content.

She was smiling at anyone who approached her. She was playing her part perfectly.

He returned with his supervisor. At least, we assumed it was his supervisor. Now everything had to be translated from Chinese to English and English to Chinese.

We thought perhaps the complication of translation might be an advantage.

The supervisor spoke a brief sentence in Chinese. It was translated:

"Where's the baby's passport?"

We took off into a rush of English explaining everything all over again, even though the man translating already knew all of it. I guess we thought that if we talked fast enough and long enough, we could convince them that Mei Mei should take a little ride on the ship to Hong Kong that night.

After patiently listening to our explanation again, the man translated our speech with about five words. We thought he said, "She doesn't have a passport."

That set us off on another explanation, basically repeating everything.

"Please have a seat in here," the officer told us as he pointed to the waiting room where David and Marianne were. They wanted to get us out of the way. Apparently they did not know what to do. But we believed that it was quite positive that they had not simply turned us away.

Hope was building. We were praying. Mei Mei was smiling.

We whispered among ourselves, saying encouraging words. David and Marianne still looked confident. I was beginning to believe that it would happen. LeRoy was saying positive words. "They've let us come this far. That's a good sign. They're talking to someone about this. They have taken it to a higher level. That's all good."

I agreed with everything he said.

The last of the passengers passed through immigration

and went quickly onto the ship because it was nearing nine – the departure time. We were anxious to board the ship and settle in.

The departure time came and went, and we were still waiting. Some of the passengers were looking over the railing on the ship, waiting to cast off. By this time we had wandered out onto the dock. We were getting near the gangplank so we could board as quickly as possible.

We were walking on the dock, praying, trusting, and believing.

Mei Mei was still being the perfect baby.

"They can't turn us away because she's a nuisance," I thought. "This is the best she has ever been."

Suddenly I heard someone call, "LeRoy."

LeRoy had walked off about 20 yards. I could not imagine who would be calling his name. Then I saw him. It was another American teacher that we had known for a few years. However, we did not know he was on the ship.

"I saw you waiting down here," he said. "Is there a problem?" He was one of those looking over the ship railing, waiting.

By now the ship's departure had been delayed for an hour while the immigration officials apparently conferred with other officials over the phone. At least, that is what we assumed they were doing. We only knew that they had told us to "wait" again and had disappeared into their offices.

"No, no problem," LeRoy told him. "But we could sure use your prayers."

LeRoy then told him briefly what was transpiring. He stayed with us on the dock and prayed with us. He seemed very positive that Mei Mei would be allowed on that ship.

As the minutes ticked by – now approaching 10:30 p.m. (almost 90 minutes past the departure time) – we looked upon this delay as most positive.

"They must be seriously considering this," I said.

We all agreed that it was a hopeful sign, especially if they were willing to delay the ship for so long.

We continued to walk and pray and encourage each other. Mei Mei continued to be all smiles. By this time she had been given the moniker "The Amazing Mei Mei" which had been abbreviated to "'Mazin' Mazer". That is what she was to us – amazing.

We saw the captain coming down the gangplank. He did not look happy. He strode purposefully into the building, looking as if he were ready to make things happen.

He must have done so, because the immigration officials followed him back out.

"You are not allowed to take this baby to Hong Kong," the supervisor told us through another interpreter. "She has no passport; she has no papers of any kind. It is against Chinese law for you to take her out of China."

We said nothing. What was there to say?

Amidst tears, I quickly took Mei Mei's bag and stuffed some of my clothes inside. After tight hugs and quick kisses, I watched my family board the ship.

There I was, feeling like a fool: a foreign woman holding a Chinese baby while the Chinese officials stared and wondered what I would do next.

Joshua 1:1-9

Chapter X

Our Daily Lives

It might appear that everything we did during the school year of 1991-92 revolved around the life of one Chinese baby. That would be fairly close to correct.

But our daily lives continued – with all that this meant in the People's Republic of China. For our family, it meant home-schooling our children, teaching English at the medical college, interaction with colleagues and students outside the classroom, two weekly Bible studies in our home, and just the daily existence of cleaning, shopping, and preparing meals.

David and Marianne continued their lessons. They worked at home, with a few outside projects to keep school more interesting. David was at the high school level, and it was becoming more difficult to stay up with him and keep him interested. Marianne was charging through her sixth grade workbooks – needing only a little motherly prodding and assistance.

I had never planned to home-school my children. It was becoming popular in the mid-80s, but I was not interested in doing so at that time. I had told people that as long as there was a good Christian school available, I would never home-school. I have heard people say, "never say never," because that very thing is what will happen. So in August of 1985, we were living in the middle of China in Wuhan, a city of 4 million people, with no Christian school and not even an English-speaking school. All three of our children, Chad, David and Marianne, were with us that year. All three needed to continue their education.

Many times I have had to thank God for his preparation in my life when I was not even aware I was being prepared. Prior to moving to China, I was teaching elementary classes at a Christian school. Before finally obtaining my college degree in sociology, I had been an education major and had taken all the necessary courses required for teaching. In fact, I lacked only my student teaching and two courses to be state-certified at that time.

As we had prepared to move to China, I gathered all the books and materials I would need to teach kindergarten, fourth grade and ninth grade and mailed it to our new address in Wuhan in July 1985. We were told that packages sent by surface mail would take 3 months. I wanted our children to adjust to life in China before beginning their classes, not to mention the fact that shipping such a load airmail would have cost enough for us to eat on for the next three months.

The book box arrived April 1986, nine months after I had mailed it in Texas. We were not prepared for that. Another of China's little surprises! One of our fellow Americans in China our first year used a certain word over and over when we were faced with any inadequacy. She always said, "Improvise."

With no textbooks, our first experience in home schooling definitely was one of improvisation. Teachers will sympathize with me knowing that I was teaching three very diverse grade levels. Even though I had only one student in each grade, I still had to make lesson plans for each subject.

Since Chad was high school level, it was imperative that he be diligent in his work. Thankfully, from among the foreign teachers in Wuhan, we were able to gather a small library of classical books. LeRoy had Chad read about 20 books and write a short essay on each. When our textbooks finally arrived, I just handed the books to Chad and David and had them read them. Marianne had attended a pre-kindergarten program before leaving for China; so we did very little in regards to her education.

All three children were sent to Chinese school a half day at the beginning of our first semester. Chad was the only successful one in this respect. He attended classes in English, art, and sports. David took math, music, and sports, but had a very difficult time.

Chad had an English-speaking teacher (the teacher of English) and some of his fellow classmates spoke limited English. David had no one. His teacher was a man and had no idea what to do with a blonde, blue-eyed foreign child in his classroom. So he decided to just ignore him. David's seatmate would try to keep David on the right page in the math book. Soon David was inventing all kinds of health problems as excuses not to attend classes at the Chinese school. In addition, winter was coming on, so we decided to take him out of classes. There was no heat provided for public buildings or for most homes in cities south of the Yellow River. We began to wear several layers of clothing as our Chinese neighbors did, but it was difficult for an American child who was not accustomed to attending classes in freezing classrooms.

Marianne's attendance at Chinese kindergarten lasted only two days. I went with her. She practically stayed glued to my right thigh. It would not have been so bad if the older woman who was the teacher's aide had not insisted on picking Marianne up every time I tried to involve her with the other children. The woman was fascinated with the foreign child in her midst, and she was making the most of it. That was just one of the terrifying experiences our children faced because the majority of Chinese had never seen a foreign child.

I think Marianne was probably traumatized from an experience we had shortly after arriving in Wuhan. Our school officials took our whole family to a bank to sort out our money. At first, the school officials seemed to be squiring us around to show off "their" foreign family.

A woman suddenly appeared from behind a curtain at the bank. This bank resembled those you used to see in American Westerns. She came from behind a curtain, walked straight over to Marianne, quickly picked her up, and whisked her behind the curtain. We were all in shock initially, so no one moved. Then Marianne started crying, "Mama!" at the top of her lungs.

The lady thought that was great because now she thought her "prize" also spoke Chinese. "Mama" is also used in Chinese for "Mother."

We finally started our feet moving and chased through the curtain. On the other side, the woman was showing off a screaming Marianne to her colleagues. I was able to retrieve my baby and calm her down. We all finally calmed down when we saw that the woman was just being friendly – a little too friendly for us foreigners, brand new to the country, and exceptionally friendly, as Marianne saw it.

The fact that all five in our family have blue eyes was also an attraction. We were told that Chinese believe that blue eyes are "mystical."

David's blonde hair was also a big attraction. He was nine years of age, when we first entered China. His hair then would be described as "cotton-top." Imagine a blonde head in a sea of black hair. It was like a fishing cork bobbing on the ocean. One time he received more attention than usual. We were walking down the street in Wuhan when a man backhanded David across the side of his head. We did not even see it happen. David was suddenly crying, holding his head and telling us what had happened. There was no recourse on a crowded street.

We assumed that the man had some sort of mental problem, because usually the Chinese would only stare and point. We were walking entertainment on Chinese streets, and free entertainment, at that. All we had to do was stop on the street for a few minutes and we would gather a crowd.

LeRoy often said, "If I charged just a nickel for every Chinese that stops and stares at us, we'd have enough money to support our whole family for a year."

By the time we were beginning our second year in Nanchang in 1991, we had refined our home-schooling program and had worked out a smooth routine. Chad was back in the U.S. He had graduated from high school and decided to join the American workforce. David was working on tenth-grade material and Marianne was doing sixth-grade work. For David's high school level, we tried to provide outside experiences to complement his education. We had no laboratory equipment, but David wanted to do some of the experiments in his science book. LeRoy and I discussed the possibility of capitalizing on the fact that we were teaching at a medical college. LeRoy was teaching a class of doctors from the hospital affiliated with our college. Some would be the very ones who would later help us when Mei Mei was hospitalized. LeRoy broached the subject of David's using one of the college's labs to do an experiment. They were more than willing to help us and found a research scientist who spoke English.

The scientist was doing DNA research. We had chosen a fairly simple experiment that involved preparing a slide of chicken meat in order to study the cells. We gave the book to the scientist so he could prepare. David went at the appointed time for his lesson. The doctor had bought a live chicken in the market and proceeded to kill it and prepare the flesh for the slide. David received quite a bit more of an educational experience than we had planned. How many students have a research scientist teach their lesson on cells? After the lesson, the doctor offered David the chicken to take home to cook and eat. David politely declined.

Another provision for our children's education came from the other foreign teachers and their spouses. The husband of a college teacher was an inventor and computer whiz. He taught David computer programming one afternoon a week. Another spouse was a nurse and offered a one-day workshop on first aid.

Besides their American educational activities, we also hired teachers to give the children lessons in Chinese language. David had been interested in martial arts, and we found the appropriate teacher for him.

Much of my time was spent being mother/teacher/administrator for our family.

I also taught part-time at the medical college. LeRoy was teaching full-time and involving himself with students in extracurricular activities like attending their parties and playing basketball. It was good that he was taller than most of his students, because by then he was in his mid-40s, playing against 20-year-olds. Of course, being taller did not always help, as he would frequently get elbowed in the ribs. He struggled on.

He once had a student ask him, "Why aren't you any better in basketball? After all it is an American sport."

Young Chinese men, especially college students, have made basketball a passion. They know all about the NBA. They play on outdoor cement courts with netless rims. They play in the rain and the cold and the blowing wind. They love the game. But it is an American game. So this college student could not understand why LeRoy's skills were so limited. Chinese often ask very blunt questions like this.

"What did you tell him," I asked.

"I explained that I'm old – that seemed like a good answer since they are supposed to respect the elderly. I also told him that basketball was not a sport that interested the young lads of Texas in my growing-up days."

"And, did he accept that?"

"He looked at me like I was searching for excuses. Of course, he was right."

LeRoy was just happy to be able to survive on the concrete courts. David would also participate, and he would be knocked around too. But, it was a good way to interact with our students.

We also had a Bible study group that met weekly in our home. There were 4-6 members – all new Christians who knew very little of the Bible, but who were hungry to know more. They had been meeting with Shelly before we arrived. We were able to continue that study, and members of that group became some of our closest friends. Tom was in the study group. The pediatrician who first attended Mei Mei was in the group, as was her boyfriend that she liked to hit. I was also discipling two Christian ladies on a weekly basis, studying Genesis.

Of course, in the middle of all this, we were involved in a full load of teaching English classes at Jiangxi Medical College. We wanted to do a solid job of teaching our students. They ranged from 16-year-old first-year medical students to doctors/nurses/ medical technicians in their 30s, 40s, and even a few in their 50s. Our oldest students had a good command of the Russian language. Knowledge of that language meant nothing to them now, and they were struggling hard to learn English.

Along with all of this mix, we had daily living – and that alone was often a challenge – other interesting challenges were brought our way as well.

Just a few weeks after Tom introduced Mei Mei into our lives, he introduced us to a 16-year-old girl from the countryside. Her name was Liu Hua Lan.

Tom had just been introduced to Liu Hua Lan himself. Tom had helped several different doctors with English – translating documents or helping them understand a medical article in an English-language publication. Because of that he had *guangxi* with several doctors.

Hua Lan's parents had tried to get their daughter into the hospital in Nanchang. They were told that there was no room. They had no contacts and were therefore unable to obtain an appointment to see a doctor. Tom heard of their plight through a friend of his. He made it his business to find them and talk to them.

The parents had come from a city approximately 100 miles outside the capital, looking for better medical care.

Tom talked to them and then talked to some of his friends, and in a short time he had Liu Hua Lan in the hospital. The doctors there reported that she had cancer in her leg and that the prognosis did not look good. That was when Tom told our Bible study group about her.

"We often read about God doing miracles in the Bible," he began. "We see that all the time as we read about Jesus."

We all agreed that this was so.

"Does God still do miracles? I have never seen one." And then he told us the story of Liu Hua Lan. He concluded by saying, "I want to see God do a miracle in her life."

When Tom involved himself with people he really got involved. He wanted this family to know Jesus, and he wanted to see Hua Lan healed.

We prayed for her that evening. After our prayer time, LeRoy quietly asked,

"Would it be all right for us to go see her in the hospital?"

"Sure," Tom replied.

"What do you think about our going and praying for her to be healed?"

He offered this in a way that would leave the decision up to them. This was something that they had never done. Plus they were going to be walking into a ward where there were other people. And Chinese are always curious. For LeRoy to walk in with them would naturally draw additional attention. LeRoy was asking our Bible study group to publicly show their faith. For us, praying for someone in public could result in our being asked to leave the country. For a Chinese, it could mean loss of jobs, being ostracized from their family, being beaten after being arrested, or possible prison time.

We always approached such things with all of the above in mind. We also always let the Chinese believers make these decisions, knowing that it was they who would face many more difficulties.

According to the Chinese constitution, there is freedom of religion in China, but it must be adhered to according to the current dictates of the government; local government officials often have various interpretations of national law.

You are not allowed to publicly proselytize, and you are not allowed to tell, teach or otherwise instruct anyone under 18 anything about religion.

We were about to violate both.

We decided that it would be unwise to take Mei Mei to the hospital so she and I remained at home. David and Marianne did not go either. They would not only have had all eyes focusing on our group, but they probably would have caused a great commotion. Everyone would have been trying to get a look at them.

Tom had gone ahead of the group to talk to Hua Lan and her parents – to basically obtain their permission for us to pray with her. They were people from the countryside who had no belief, but they were becoming desperate to see their daughter healed. Doctors had offered them little hope.

Our group entered the hospital as quietly as possible. LeRoy had dressed as inconspicuously as possible. He tried to look more Chinese than usual, and he quickly went to

Hua Lan's bedside. Her parents were there, as well as an uncle and one or two of her older siblings.

Tom served as interpreter. Introductions were made. The parents seemed happy to see LeRoy.

"Is it okay if we visit with Hua Lan?" LeRoy asked the parents.

"Oh, yes, that's fine," they replied in Chinese.

There was general talk of getting to know each other a little better, and then LeRoy had Tom ask her, "Do you know about God?"

She said that she had heard some things, but did not really know anything about God.

"Would you like to know about God?" he asked.

"Yes," was her quick reply.

LeRoy gave her a simple presentation about God and told her about Jesus. Tom was interpreting throughout and probably throwing in any additions that he thought she needed to help her – a teenage girl from the countryside – to understand that Jesus had come to die for her so that she might have life everlasting.

For some reason, she seemed to fully grasp the concept right there – right then.

Our experiences in the past had almost always been to receive a good laugh from people when we told them that we believed in God. Others were astounded that we – people with college degrees and from the most technologically advanced country in the world – could believe such drivel. Only occasionally one would listen seriously and then just as seriously reply, "I'll think about that." We believed that we were making inroads whenever we heard a Chinese say, "I'll think about that."

LeRoy was very surprised when Hua Lan answered, "Yes, I understand."

He had Tom present the Gospel to her again. He watched her as Tom repeated it all. Her eyes responded that she understood.

Of course her parents, uncle, siblings, and the person in the next bed, and their family members were all hearing this.

"Do you understand what we're telling you about Jesus?" LeRoy asked her again.

"Yes."

"Would you like to know Jesus personally? Would you like to become a member of God's family?"

"Yes."

LeRoy, through Tom, then led her in the prayer of salvation.

There, in that hospital bed in Nanchang, Jiangxi Province, a very sick 16-year-old girl was born into the Kingdom of God.

"Jesus is the one who brings life to us," LeRoy continued after the prayer, "and He is also our Healer. He is the Great Physician."

He then gave her some healing Scriptures that Tom had translated into Chinese.

"Read these every day. Read them three times a day. Believe that Jesus – who is the Mighty God – can heal you.

"We will pray these same Scriptures for you, believing with you that Jesus will heal you."

About that time her uncle asked, "Do you have to be sick to know God?"

"No," Tom answered. "God wants you to know Him and to know His love."

He nodded. That was all he wanted to know.

Our group left shortly after that, but they left rejoicing.

Hua Lan and her family had become a part of our Christian family. One, two, or more of our group would go and visit her from time to time.

At one point, the doctors decided to perform major surgery on Hua Lan, in which they actually removed the bone from her left leg, did treatment on it, and then replaced it. She was in an almost full-body cast after surgery.

That of course made things even more difficult for her. During her hospital stay she remained in contact with her main teacher and her classmates from school. She showed us letters that she was writing to her teacher to share with her classmates. In the letters, she was telling them about Jesus and what a difference He had made in her life.

Our group decided to help Hua Lan celebrate her first Christmas. Everyone had purchased one or more presents for her, and we merrily headed for the hospital on Christmas Day. When we arrived, we found out that the officials had decided our group had been there too many times. We were refused entrance. They would not let us even enter the hospital grounds, much less go to Hua Lan's room.

Different members of our group tried to make some headway with the officials, but we were turned away along with our presents for her. We never did get to celebrate Christmas with her. We kept our foreign faces away from the hospital, because we were concerned we were drawing too much attention.

Our Nanchang days were full, and we were most assuredly ready for the winter break that took us to sunny Guangzhou— and found us facing another crisis on the dock of the Pearl River.

Chapter XI

Abandoned

Faith – foolishness – stupidity – abandoned –
forsaken – left behind – alone – very alone –
answers – many questions— alone

There was an aching in my heart as I sought answers. To be so ignorant of God's will at this time was proving to be almost more than I could stand. I was not bearing up well as I stood on that dock in Guangzhou and waved goodbye to my family.

"I will never leave you. I will not forsake you." I repeated those words over and over under my breath. I *was* feeling forsaken.

"I will never leave you. I will never forsake you."

The workmen on the dock and the immigration people were quietly ignoring me. Most likely, they were willing me to disappear. Foreigners have been known to cause scenes and make life difficult for everyone else when they do not get their way. They were hoping I would just disappear instead of exploding in such a way that would cause them trouble.

I honestly did not know what to do.

My family was sailing away to the bright lights and Western comforts of Hong Kong. I was alone on a dock in Guangzhou, and it was getting darker there by the minute as they turned the lights off. They were closing down for the night.

Mei Mei was perfectly content. She was close to me and was secure. I had her strapped to me by a cloth baby carrier that is very common in southern China. She was facing me. When she tired, she would simply lay her head on my breast and rest.

I did not know where to go for comfort. I truly knew the feeling of being deserted. My family was sailing away; we had not seen "eyes blinded" so we could walk through immigration and onto the ship.

I was already doing a mental search to see what we could have done wrong. Was keeping our hotel room an act of unbelief? Did we fail in that we did not fully trust God?

Was this His plan to keep us from even more trouble when we docked in Hong Kong?

I only knew the questions. I found no answers while standing there on the dark dock in Guangzhou.

"Well, Mei Mei," I sniffed. "We have a room. Let's see if we can find a taxi and get back to the hotel. There's certainly no reason to stay here."

She smiled at me.

I gazed toward the ship slowly slipping farther away from me and that sinking feeling of being abandoned almost smothered me. I waved toward the ship again and turned to leave.

Abandoned.

By the time we returned to the hotel, we were both exhausted and ready for bed. Before retiring, I made a mental checklist of what needed to be done the next day. I had to get a train ticket to Nanchang, contact someone to meet me, and figure out how I would get to the train station late the next evening with all of Mei Mei's paraphernalia. The baggage did not seem like much when I had LeRoy, David, and Marianne to help. I had a suitcase, a baby stroller, and a baby. I could not use the stroller because of all the steps at the train station. I would have to strap her to me and then carry the suitcase and stroller through crowds of rushing people pushing and shoving their way to the train. I was so tired I fell into a deep sleep, as did Mei Mei – thankfully.

The next morning was another beautiful day in southern China. I just wish my outlook had matched the day. The first order of business was getting a train ticket. It sounds like an easy assignment, but the Guangzhou train station is an infamous place. We have heard several personal tales from our friends. One was jerked back by her neck and choked as a thief tried to steal a necklace that would not easily break. Another friend was standing in the long, sweltering line at the station thinking he had his billfold secure in his front pocket. He was practicing the art of patience and experiencing the cultural closeness of the Chinese people. That means he was jammed in the line with hundreds of people, waiting, waiting, and wondering if the line was actually moving. As he was waiting, he suddenly realized that someone was cutting his front pocket to get to his billfold. He managed to thwart the thief and was thankful that the man's razor did not slip.

The Guangzhou train station: not a place I wanted to go; and how was I to manage fighting through the masses to the ticket window with Mei Mei and all our baggage?

I decided to try a special office where they would sell certain tickets on certain trains for foreigners. I prayed that I was that certain foreigner who could get a certain ticket on the certain train that *I* wanted to be on.

First problem: I had not chosen the correct train.

"No tickets to Nanchang," the man said very distinctly as he looked at me with a bored expression. I gave him my best smile, readjusted Mei Mei on my hip, and stood my ground.

I could not go anywhere else. I had nowhere else to go.

The ticket seller was ready for me to move on – get out of his window – so he could deal with the next person. But I could not give up so easily. I remembered the train to Shanghai, which stopped at a small station approximately 30 miles south of Nanchang. Many foreigners take the train to Shanghai. Surely he would have a ticket for me on that train. Bingo! I had finally picked the right train.

"Okay, there are tickets available on that train," he said, still maintaining his bored expression. I smiled even more brightly.

Then, I bowled another strike; I picked the right kind of ticket – soft sleeper— and he would sell me a ticket that would let me off just south of Nanchang. I was thankful and almost leaned over and kissed his hand. Of course, I realized that the only ticket he would sell me or any other foreigner, at this window, would be the most expensive – the soft sleeper. There are four kinds of tickets available on Chinese trains. A person can buy a "get-on" ticket and hope to find a seat that someone has vacated or buy a hard-seat ticket. There are two types of sleeping accommodations for long-journey trains. The one we usually tried to buy was called hard sleeper. There were six bunks in each cubicle with three on each wall. The soft sleeper compartment has only four beds, two on each wall, and a door for privacy.

I was able to purchase a ticket for the train that left that very night. I was feeling better already. I had done something positive, and with only a little difficulty— a major accomplishment in China.

When we returned to the hotel, I checked out, and then we took a taxi back across the city to a hotel directly across a main thoroughfare from the train station. I arranged with the management to rent a room for a half-day rate. We would be able to stay in the room until 6 p.m. This development was a major blessing; however, I did not know what Mei Mei and I would do for the 4 hours before our departure time or how we would get to the station; but I would just have to take one thing at a time. I was too emotionally spent to worry about everything!

Our experience at the train station had proved that God had not abandoned me or our precious "daughter."

I was feeling so much better after Mei Mei's nap (I joined her in napping) that we took a little excursion. The weather was still very pleasant, so we walked up to a small store and bought some *suan ni* (yogurt). It was one of Mei Mei's favorites, and I found it very refreshing also.

As we were passing through the hotel lobby on our return, I recognized a couple who were checking in at the main desk. They were American friends also teaching in China. They had traveled to Guangzhou and were going to stay a couple of days before going on to Hong Kong to attend the same conference that LeRoy would be attending— the one I was supposed to have attended. Timing is always an important factor with God, and this incident was no exception.

After our greetings and my brief explanation of everything that had happened, Gayle said, "You and Mei Mei come stay in our room until it's time for you to go to the train."

"That would be great," I quickly replied.

"And we can help you get to the train station," David offered.

"That would be great," was my agreement again. They probably thought my vocabulary had been stunted by too much baby talk; but I was so thrilled at what I was seeing God do through the sudden appearance of this couple that it was difficult for me to say much else.

Instead of sending one guardian angel to help us, God had sent two!

The Wilsons had heard through the "little alley" that the Ramseys had a Chinese baby. The term "little alley" in Chinese is equivalent to the American term "grapevine."

The Wilsons were anxious to hear the whole story, and I was thankful to have someone to tell it to. Just sharing problems with sensitive hearers made a big difference and greatly encouraged me.

The other important thing was to have someone meet me at the little countryside train station. There were no official taxis in that area back then. I would have to negotiate with a driver and have him take me to Nanchang. I could do that, but did not want to have to go through the hassle or pay the exorbitant price that he would try to make me pay him. I called Dominick, a friend in Nanchang, and asked if he could meet us. He had been trying to help us with Mei Mei through his mother, a government official. He said that he would try to get a driver from his father's work unit and meet me. That was easier said than done. In 1992, official drivers were the only individuals with access to a car. Still, I had done what I could do and left the rest in God's hands as I continued to ask for His guidance. I was feeling more and more as though I was under His personal protection. Even though our plans had gone awry in Guangzhou, His plans were apparently still right on track.

At the appointed time, we left the hotel to walk to the train station. David carried the suitcase, Gayle the stroller, and I had Mei Mei strapped to my chest. I don't see how I would ever have made it to the special waiting room. The attendant even allowed the Wilsons to go in with us while we waited. Finally, it was time to board. I hugged David and Gayle and told them to tell LeRoy that they had "found" us and that God was truly taking care of us.

On the train, we shared the compartment with a young Chinese couple. The man did not smoke, so it was a nice arrangement for us. The only problem was that they constantly wanted to play with the baby. I had a difficult time getting her to sleep what with their trying to get her attention. I had set the stroller up in the small aisle between the bottom bunks and then laid its back down for sleeping. The Chinese thought that practice quite strange. Usually babies slept with their mothers. I suppose babies could fit with Chinese mothers on those narrow bunks, but it would have been more than snug with Mei Mei and me on a bed that was only slightly wider than my body.

When we arrived at our destination the next morning, I watched anxiously out the window as the train began slowing. I saw no one I recognized. I was poised at the door when the train stopped. It stopped for only a few short minutes, and they expected you to be off and out of the way quickly. I was ready, even though I was loaded down. Mei Mei acted as if she was ready, too. She was still a contented baby – another sign to me from the Lord, I thought.

The train stopped, the door opened, and I prepared to make a quick escape. Hands reached out to grab the baby stroller. I looked up and into the smiling face of Dominick. He was right there, right on time, exactly when I needed him.

"Hello. Did you have a nice trip?" he asked as he helped me down from the train.

"It was very nice," I replied, "but it is even nicer to see you here. This certainly makes everything better for me."

He just smiled his big toothy smile at me again and said, "No problem."

Dominick was there, the driver was there, and Dominick's father was there – all just to help Mei Mei and me. God was just continuing to send angels.

They drove me straight to our apartment and quickly settled us into our home.

"Do you need anything? Are you okay? Anything else I can do for you?" Dominick wanted to make sure we were okay. He obviously knew that I was upset by the events in Guangzhou.

"I'm fine – really," I emphasized.

His father and the driver had returned to the car by this point.

"I just want you to know that I'm working; my mother is working to get Mei Mei's papers moving. I think there is progress. Something good is happening." He gave me another wide smile in an attempt to transfer some of his confidence to me.

We had been in contact with Dominick while in Guangzhou as he tried to expedite the paper work while we were gone. He always had positive things to say, but we had yet to see any positive results.

At our apartment, they said their good-byes, after receiving my assurances for about the tenth time that we were fine.

As Dominick closed the door, my mind immediately started cataloguing what was needed to be done for Mei Mei and me to make it through the next few days.

Chinese New Year was just one day away, and the whole city would then shut down for three days. Since we had planned to be gone several weeks, our cupboard was bare. I arranged for the woman downstairs to watch Mei Mei while I ran errands and bought groceries. It would have taken too long with a baby, and she seemed to be coming down with a cold.

I was back in a short hour, and it was then that I sat down and offered Mei Mei her simple supper. The adrenaline flow slowed, and the reality of our situation slowly settled in on me. The cold dampness of the apartment in mid-winter also had a chilling effect, physically as well as emotionally. You know there is an insulation problem when all the doors and windows are closed and the north wind *still* blows the pages of your book.

I realized that this was not going to be an easy time. I had no idea what I was going to try to accomplish now that I was alone with Mei Mei back in Nanchang.

I was truly feeling the "bleak mid-winter" in my apartment; yet, for some reason that I really did not fathom at the time, I no longer felt abandoned. I did not feel that I was alone. There was a calm assurance rising up within me that somehow, some way, this was all going to turn out well.

"I will never leave you. I will never forsake you. I will not leave you an orphan. I will come to you."

I knew that it was true. I knew that this was God's word to me and to the sweet baby that was beginning to doze on my lap.

Sleeping in my own bed was pleasant but it now seemed to be a very large bed. I snuggled Mei Mei into her own covers in the bed with me, then settled into my own cocoon of comfort and went to sleep.

The first day of Chinese New Year was upon us, and the celebrations had already begun. Folks did not let the cold, rainy weather dampen their holiday spirits in any way. The fireworks popped and boomed and fizzled throughout the night and blasted out with particular authority around midnight.

And now on the first day of Chinese New Year, the people were out and about to visit relatives. Since we were not related to anyone, we received no visitors. As we sat in our apartment, as winter sneaked in through various cracks and crevices, the cold and dampness began to seek us out through our layers, and my spirits began to dip deeper into depression. Layering in China, especially anywhere south of the Yellow River, is just part of the Chinese winter. How many layers you had on depended on how cold it was; and that was true whether you were inside or outside. I had on a pair of long johns that I had brought from America – they were pink to give me that feminine feeling— then I had on a long woolen gown, and on top of that was a long cotton housecoat, zipped up to my throat. Mei Mei had additional layers also. That kept us warm enough inside our apartment. But I was feeling the bleakness of "winter on the inside" as they day wore on.

I had talked to LeRoy, as well as David and Marianne, briefly after they arrived in Hong Kong but LeRoy and I had not *really* talked. Now was when I needed to *really talk*. When Mei Mei went down for her nap, I called the number in Hong Kong and prayed that I would be able to get through and that LeRoy would be there.

He answered the phone at Bethany Cottage on Cheung Chau Island in Hong Kong, and I could not keep my voice from catching and the tears from falling.

"LeRoy," was about all I got out before the tears started.

"Jane, what's wrong?" was all he said. It seemed like a foolish question to me, since it was pretty obvious that there were many things wrong. During the times that we had already talked over the phone since we parted, I had managed to sound upbeat. I did not sound upbeat this time. I did not feel upbeat.

"Everything's wrong. I'm here with Mei Mei in a cold, damp apartment all by ourselves. No one has been by all day today. It feels like we're all alone in this city. I look outside, and all I see is the darkness of a winter day. It feels like February in Nanchang. You and the kids are in Hong Kong – where it's warm, and the sun is probably shining— and Mei Mei and I are stuck in this freezing apartment. And, who really cares?"

I really let the tears flow after that outburst. It was surprising we were not cut off after I said so many negative things. Maybe no one was listening in on our conversation, since it was the holiday.

LeRoy was quiet for a little while before he spoke. He was trying to sound as if he were full of confidence, but his positive approach, when I was in such a down mood, did not help the situation at all.

"Jane, it *is* February in Nanchang," he said. I think it was supposed to be some kind of joke to make me feel better. He failed miserably.

"Yeah, and it's February in Hong Kong, and it's Chinese New Year in Hong Kong, and you're not alone and you're not freezing indoors."

I was sure that he was beginning to feel as miserable as I by this time.

Actually, when we spoke face to face later on, I found out that he was feeling pretty miserable all along.

While I had felt abandoned, he felt that he had abandoned Mei Mei and me, that he had just walked away and left us all alone on a darkened dock in Guangzhou.

"I felt like the biggest fool," he would tell me later. "To think that I knew God's will and acted on it accordingly, and then see it all fall apart was so disheartening.

"To leave on the ship for Hong Kong and see you and Mei Mei still standing on the dock in the dark was most disturbing. I believed that God wanted you to stay with Mei Mei," he continued, "but if I had missed God so badly on the first point, was I also missing Him on this one? How much a fool was I?"

He related that he and David and Marianne had retired to their cabin and prayed together for Mei Mei and me and then went to bed rather quickly. But his mind would not be still as he kept thinking of what he had just done.

He told me later, "It was three days later when I felt like I was finally able to put the whole situation back into God's hands. It took me awhile. I felt I had failed as a husband and a father in one giant sweep of failure when we left on that ship."

Of course, I did not really know how he was feeling when I called him from Nanchang on the first day of Chinese New Year. I just knew how I was feeling at the time.

Eventually we did talk more that day and share a little

more of our true feelings. I did feel a little better after I hung up the phone. I was not feeling so alone, even though the apartment was still empty except for Mei Mei and me on a holiday evening in Nanchang.

Chapter XII

Paper Wars

With all the battles being waged – and the biggest was within me – there still remained a certain peace. It seemed to settle over me. Yes, there were still times when I panicked and when I looked too far in the future, which often would give me bad dreams. Yet, during all the external and internal battles taking place over this one very small child, I knew – I just knew— that somehow, some way, God would win this victory.

There was no evidence that I could see "in the natural," but each day I would reach out to the promise that I believed God had made to me back in December – "I will not leave you an orphan – I will come to you." I knew deep inside my being that it was true. It simply had to be true.

While we had been trying our espionage method of moving Mei Mei to another country, there were papers languishing on desks in Nanchang, in Portland, Oregon, and eventually, in San Francisco, California, and Beijing.

We were attacking with legal papers wherever we saw an opening, and John and Lynn were also moving forward with the paper work needed in the United States and in China.

We had friends carrying papers for us in at least two of those cities.

In Nanchang we had a friend – Dominick (the one who

met me at the train station) – who was doing his best to assist us with papers to make Mei Mei legal.

I well remember the day we decided to call John and Lynn to see how serious they were about adopting. It was just a few short days after I brought Mei Mei home from off the streets of Nanchang.

"Hello."

"John, are you ready to adopt?"

"Wh – What? Who is this?"

"This is Jane Ramsey. I'm calling you about a baby."

"A baby? What baby? What time is it?"

"I don't know; it's about 4:30 I guess. Why? I'm calling you about a Chinese baby that I found on the street. Lynn contacted us about adopting a baby. We have one in our home. Do you still want to adopt?"

"I guess so. It's 12:30 in the morning here."

It suddenly dawned on me that we had miscalculated the time difference. We thought we were calling at about 10:30 in the evening there. We had done to John and Lynn what people had often done to us – called in the middle of the night.

John eventually managed to get awake so that we could have a conversation.

"Yes, we still want to adopt," he assured me.

"Well, now is the time to start moving on it," I prodded him. "Get your paper work moving, and we'll see what needs to be done over here." They said they would fax to our school all the information we would need about them.

And so in October, about two weeks after Mei Mei joined our family, began "The Great Paper Shuffle" that seemed to have no end.

While John and Lynn began filling out forms in America, we were busy filling out forms in Nanchang. Within just a few days, John and Lynn had completed forms and faxed them to us.

Our first stop was the Foreign Affairs Office at our college.

That was also the beginning of our chasing paper trails. It could be compared to a dog chasing his tail. We were just as determined as that dog to find the end of the paper trail. But the authorities seemed just as elusive as that dog's tail.

Go here – go there – talk to this one – do this – do that – go back there – you didn't talk to the right person there – write this letter – get this person to sign it – write another letter – get that person to sign it – get more papers from your friends in America – go here – go there.

We chased that same paper trail no matter how many times we circled. We continued the chase with our teeth set, because we were dealing with the life of Mei Mei – a precious child whom we loved.

"It's just typical of most governments," LeRoy offered on one of his most negative nights. "The whole purpose of governments – any government – is to harass the people. And since we're Americans we should expect double the harassment from a Communist government."

"I don't really think that's true," I said as he caught me in one of my more positive moments. "This is a new situation for everyone involved, and they just don't know procedures, plus they are concerned that they might do something that will get them in trouble with a higher authority."

LeRoy scoffed at that.

"I experienced something similar in the Army," he said.

"What does this have to do with anything that happened to you in the Army," I asked. David and Marianne happened to be hanging out in the vicinity at the time. Their expression seemed to say, "Where does he get these army stories from?"

He was not to be deterred. Something had set him off down a negative trail, and he was going to go there no matter what the rest of us thought.

However, we did manage to encourage him to tell it quickly.

"I had a pain in my foot and didn't know from whence it came.

"I went to the doctor on the base. They poked, prodded, took X-rays, couldn't find anything, but said, 'You must have a hairline fracture; here take this crutch and try to keep from putting weight on that foot.'

"Okay. I did what I was told. My foot only hurt worse, and the pain increased.

"I went back to the Army doctor. They poked, prodded, took X-rays, couldn't find anything any different than before, so they gave me another crutch. I now had two crutches. And my foot still hurt for no discernible reason."

"And the point of this lovely story?" I nicely inquired.

"Governments are all the same. They run you in circles. Some run you on two feet, some run you on one crutch, then they'll give you another crutch; all in hopes that you'll go away and leave them alone."

The kids laughed because they thought they were supposed to laugh. I tried to laugh a little just to get LeRoy out of such a negative thought pattern.

But, we *were* running in circles. At times we did not realize we were circling. At other times, we were happy to be circling just because we saw something happening. It was those dead times when nothing was moving, when we were hearing nothing, that most frustrated us.

Circling with no victory in sight would often take us in a downward spiral, but that was usually when our Heavenly Father would drop in one of His encouraging verses from His Word. Or He would send someone our way who would offer a bit of good news or have some encouraging word for us.

Dominick was often the one who came with a new word for us. He always came in smiling – he had very white teeth, and he loved to show them in a wide smile – whether he had good news or bad news. Even when he had bad news, he seemed to have another possibility in mind.

For no discernible reason he was really working hard to help us. He professed to be a Christian, but would not join us for Bible studies. We were unsure of where he was spiritually, but could not understand why he would quietly tell us that he was a Christian if he were *not* a follower of Jesus. Of course, he could be sent by the Public Security Bureau (similar to Russia's KGB) to keep a close eye on us during all this time.

There seemed to be enough of those floating around us.

Tom was hauled in to the PSB station one day for no apparent reason. The main thing they wanted to know from him was "Why do you go to the home of the foreigners so much?" They told him directly, "We saw you enter their home four times" on this one particular day.

From all indications they had our phones tapped, and we now knew beyond any doubt that they regularly watched our apartment to see who entered and how many times they entered.

People who came to visit us were supposed to sign in and sign out with the woman who lived just below us. Our students and colleagues did not want to register their attendance with us, so they tried to avoid the sentry downstairs. I would often assist them, especially if it was Christian friends coming over. I would turn off the light in the hall. If they got past the woman downstairs, then maybe whoever else was watching from whatever vantage point would miss them also.

Usually I would turn off the hall light. Before long it would be back on. It was one of the games we played. We knew they were watching. They knew we knew they were watching. Our trying to thwart their watching made the game more interesting for them, I think.

Tom was the only one we knew who was taken in for questioning, and they released him that day, so there apparently were no serious repercussions.

This woman who lived downstairs and was supposed to take note of anyone entering or leaving our apartments (not just ours but also Shelly's) took her job seriously. More than once we were visiting with friends in our apartment and our door would suddenly open and there she would be. She would make some excuse for opening our locked front door, take a quick look around to note who was in attendance, then close the door. That was taking the game a little too far, according to LeRoy's rules and regulations. One time she did that when we had an apartment full of people. LeRoy quickly grabbed her arm and escorted her back to her own apartment, making it very clear along the way that he did not appreciate her intrusion into our home.

One time this lady entered – using her key – looking for one specific person.

"Where is the woman in the black and white coat?" she asked.

We had no idea what she was talking about. There were five or six of our Chinese friends present at the time – and no one was wearing coats then.

"A woman wearing a black and white coat came in a few minutes ago," she stated emphatically in Chinese. "She failed to sign in."

No one owned up to being the "woman in black and white," so our sentry left after giving warning: "Everyone must sign out when you leave."

They left one by one quietly after I turned the hall light off.

Things could have been considerably more difficult if we had been a little more gullible.

A few days after Mei Mei returned from the hospital a man appeared at our door whom neither of us had ever seen before. LeRoy opened the door to him. Chinese appear from time to time with a variety of inexplicable requests. This one was most unusual.

"Mr. Ramsey?"

"Yes, that's me. LeRoy Ramsey. How are you?"

"I'd like to speak to you in private, please," he said in very acceptable English.

"What would you like to speak to me about?" LeRoy replied.

"Well, could we speak in the hall?"

"I guess so."

Once they were in the hall, he started to pull a small packet from his overcoat. As he was taking it from his coat, he was explaining to LeRoy what he wanted him to do.

"I used to be in contact with the CIA," he explained, "but the government has stopped the contact. I don't know where he is." He did not explain which government had stopped the contact.

"He was to take this package to the American embassy in Beijing for me. I need someone to help me with this. Please help me."

LeRoy did not have to do any deep thinking to realize that this was most likely a set-up of some sort. Still, he did pause briefly, hoping the Holy Spirit would lead if he was to take steps to help this fellow. He did not feel any nudging from the Holy Spirit to go forward with this, so he told the man, "I don't know you. I've never seen you. I don't know anyone who knows you."

"But, who can help me?"

LeRoy was not going to give him any names.

"I'm sorry I can't help you. I hope you find someone who can, but I can't."

The man seemed to accept this word and turned to leave.

We were almost positive he was with the PSB.

We were telling Shelly about the man the next day, in case he decided to drop by and visit her with his tale.

"I talked to him this morning," she said. We were too late. "He followed Melinda and myself when we went downtown today. He stopped us and asked us to take a packet to the American embassy in Beijing. We told him 'No.'"

"Good thinking," I commented.

Dominick – we really did not know the truth about him, but he had a great smile and he was the one person who was ready, willing, and able to help us obtain proper documentation for Mei Mei. We decided to trust him implicitly.

Meanwhile John and Lynn were also assembling a plethora of the documents required by the Chinese government. Within a matter of days they had faxed us copies of certificates proving that they had been born, were now married to each other, were both in good health, and that they were either infertile or there was some other reason why they were not having more of their own children. They also had to provide documents of Kristin's birth, and her condition of health.

We had to have those before we could begin anything in Nanchang.

Meanwhile we were instructed that there must be "proof of abandonment" on Mei Mei. They wanted some type of evidence that I did not buy her or make some type of trade with the mother. They had to be sure that she had truly been abandoned.

This all sounded like a most difficult assignment for a foreign woman with limited Chinese. However, since that was what was requested, I went after it determined to complete any assignment the Chinese government gave me.

Each process would mean that we were one step closer to having Mei Mei adopted by our friends.

On a Saturday in mid-November, 1992, I went out on the street with Wen San Li, a doctor friend of ours. We started from the point where I found Mei Mei on the street, a month before, and started asking questions of shop owners and of people who lived nearby.

I had not entered into this with the greatest of confidence. Chinese are notorious for not wanting to be involved with anything official. They are especially reluctant if it involves a foreigner. Thus, I believed that God was definitely moving on our behalf when on our first day out we were able to find a man who told us that his wife had seen the whole thing. Then he offered to take us to her.

She wrote out and signed a statement that she had seen a baby in a box at that location on her way to morning exercises and that the baby was gone when she returned home. A lady sweeping the streets told her that a foreigner had taken the baby.

My friend read the statement and said that he thought it would suffice. I left that Chinese home feeling a great deal better about everything.

Yet, one month later I was again feeling quite discouraged. Mei Mei had almost died in the hospital in December. We had seen God rescue her. She was healthy and back in our home, but it was the paper work that was going nowhere.

I went to the *wai ban* at our college determined to get something going.

"What can we do to get the papers moving for Mei Mei's adoption?" I asked with as much kindness as I could muster for that day.

After talking awhile, I realized that nothing had happened at all. I was about to lose all my kindness when the *wai ban* suggested, "Why don't you go talk to Mrs. Hu at the Jiangxi

Provincial *wai ban*."

I gladly accepted the idea and agreed to go "bother" them. It was a step up, and maybe something would get done. Everyone had been telling us that we had to go through our college *wai ban*, and now they were telling us to talk to the people at the provincial level.

We were willing to go anywhere – try anything – talk to anyone, in order to see some progress on Mei Mei's adoption. I explained everything to my class of doctors one day. I thought they might be able to exert some pressure somewhere. It was worth a try, I thought. Wen San Lie was in the class. I thought he would most likely further explain the situation.

We chased down many alleys and main streets – over mountains and through valleys; getting a variety of responses.

Our main contact in the school *wai ban* was a woman who had been an English teacher, but had recently transferred to the *wai ban*. We were pleased to be working with Alice as we trusted her. We thought that she would be honest and forthright with us. We had been colleagues in the English Department. That bonded us to a certain extent.

After the visit to the provincial level government authorities we were back to working mostly with the school officials.

December 12 – Thursday

We went to see Ms. Hu at the Provincial *wai ban*. She said the authorities in Beijing had not formalized a new adoption law. They were instituting new law because articles in the Western press recently had said unkind things about China's birth control and adoption policies. They told us to contact the Civil Administration Bureau – they apparently would have to approve any adoption after the law is decided.

December 16 – Monday
Zhou Li came by to tell us that the latest on Mei Mei was that we cannot adopt her. We can adopt any other baby; but Mei Mei needs to go to the orphanage. That was extremely upsetting for all of us; but later we realized that this was nothing new – as we had we learned at first. God is bigger than any government.

December 17 – Tuesday
Fax from John and Lynn sounded good; they are both upbeat on the adoption. We needed to hear that. I told Wen San Li that I was very upset over the news the government told us Monday. I did not share this news with the rest of the class.

December 20 – Friday
Dominick came by in the afternoon to tell us that we should not mention his name in connection with Mei Mei. He said a friend of his had told him he had better be quiet about helping Mei Mei – so he cautioned us to be quiet. He also told us not to let anyone have her picture. He is trying to work through the orphanage.
A fax from John and Lynn said they still had some things to do on the

American side. But the letter from the Guangzhou consulate sounded as though everything was clear.

I talked to Alice again, and all she said was "This is going to be difficult." Our response was "Praise God – He is the God of the difficult – nothing is too difficult for Him."

December 25 – Wednesday – Christmas Day

Dominick came marching in when some of the foreign teachers came to surprise me with a birthday party. He told us he had good news about Mei Mei. He said that he knows someone who can get a high official to put his stamp on the papers – and if he approves it, it will go through – he has the power. Dominick looked at the papers and said that he is pretty sure that his friend knows the witness that Wen San Li and I found. God put His plan together long ago. Dominick took all the documents and headed out to see his friend. He said he would probably have to take Mei Mei to the orphanage to complete the transaction.

A few days ago Dominick told us we might have to find another baby, take two babies to the orphanage and pull a switch. That didn't sound like God's idea, so we are praising Him that He has a better idea.

December 27 - Friday
　　Saw Dominick on my way home from class. He gave me a confusing message that his notary public friend had told him - he had to wait for the new law to come through from Beijing. Dominick said it may take 3-4 months and that Pat King should work on the PSB to get a temporary visa for Mei Mei to go to HK. I think he also said that he had not given all the information to the Big Potato yet.

December 28 - Saturday
　　Got the Dec 25 *China Daily* today - it had an encouraging story on adoption; said the law was to be decided by the end of the year. That's great news! Praise Jesus, we're thankful to hear that.

So the paper merry-go-round went round and round, and we were not enjoying the ride. We were at the point that we wanted to get off and make a run for it. Perhaps that is what led us to Guangzhou and took us to the dock of a ship bound for Hong Kong.

Our last stop prior to trying to make our "dash of faith" onto the ship for Hong Kong was stopping by the U.S. Consulate in Guangzhou. As we approached the gate, we saw the American flag flying. That gave us a little more confidence and made us feel better about the whole situation. Inside that building were people like us. People who would understand the importance of rescuing a baby off the streets; compassionate, understanding people.

We showed our passports to the Chinese guard, then to the American Marine, who smiled and greeted us cordially.

We were able to go straight to the division we needed, and within just a few short minutes we were visiting with Sharon Long. Slam. Another door was rudely shut in our faces.

Another government. Another rebuff.

We were shocked by what this official of the U.S. government was telling us.

We had told her the whole story. As we related the story she took down notes. We later believed she was taking down the notes to use against us.

From the moment she opened her mouth, negative words flowed out.

"You shouldn't even try to get her papers to go to Hong Kong. I'd have to send the papers to Hong Kong, and it would take at least seven days for them to reply. I can already tell you what they'll reply. They'll tell you "No!"

We tried to keep a confident look on our faces but I could feel it draining from mine. I did not look at LeRoy because I thought I might see anger coming up which could mean his saying something risky to this woman who currently held Mei Mei's fate in her hands.

"Why did you pick this baby up from the street, anyway?" she asked, looking at me as if I were the biggest fool to ever cross her threshold. Thankfully, she did not give me time to answer, but continued, "You are going nowhere with this. I don't know why you even bothered to get involved. This will be just one big mess if you try to continue with having that baby adopted."

We decided to get out of there as quickly as possible. We did not enjoy being lectured by a U.S. government official who was basically telling us, "You are two really stupid people."

Of course, we talked when we were out on the street. We had to do something to let our emotions loose.

"They don't care anything about her," I said.

"It's like she doesn't exist," LeRoy agreed.

"She's telling us to just throw her back on the street. This is a child we're talking about here, and that woman talks like she's a rag doll."

"Both governments are against us."

We continued to say unkind things about both governments, until we calmed down a little while walking back to the youth hostel.

I finally got it back in perspective and told LeRoy, "I think it's dangerous for governments to fight against God. He rules and reigns in our lives. He has decided <u>for</u> Mei Mei, and everything must line up according to God's plan."

We were not giving up this battle just because some government official thought we were "loony tunes!"

Remember the Lord's deeds
Ps 77:10-15

You need only to be still
Ex. 14:13b

Chapter XIII

Into the Valley of the Shadow

"Everything must line up according to God's plan."
A bold statement of faith on my part. Now that it was just Mei Mei and myself alone in our cold Nanchang apartment, my boldness was totally gone, and I could feel my faith slipping away. I was not encouraged by knowing that my husband and children were in free and gleaming and foreigner-friendly Hong Kong.

Mei Mei was not being such the perfect baby any more; as she now had a full-fledged cold with a fever. That meant taking her to the doctor to get medication.

It was dark. It was dreary. It was cold. It was lonely. And my bold statement of faith proclaimed so recently seemed to have been blown away by the cold north wind that walked through our apartment on a regular basis.

Was this God's plan?

I was right back where we had started, but now I was trying to walk this path alone – in the middle of Chinese New Year – when all offices were closed and people did not want to have to bother with a foreigner.

However, the Lord knew I was about to cross over a line taking me into depression. The next day He sent friends – He sent Christian friends – He sent encouraging Christian friends. And He continued to walk us through this process day-by-day with assurances from His Word.

Different Scriptures appeared at appropriate moments to encourage me. I certainly needed some encouraging.

> Isaiah 49:25— *...for I will contend with him that contendeth with thee, and I will save thy children.*

> Exodus 14:13 – *Fear not – stand still – see the salvation of the Lord.*

Chinese Christian friends began to appear, then Shelly and Melinda (yet another foreign teacher in Nanchang) and Shelly's sister – Kim (who had come from the US to visit)— returned from their travels. It was heavenly to see them and have them nearby. They were stopping over for a few days prior to heading south to attend the conference that I was supposed to be attending.

Being able to visit with Shelly in particular really encouraged me. She had walked down a good portion of this path with us and had a better understanding of my feelings than the others did.

Still, those days in our Nanchang apartment with Mei Mei were a roller coaster ride of emotions.

The news of progress toward Mei Mei's being adopted continued "Yes" one day and "No" the next.

It was always good to see Dominick come walking in the door, which he did often. He always had that wide smile of his, and he always offered hope. Even when his news was bad, I knew that he was not giving up. He was in this fight with us to the end.

In the morning he came in with his smile set, but it looked more pasted on.

"I checked with different people yesterday," he reported. "I think everything is off. Everyone I talked to has told me, 'She can't be adopted', 'Don't try', 'You need to stay away from this'.

"They say, 'People can get in trouble for helping you'. It looks bad.

"Maybe you should take Mei Mei to the orphanage." He said that with a look that said he was surrendering. I in turn looked at him in a way that conveyed, "How could you even suggest such a thing?"

"Many people have tried to help you," he continued. "They might lose their jobs if they get involved in this. They have tried, now they are afraid. The man who told me 'No' today can cause trouble for everybody. You should at least think about taking her to the orphanage. What else can we do?"

My emotions were dropping, but I just kept looking at him and repeated to myself another of the verses that the Lord had impressed upon me over the last few days. I had to reach back and pick up the Word of God that the Holy Spirit had placed in my mind a few days back. I had no one else who could help me. I had nowhere else to go. My own strength was ebbing. I felt I was losing this battle.

I reached far back. I pulled from the recesses of my mind, *Great peace have they which love thy law, and nothing shall offend them.* [Psalms 119:165]

And again, *I will not leave you orphans, I will come to you.* [John 14:18]

There it was— the truth from God's Word. So, I just smiled toward Dominick. I am sure my smile looked just as forlorn as his did, but still I smiled.

Later that night I called LeRoy and sobbed over the phone. There had to be a release somewhere. I thought he should be able to handle it since he was in Hong Kong.

I told him all that Dominick was telling me and related

about Mei Mei's illness and how I had to take her to the doctor morning and afternoon for an injection, and that the weather was still lousy, and that I was not sure how much longer I could ride this emotional roller coaster.

By the end of the conversation he was telling me that he would make arrangements to return to Nanchang. I was certainly not going to tell him "No." He could make arrangements for David and Marianne to stay with our good friends in Hong Kong, Rob and Elaine Hartland. They and other members of their staff at Bethany Ministries were already praying for us. LeRoy had shared everything with them.

"I'll call tomorrow and see if I can get a flight up there," he told me before we finished talking that night. That was reassuring news to me.

After I got Mei Mei to sleep and we were all alone, I went back over the promises of God and forced them into my spirit and into my mind. God's Word was all that I had to cling to. I went back to Psalm 37: *Fret not...trust in the Lord, and do good...delight thyself also in the Lord, and He shall give thee the desires of thine heart...commit thy way unto the Lord; trust also in Him, and He shall bring it to pass...rest in the Lord, and wait patiently for Him; fret not thyself...cease from anger, and forsake wrath; fret not thyself in any way to do evil...but those who wait upon the Lord shall inherit the earth.*

As I lay in bed, the battle continued in my mind. It wanted to review all that Dominick had told me that day. I had to grasp at the Scriptures to keep them at the forefront, to overpower the negative thoughts. I kept the verses playing across my mind until I finally slept.

LeRoy called the next morning, after I had returned from taking Mei Mei to the clinic for her injection.

"I'm having trouble getting a flight," he reported. "It's hard to get flights anywhere during Chinese New Year."

"So?" was my response. That was a bit of an angered

exclamation, but also a question.

"So, I'll check about train tickets and keep bugging the travel agent about getting me a flight."

I was not very encouraged after talking to him.

Within a few hours Dominick was at my door. He was smiling, and this time the smile looked legit. Also, he did something similar to a waltz when he came in the door, leading me to believe that he had another plan. I did not always like his plans, but at least he was working at it. That was always good to know. He had brought his wife and 5-year-old son with him.

"I was very upset last night because of what I told you. I prayed after I went home. After I prayed, the very first thought that came to my mind was to get my mother to talk to the governor." And he smiled even more brightly, as if he had really locked onto something good now.

"The governor can override the man at social services who said 'No.'"

"Where does your mother work?" was my question. "Is she in that powerful a position?"

"Yes, she is respected by people in high positions." was his response. "There were some things that happened during the Cultural Revolution that cause people today to respect her. She doesn't talk about it much."

Again, all I could do was look at him. What was going on now? He had connections that reached as high as the governor of this province. It was possible that the papers could actually go forward if the governor became involved. But would the governor get involved? There were political questions all around; as relations between the U.S. and China were still at a low point after the Tiananmen Square incident of June 4, 1989. And Beijing was still trying to formulate that new adoption law. I was unsure of what could be done, but to me, his was most positive news. Dominick himself viewed it as so good that he was dancing around my apartment. He even scooped up Mei Mei to dance with her. It pleased her also.

Then it entered my mind that Dominick could experience trouble if he had his mother ask for this favor. He was just telling me last night how many problems people could encounter if they tried to help me.

"But you may get in trouble," I said.

"Maybe I will, and maybe I won't," he said lightheartedly, "but I have asked my mother to try this and see what happens. The man at social services is the governor's son. Surely we won't get in trouble if his father tells him to do something."

That was a revelation. I cautioned him one more time that I did not want to see him hurt trying to help us.

"I don't think I'll get in trouble. I've already asked my mother, and she says she'll do it." And with that, he waltzed out my door with his wife and son.

I decided to call LeRoy. After telling him this new development, we agreed that he should postpone trying to get to Nanchang. He was still not making any progress on that one anyway.

The next day was quiet. Dominick failed to appear. Shelly, Melinda, and Kim were trying to buy tickets on the train to head south and were having no success. It was okay with me if they continued staying in Nanchang. Melinda slept in Marianne's room one night to keep me company. I was happy to have them nearby.

They did finally manage to secure their tickets to "get on the train." That kind of ticket is very cheap and it does literally mean to just *get on* the train. They had to negotiate for a seat after boarding. But sometimes there is no seat to be had, and you end up sitting on the floor or standing for the whole journey. They were going to Guangzhou – 24 hours away by train.

I was feeling more and more under attack. With everything else going on with Mei Mei, Tom dropped in one day to give me more bad news.

"Liu Hua Lan's parents brought her back to the hospital," he told me. "They examined her, the cancer has gone too far; they can do nothing for her. They sent her home to die."

All I could do was look at him in silence and wonder how much news of this type I could handle. I debated telling LeRoy this, but decided against it for now. He had invested too much and believed too much for Liu Hua Lan. I decided he did not need this type of news now.

Mei Mei continued to battle an infection. I thought she should have been over it, so I was becoming more concerned about her health. Memories of totally misdiagnosing a disease in December began to haunt me.

It seemed as though the devil was attacking from different points trying to drive me under. Some days it certainly seemed that he was making progress.

This day was one of those; Mei Mei's temperature suddenly increased late afternoon. I was able to get in touch with Wen San Li to have him look at her. We ended up at the hospital at 9:30 that evening. I was concerned that we would have to stay overnight, but they checked her over, gave her another injection, and sent us home. It seemed to me that she was receiving too many injections for one so small.

I returned to the hospital the next morning for yet another injection. Her temperature was down, and she was apparently feeling better. I consequently felt better, too.

It was a few days before Dominick returned with any news. He reported that the governor had approved his mother's proposal, but that they would have to wait a few more days until everyone returned to work after the holiday. They would then have an official letter written that we could use.

I was excited at this news. To have an official letter from

the governor of the province meant that something would have to go forward with the paper work now.

However, Dominick had an addendum to his news that made me wonder just how much could be done through the provincial offices:

"Beijing is not very happy with the government here," Dominick told me.

"The report is that 52 babies had been adopted from this province – mostly by Canadians – and that they had paid US$3,000 for each baby. In Beijing they are saying that such things make it appear that they are selling babies in Jiangxi Province. That does not look good to the rest of the world."

Then Dominick told us something that made us both smile. "The officials in Beijing told the government here that they can charge only 100 yuan – that's just enough to pay for the paper work."

It looked as though the paper work would actually begin, that some progress would be made. I went to bed that night feeling very positive. I knew that God was moving and that our prayers were being answered.

Over the next few days Mei Mei's fever disappeared, but she continued to have a runny nose and was still coughing at night. She appeared to be feeling much better since she enjoyed every guest who came by; and we were having an increasing number of Chinese friends visit. Of course, all our foreign friends who were all teachers in the city had left to enjoy their mid-semester break. I continued to wait, patiently waiting for God to answer our prayers.

On Thursday Dominick came to take me to the social welfare offices in order to talk to the officials there. They were ready to get to work on the adoption.

"We will do everything in our power to help you get this baby adopted," is what Dominick translated to me from our conversation with the two officials. This was the most positive news I had received from anyone in a position to actually get something done. They told us they had all the papers they needed. Everything that we or John and Lynn needed to do had been done. They were satisfied with the papers they had to work with for this part of the process. They smiled. I smiled. Dominick, of course, smiled.

I was elated as we left their offices. Mei Mei even seemed to be back in her "happy mode," even though her little body was still fighting a cold.

All of this certainly made for a brighter weekend for me. I knew that the process could still take weeks or possibly even months, but I had the word of officials in the social welfare offices – people with power. I was ready to charge forward.

On Monday I was asked to come to the president's office and bring Mei Mei with me. I was not sure why I needed to go to the office of the medical college president, but I viewed it as another step that needed to be taken to see Mei Mei adopted. I was more than ready.

Dominick happened to be there when the *wai ban* called for me to meet them there, so he went with me.

When I walked into the president's office, the president was not there. Two of the *wai ban* staff were there. The two men I had spoken to on Thursday from social services were also there.

I was beginning to feel that the news I was about to hear was not going to be positive.

They dispensed with all the typical Chinese niceties – they offered me no tea, and we did not have the usual meaningless conversations prior to moving on to the agenda.

They told me directly that the men from the social services needed to tell me something. They spoke in Chinese, and Ms. Hu translated.

"You cannot adopt this baby. Your friends cannot adopt this baby. You must put her in the orphanage. It is illegal for a foreigner to pick up a baby off the street. It is illegal for you to have a Chinese baby in your home."

I was hearing this from the mouths of the people who had told me that they were going to do everything in their power to help me. All the government agencies, the people at our *wai ban* office, and the provincial *wai ban* office had previously extolled my virtues because I had taken a Chinese baby in my home. Now they were calling me a criminal. This was my breaking point. It had finally been reached.

I turned to the men from the welfare office and told them firmly. "That's not what you told me last week. You lied to me. You told me you were going to help me." As I told them what they had told me, my voice continued to rise, and I could feel the tears welling up in my eyes. "When I took this baby home in October, no one said it was 'illegal.' You're liars. No one even wants this child. You're all liars. Nothing but liars." No one bothered to translate. I think they understood without the translation.

I was practically shouting, which upset Mei Mei and she started crying. I got up and walked out. Dominick went with me, but he said nothing.

"I have to put Mei Mei in the orphanage."

I made it a simple statement. I spoke calmly and said it as if it were something people did on a regular basis. It set off a firestorm. Several of our Chinese Christian friends were visiting in the apartment when I made this announcement later that night.

"You can't do that." At first Tom spoke as calmly as I did.

Then, "You <u>can not</u> do that," he emphasized. "Do you know what will happen to her there? Do you know what the orphanage is really like? How can you think about this? Bad decision!" The more he spoke, the more agitated he became, and the worse his use of the English language.

"She'll die in orphanage. You know she'll die in that

orphanage. No! I will stop you. Take she to other province from here. No!" Tom had every reason to be adamant. He and his sister were put into an orphanage in Jiangxi Province when his parents were killed during the Cultural Revolution. He knew the horrors of such a place. He knew the truth about Chinese orphanages. Over 90 percent of the babies in Chinese orphanages die there. They even have "dying rooms" where they place babies to die. He was not going to allow me to take her to the orphanage.

"Tom, I have to do it." I was about to stare directly into the face of the most difficult thing that I had ever been asked to do in my life, and Tom was making it all the more difficult.

The authorities had finally come forth with the truth – there would be no adoption, there would be no papers moving, nothing was going to happen. After all these months of trying every avenue that opened before us, it had come down to the fact that Mei Mei still did not exist in the eyes of anyone official. She was still a nonentity. So, how could there be any paper work on someone who did not exist?

The provincial authorities had not *asked* me to take her to the orphanage. They had *told me* that I must place Mei Mei in the orphanage.

Tom continued to berate me and was now telling me exactly what he thought of me for even suggesting such a thing. "A Christian would never do this," he said as his final statement.

"Tom, I must. I must obey the authorities over me."

That set him off again on "how could a Christian obey Communist authorities?" I did not really have the answer to that except to tell him, "It's in the Bible."

"No. Show it to me. I don't believe it."

I showed him the verse where it clearly says that we must submit to those in authority over us.

It made no difference to him. He still equated what I was about to do with murder; nothing less. It was that simple to him. Nothing was simple to me. It was not a decision I made because I had run out of options. It was a decision made after much prayer and the urging of the Holy Spirit that this was something I had to do. That did not make it any easier.

I had spent over two weeks in Nanchang, still chasing paper work, which continued in circles – going nowhere. I had been patient. I had been persistent. I had been praying.

I had been ordered to put Mei Mei in the orphanage, and all I was hearing from God now was to be obedient.

I had been told that morning to put her in the orphanage. I told them to come at 2 p.m. and get her. They did not show up. They said that we would go tomorrow morning.

I had called LeRoy that night after Tom and the few other friends who were there had left. Almost all of them were convinced that I was making a grave mistake.

I called LeRoy again the next morning. As I was talking to him, I saw the women from our *wai ban* office coming with officials from the social services office. I started crying as I told LeRoy, "They're coming. I have to go now."

When I opened the door for the officials, they found a woman with tears in her eyes and a baby ready to be taken to the orphanage. I had surrendered; but I had not surrendered to them. I had surrendered to God's will. It was not my choice. It was not what I wanted to do. It was what I believed God wanted me to do.

Hear my prayer and answer.
Is this your answer?

Chapter XIV

My Doubting Steps of Faith

W hen you put your faith in God, when you totally trust Him; when you know that you have assurances from His Word, when you know in your heart that you have heard from God, and still everything falls apart, when everything that you know He told you disintegrates before your eyes, and you have nothing left to cling to, where do you go?

What is left when your faith is wiped off the board? I had reached that point. I was reaching out to find something that I could cling to in order to maintain my sanity. Mei Mei was still in my home, and some how, some way, I knew that God was still in charge. But I could not imagine that God would send me down this road. How could this be of God? Why would God want me to put this precious child – who had already been abandoned once, who had almost died in December— into an orphanage where death stalks the halls daily?

Surely this was just another one of those twists and turns, and God would set it right before they came to take us to the orphanage. I wanted that to be the truth, but somehow, deep inside of me, I knew that they would come on that fateful morning – Monday, February 17 – and Mei Mei would be taken from me and placed in that horrible orphanage.

I had made this latest decision without consulting LeRoy. I knew what David and Marianne's reaction would be. I did not want to think what would course through their minds about their mother after LeRoy told them what I was about to do. I was also very unsure of what LeRoy himself would think of me. He had said little over the phone; just that he was praying, and he was enlisting others to pray.

What if my family decided to abandon me over this? If Mei Mei suffered harm in the orphanage, if she did die there, would my husband and my children ever speak to me again?

These were thoughts that I had to put to the back of my mind. To even think about what I was about to do was just too difficult to ponder, too much to comprehend. I did not know where all this would lead; I just knew that I needed to take this next step.

The ladies from the *wai ban* office were at my door, waiting for Mei Mei and me to go with them. They would not even walk inside our apartment. I guess they wanted to have this thing over with quickly. I had Mei Mei's clothes packed in a small bag and also had her bottle, extra milk, and a few toys. The school had sent the Beijing jeep for us to ride in. That was their best, and newest, car. That was the first time I had ever been allowed to ride in it. Always before, we had been taken in the black sedans that looked like something out of the 1950s. Of course, that was only when we were able to ride in a car at all. We usually biked around Nanchang.

I remember little about the trip to the orphanage. I just remember holding Mei Mei tightly, praying, crying a little and trying to keep my thoughts reined in.

They wanted to run in dire directions, such as thoughts of all that could happen to Mei Mei at this place where I was taking her. Perhaps that is what hit me hardest of all. I, myself, was taking this precious child to a place of horror. I was doing it.

The others were stoic during the ride over. That was just fine with me. What could they say? What could I say? Just driving into that part of town depressed me even more. When we pulled up at the gate, it was all I could do to keep from breaking down totally right there.

We were ushered into the same office where Tom and I had sat last September when we had biked to the orphanage to obtain information about a foreign adoption. I was numb with the impact of what I was doing. Mei Mei was being her adorable self and giving everyone her beautiful smile. My heart was wrenched knowing she had no idea what was happening. She knew nothing of the momentous decisions that were being made concerning her future.

The orphanage officials asked if I would like to tour the facilities and see the babies. I declined. I had refused in September, and I was not about to change my mind. Ms. Kong and Alice accepted their offer, whether out of courtesy or curiosity, I did not know. I stayed alone in the office with Mei Mei, willing for as many minutes as possible before I had to hand her over.

My request to God the day before had been "Hear my prayer and answer!" That was before I was called to the president's office. Last night I wrote a postscript under my plea: "Is this your answer?" For today I had written "DELIVERANCE!!" So far the deliverance I was looking for had not come.

When Alice and Ms. Kong returned looking very solemn and upset, we said goodbye to Mei Mei, and I held her tightly to my chest. I was clinging to her the way she had clung to me when I picked her up out of the cardboard box last October. The time had come.

I hugged her very tightly, kissed her one more time, handed her to the director of the orphanage, turned and walked out of the door. I walked directly to the car without looking back. I was trying to somehow turn myself into a robot because I did not want them to see me fall apart.

"Alice, will Mei Mei like it here?" I asked as we drove away from the orphanage, leaving a crying Mei Mei behind.

"Will she be happy here?" I was unable to phrase my real question – "Will she die here?"

Alice just looked at me and shook her head slowly. She knew the truth of the place. Most Chinese have never been to an orphanage. They could not tell you anything about one. Those who abandon their babies on the street assume they will be picked up and taken to the orphanage. They assume that their babies will be taken care of there and will grow to become adults.

I already knew so much more than I wanted to know.

Again, it was a quiet trip on the way back. I could not manage any conversation. I was crying and could not look anyone in the face. There was nothing to be said. We had done what we had been ordered to do. Trusting God had taken on a whole new dimension in my life, and I was not pleased with the lesson I was learning.

They dropped me off near our building. I could not say anything. I was not about to thank them for going with me. Not only was I upset, but also there was an anger building within me. Everyone had seemed like the enemy that day. I could not trust myself to keep from saying things I might regret later. I wanted to get away from them all.

The apartment was empty. I walked into our bedroom and saw one of Mei Mei's toys lying on the bed. Her crib was empty. Empty. No more would that cute little head pop up over the edge with her beautiful smile. I fell on the bed and wept until there were no more tears. There was just a terrible gut-wrenching pain in my middle that nothing seemed to alleviate. I could not pray. I could not think. I had never experienced anything like this. It was raw grief. It was as if she had died, and the impact of it hit me like a rock.

I do not know how long I lay there, but I had such a sense of loss and of being alone facing something that was beyond my ability to cope. At some point I turned on the tape player. It was a praise tape. The song that was playing was <u>Wounded Soldier</u>. The lyrics hit me as I listened to the music:

> "I am a wounded soldier, but I will not leave
> the fight…….."

I was truly wounded. That was why I hurt so badly. A living part of me had been ripped out, and I was bleeding. I had almost lost her last December when she had been so seriously ill, and now I was really losing her. She was entering a place of death for unwanted baby girls. But the words of the song also gave me a glimmer of hope that God was trying to speak to me in my grief. I was not to leave the fight. Many months later, I realized a very important truth in God's kingdom: "We cannot be defeated; we only lose when we surrender!" I was NOT to surrender.

I do not remember much of those first hours alone in the apartment. At some point I went to the bathroom and washed my face. I looked as terrible as I felt.

In the afternoon two American teachers, who I assumed were still out of town, arrived at the apartment. I briefly told them what had happened and that I had made a decision to ride back out to the orphanage on my bike. Brad and Pamela said they would go with me. As we were leaving, Dominick appeared. He told me that he would go with me also. I had quite an entourage as I returned to the orphanage. I had to see her, had to see what they were doing to her, had to see the conditions where she would live. I had to hold her again just to know that she was all right. Some how, some way, I had to convey to her that I was not abandoning her; that she was not being thrown out like a piece of garbage again. But I did not know how I could reassure her of that when I felt as though that was exactly what I was doing. Yet, I needed to hold her. Whether she needed me to hold her or not, I needed to hold her and assure myself that she would be all right.

Dominick quickly found where she was and took me to her.

The attendant brought her out to us on a long covered porch that went the length of the building. She flashed the most beautiful smile when she saw me. The officials soon noticed our arrival, and they came quickly to find us. On the long bike ride to the orphanage, I had determined that I would ride out to the orphanage every day to see Mei Mei. She had to know that I had not abandoned her. It gave me purpose and a resolve to have a plan. I was not to give up. I would not give up.

Brad and Pamela had their camera. They snapped a photo of Mei Mei and me. Later when I saw it, I could barely recognize myself. I looked like death warmed over. It had been the worst day of my life, and it showed clearly on my face. In fact, it caused the foreign community to really worry about me. It later seemed as if they had organized a schedule for someone to always be with me the first few days.

The orphanage director spoke rapidly and pointedly. Dominick translated, saying, "They don't want you to come to the orphanage again."

I could not believe what I was hearing. It sounded so ludicrous to me. There was no reason for this. I told them I thought it was ridiculous.

They responded by saying, "You should not come back for at least 2 weeks. It will just make things more difficult."

I was drawing a breath to respond when Dominick quickly cut me off. "You should do what they say. It may cause serious problems if you don't." Later, when I had time to think about it, I realized that Dominick was probably only translating part of what they were telling me. And he was trying to get me to leave before I actually did make things worse for Mei Mei. I did not realize all of this at the time since I was frustrated and could feel anger welling up in me again. It seemed that everywhere I turned, I was thwarted. Every time I took a step to do what I believed I should do, I was slapped in the face. I was not sure how much more of this I could endure.

I returned to an apartment that seemed to be void of life. When Dominick left, I sat down and cried. I just let the tears fall. I had failed. I went through the pain of loss again – the second time that day.

Finally I was able to rouse myself. That afternoon I called John and Lynn and asked them to send more information. I wanted to make sure that we had every document, no matter how insignificant, so that we would see the adoption go forward – quickly. I was determined to scratch and scrape, if necessary, to get everything done and done quickly.

LeRoy called at 6:30 to say that he was returning to Nanchang. He knew that I had been pushed farther than I could go. He said that he would get a ticket on a plane somehow. He was prepared to go to the Guangzhou airport and wait until they could put him on a plane. I was more than ready for him to be with me, even though I was still unsure what he was thinking about what I had done that day. Maybe he was coming to take Mei Mei out of the orphanage and try another tactic, like taking her to another province, as Tom had suggested.

In the meantime, the Chinese community was finding out what had happened, and they began to appear at my door. Ingrid, a Chinese Christian friend who is a coach, called to see if I was doing all right.

In the afternoon a young Chinese woman, Melissa, came over to stay with me for a few hours. Her English was very good, and she had been helping in the adoption paper work. She and another young woman, Betty, had been translating all the papers that John and Lynn had sent from America. Thus, they had been in the middle of the adoption process and were well aware of everything that was going on. Neither one of them was a Christian.

Melissa was a quiet woman, so she did not say much, but just her presence was comforting. She had become fairly close friends with Shelly, so we too were friends of hers.

Ian, an American Christian friend, who was teaching in Nanchang, called that afternoon to assure me that God was in this and that I could lean on Him. About the time Melissa was leaving in the evening, Pamela, appeared at my door again. After she visited awhile, she told me that she would spend the night with me, if that was okay.

I readily agreed. I do not know if I looked so haggard that these people thought I was about to go over the edge or if the Lord was sending them to reassure me that He could take me through this if I could just continue to trust Him. On that day I was having many doubts about just how trustworthy He was, because this was certainly not the way I would have written this story.

I was most thankful for the support. Having someone to talk to, someone who understood English without a problem, someone who knew some of my heartache at that time, was a great blessing. It certainly did not allay the hurt any, but helped massage the ache in my heart and at least make it bearable.

LeRoy called around 10:30 that evening.

"I think you should come to Hong Kong," were almost the first words out of his mouth.

"I thought you were coming here," I moaned.

"I've been praying, and I've had the Hartlands and

Heather Tardiff praying with me. They have encouraged me to take you out of Nanchang for now. Grace Kidwell, (a friend working in Hong Kong) called me. She thinks you should come to Hong Kong. I think it's right."

"But, what about Mei Mei?"

"What can you do for her there? You just told me they told you to stay away from the orphanage. It would only cause more problems for Mei Mei if you go back. "There is nothing more you can do with the paper work in Nanchang.

"As we were praying for you here today, we came to realize that it would be best for you to come to Hong Kong. You need to get out of Nanchang."

I finally agreed that sitting around in that damp, cold, dreary apartment in Nanchang would only drive me deeper into despair. Of course, it seemed like an impossible venture, as others had been having so much trouble obtaining tickets, even though the Chinese New Year holiday was officially over. However, this holiday actually lasts until 15 days after New Year's Day. New Year's Day that year was on February 4. They celebrate for three days, with most of official and economic China shut down during that time. Most return to work after three days, but the holiday is actually still observed until a meal on the 15th day afterward. So, many people were still traveling, and tickets were still difficult to find.

It was amazing to me that I actually slept through the night after putting Mei Mei in the orphanage. I suppose there is a point of exhaustion where your body simply must have rest. I was sure I had reached that point.

I awoke to the sound of rain falling outside. I had been hoping for sunshine. A dreary sky would not improve my disposition at all. However, I was able to obtain a ticket to fly to Hong Kong on Friday – just two days hence. That development seemed like something along the line of a miracle, making me a little more assured that I was supposed to go to Hong Kong.

LeRoy called, and I told him that tickets had been procured; he was very happy. I did not bother to ask him what he thought about my decision to put Mei Mei in the orphanage.

Tom had ridden out to the orphanage in the morning. He came to our apartment immediately upon his return in order to report to me. "Mei Mei is doing okay," he said. "She's not happy, but she's okay. She still has a cold, and they've started giving her injections."

I was disappointed to hear this news, because they have only "barefoot doctors" at the orphanage (pseudo-doctors), those who have "learned by doing," as Chairman Mao would have said. All I could do was to continue to pray and believe that God was able to keep her and sustain her and allow no harm to come to her.

Pat King came by in the late afternoon. She was preparing dinner for us when Dominick came in. He was smiling very little now. He joined us for dinner. Pat told me she was going to spend the night with me. It sounded like a good idea to me.

More Chinese Christians were calling and coming to our home. American Christians who I thought were out of town were suddenly appearing at my door and spending the night with me. It was proof again of the wonder of God's family throughout the world.

It was also evidence to me that God was trying to break through my emotions and reveal to my mind that He was still in charge whether it appeared that way to me or not. It finally penetrated deep enough for me to be able to understand a little of what God was doing by sending all these people to me; a little bit of peace began to settle into a corner of my mind.

On Thursday morning Tom called me. He had been to the orphanage early in the morning. He said Mei Mei was doing okay. She had recognized him and was happy to see him. He told me that he would often speak to Mei Mei in English. He thought that it would help her to hear English words.

In the afternoon Melissa and Dominick went together to the orphanage. Later that afternoon Dominick came to give me a report on Mei Mei. His report was also positive, saying that she smiled when she saw him. It made him smile to be able to give me such a report.

In the evening more Chinese friends visited me. Ingrid was among them. She told me that she would go to the orphanage to visit Mei Mei tomorrow. I knew that Tom and Dominick would continue to go. I also knew that Tom would take her out of there himself if he thought any harm would come to Mei Mei. I was not sure if that fact was a comfort or a worry. But at least I knew that he would be watching her closely.

It was becoming clearer to me that God had this all under control. I cannot say that I was at a place where my faith was reinforced, but I could feel it gaining strength as my Heavenly Father was showing me that this small child – so insignificant in the eyes of the world, a nonentity according to the Chinese government – was very special to Him. I was beginning to see that He was truly holding her in the palm of His hand.

I doubt that I will ever fully understand God's great love for us while I walk this earth. But there is no doubt that His love for this one small Chinese baby was well beyond my comprehension.

The school was gracious enough to send a car at 6:45 on Friday morning to take me to the airport to catch a 9:30 a.m. flight. I imagine they would have done almost anything to get me out of town. Perhaps they were hoping that we would not return. I was beginning to think that might be a good idea.

Three days after I had placed our baby in the hands of the understaffed orphanage workers, I was flying away. I was flying away to Hong Kong, which would certainly feel like a different world.

I was leaving Mei Mei behind. The questions continued to assault my mind. But I had set my feet upon this path – a path that I could not begin to understand; yet one I believed that God had mapped out for me – and I was going to walk it. I did not feel good about it. I did not feel relieved to leave Nanchang. If anything, I was even more worried since I was still not certain how my husband and children would receive me in Hong Kong. I could not imagine doing what I had done. So, how would they, who had no control over the decision, really feel about what I had done?

Chapter XV

That Freedom Feeling

Hong Kong greeted me with sunshine and the air was warm. I could only hope that I would find a similar reception from my family.

I went through immigration and was headed toward the doors that swing open automatically to suddenly reveal you to the waiting masses at Kai Tak Airport. Everything about Kai Tak was an experience. Just flying in to Kai Tak could be compared to a thrill ride at an amusement park.

A friend, making his first trip to Hong Kong, was asleep during the approach, but woke up within a few minutes of touchdown and was surprised to find he was looking into apartment windows. It shook him for a moment – he thought a crash was imminent. It was just the normal approach in to Kai Tak – where you could wave at local residents in their apartment windows as you tilted toward them immediately before the plane finally righted itself to land.

After going through immigration at Kai Tak, you would enter a long hall with doors at the end. As you stepped through the doors, there was a runway – something similar to a model's catwalk – only about double that width, and sloping down. Sloping down toward hundreds of people awaiting friends and relatives arriving from various parts of the world. People would be holding signs with a variety of names. People would be holding flowers. There would be many smiling people.

The doors swung open, and I walked onto the runway. I scanned the crowd, but did not see a familiar face among the entire crowd. I caught a glimpse of flowers being waved and eventually saw LeRoy's face, then spotted David and Marianne. They were smiling at me.

It was so good to have them reach out to me, to encircle me with their arms and their love. The tears fell once again. This time, they were tears of sorrow and joy intermingled. At times I wondered just how many tears I would cry over this one baby.

I did most of the talking on the way to our hotel room. I tried to tell them everything I could about Mei Mei and what had transpired, but I shied away from the most difficult parts. It was during that ride that I expressed my belief that papers would actually move now that she had an identity. When she was registered in the orphanage, she was given the family name Zheng. Every baby accepted into the orphanage – that looked as if it might survive – was given the family name of Zheng that month. Next month it would be a different family name. So, now she had a name. Now, she was an official person. Now she was registered with a designated unit within the People's Republic of China. Now, I had been led to believe by Chinese friends, the official adoption process could begin.

But, at the moment I was in Hong Kong, and I was enjoying the love being showered upon me. I enjoyed soaking in a bath – a luxury seldom known in Nanchang. I went to a beauty shop to have my hair cut and shampooed. More of God's Hong Kong Family reached out to me in a variety of ways to let me know that I was loved. Kim Miller, another Nanchang teacher who was visiting Hong Kong, sent me a rose. Grace Kidwell, a friend of some years who lived in Hong Kong, gave me an encouraging card and a gift of earrings. And there were others who reached out to me in special ways. Again, God's Family was showing His love. As wonderful as it was, it must be only a glimpse of what it will be like when we are walking on His streets of gold. We greatly enjoyed our time together in Hong Kong, reunited as a family. We continued our prayers for Mei Mei – mostly that God would keep her safe and that there would be real progress on her adoption.

More than ever I was now convinced that I had done what needed to be done and that the paper work would actually begin to move now that Mei Mei was officially registered with the government of China. We prayed, believing that I had been obedient and that God was now moving on Mei Mei's behalf.

We enjoyed our time together in Hong Kong, but it was a short reunion, because LeRoy had to return to Nanchang to start classes. I had arrived in Hong Kong on Friday. LeRoy flew back to Nanchang early Tuesday. He flew from the Guangzhou airport (it was much less expensive to go that route). His classes began Friday morning.

David, Marianne and I enjoyed the gracious hospitality of Bob and Grace Erickson, a Canadian couple. Bob was working for a bank in Hong Kong. They even had a special bedroom set aside for people like us. We had enjoyed their hospitality once before when we fled to Hong Kong in June 1989. They harbored our family for a week then, as we made arrangements to return to the U.S. Even though they had a family of four boys, still they made room for us. We had seen God's love at work through their family in 1989, and now we were experiencing it again.

I was enjoying spending time with David and Marianne and doing some much-needed shopping in Hong Kong. I was also fully expecting to receive the phone call from LeRoy that the papers were moving and even possibly that Lynn would soon be on her way to China to take Mei Mei home with her.

He called us our last evening in Hong Kong.

"How's the weather there?" LeRoy asked.

"It's fine— cool for Hong Kong, but the sun is shining, so it's just right."

"Are Marianne and David enjoying their time with the Ericksons?"

"Yes, David has especially been enjoying himself – with four boys! They've been getting into play fights all the time. I'm sure it's good for him. Marianne finds it sort of entertaining to watch them. Of course, we've been out doing things in the city too."

"Is everything set for your flight tomorrow?"

"Yes, everything is set. We've got the tickets. Our plane arrives shortly after five. Be sure and be there."

"Not a problem. I'll be there waiting."

We were playing a type of language musical chairs – dancing all around the subject that was most on my mind. I was not pleased, because LeRoy knew what I wanted to know. I could endure our chitchat no longer so I asked him:

"What did you find out about Mei Mei?"

"Oh, she's fine. At least one of our friends goes out there every day to check on her, and they report to me when they get back."

"Have you seen her?"

"No, not yet; everyone seems to think that I should wait."

"But, what about the paper work? May we call Lynn and tell her to come on? Is everything about ready for her to come to China?"

He paused. "Well, uh, we can't call her yet."

"So what has happened with the adoption process?"

"Apparently nothing," he finally admitted what he had been stumbling around throughout our conversation.

"Nothing!" I questioned with an exclamation point. "Nothing? Still nothing!!"

There was the truth. I had taken Mei Mei to the orphanage almost two weeks ago, and still nothing had been done toward her adoption. We had been chasing papers for four months now, and we were still going in circles. My great theory of putting her in the orphanage to expedite the adoption process now appeared to be wishful thinking.

I guess I was doing a great deal of wishful thinking. I had planned a triumphal return for myself to Nanchang. I expected to be greeted once again as the nice foreign woman who had gone out of her way to rescue a Chinese baby. I expected the papers to be signed and sealed, with Lynn on her way. I expected to walk into that orphanage and take Mei Mei out of there. I was even thinking about snubbing my nose at some of those people. Yes, I had some great plans for my return to Nanchang.

However, now I had seen all my plans disintegrating, so I supposed I should not have had such high expectations.

Still, as David, Marianne, and I flew into Nanchang, I was still waiting for LeRoy to tell me the latest "good news." It was nearing dusk when we arrived. It was cloudy, but it was not raining and was not actually cold.

I will never forget the sight just as we touched down at the Nanchang airport, which is located out in the middle of rice fields, far from the city. I was looking out the window, just letting my mind wander and thanking God for a safe trip, when I saw LeRoy standing on top of a six-foot wall that bordered the airport runway. He was waving his arms up and down like a gangly bird trying to take off. A smile came to my lips, and I quickly pointed him out to the children before we zipped past that point. I was so happy to see him there, and judging from his gestures, I hoped that he would have good news to share with us now.

We retrieved our luggage from the makeshift baggage claim – which was just a shed with a long counter. They would drive the luggage there in a truck and dump it along the concrete, unpainted counter. It was quite primitive, but they somehow still managed to do the job fairly efficiently.

We boarded the CAAC bus for the almost one-hour ride back to Nanchang. CAAC is the national airline of the People's Republic of China. For just four yuan each we could ride the bus downtown. Then downtown, we could catch a mini-bus, for one yuan, which would take us to the gate of our campus.

We were smashed into the back of the CAAC bus, holding our luggage, when I started quizzing LeRoy about what had been happening. I had thought that perhaps he had been unable to be very open over the phone, since someone always seemed to be listening. So, I was expecting to hear something that would encourage me.

He had no words of encouragement. Of course David and Marianne were listening. Neither one of them was very happy to be returning to Nanchang anyway, and hearing negative reports about Mei Mei was even more of a setback.

I felt the same way. I had a sickening feeling in my stomach about this return to Nanchang... returning so quickly to the place where I had done something I thought I would never do was most disheartening. Mei Mei was there, but she was not in our home – the place where she should be, the place where she deserved to be.

I was so frustrated I felt like hitting LeRoy just because he was the bearer of the bad news. I guess I did verbally hit him as I threw a mini-tantrum right there in the back of the bus. That set David off, and he offered up his negative opinion of Nanchang and of any official who had anything to do with Mei Mei's not being adopted.

Marianne remained quiet. Perhaps she did not know what to say after hearing her mother and brother fling out our negative opinions. LeRoy tried to offer some explanations and tell me that he had been "talking to some people," but that did not help me at all. I knew that just talking to people would get you nowhere. They would tell you anything just to get you to go away and leave them alone.

New doubts began to surface. What if we had totally missed God's plan again? We seemed to have developed a knack of doing that. It appeared that we had fallen off on the wrong side of that faith/foolishness line and were unable to get back where we should be. Being a fool was never something to which I aspired, but I could wear that title if I knew that we were truly following the leading of our Heavenly Father. But I certainly did not want to play the fool just to be playing the fool.

I was also assailed by thoughts that somehow we had been tricked into a trap that the Devil had set for us. Perhaps we had missed God so badly that we were now doing what the Liar wanted us to do. I was so flustered – emotionally, physically, and mentally – upon our return to Nanchang that I just wanted to strike out at someone. LeRoy happened to be nearby.

Tom was one of the first people to visit when we returned. He appeared at our door the following morning. I was not overjoyed to see him because he still had a very poor opinion of what I had done with Mei Mei. He had been to the orphanage to see Mei Mei every day since I left. He said that she was okay even though she seemed to still have a cold.

He then started relating everything bad that he could think of about the orphanage. Every story he told was bad. He finally concluded by stating that it was a terrible place for Mei Mei and that she should not be there.

When he had completed his lecture, I felt as though I should find myself a small hole somewhere, crawl in it, and stay there until darkness fell; then I could crawl out with all the other creatures of the night.

This was not the kind of return I had planned to

Nanchang. I had that triumphant return planned, with everything falling into place, and Lynn on her way, and Mei Mei out of the orphanage, back in our home, awaiting her American mother.

So much for dreams and for my great expectations.

I was swimming far down in the blue lagoon of doubts, depression, and frustration. But I could feel myself beginning to rally, and anger was my rallying point. I was becoming outright angry. At first I was directing it toward LeRoy because he did not bring me good news. Then my anger turned toward the authorities. As I had many unkind words for them, and I was trying to restrain myself from becoming angry with God. At times I was not winning that battle.

LeRoy shared an incident that happened prior to my return that offered something of a reality check. He told me that he had been feeling very much as I had when he first returned to Nanchang.

"I was talking to Betty just a day ago," he related. "And I was into my moaning attitude of 'Why is God doing this to me?' type of thing. I was going over all the problems and how there didn't seem to be any solution. I was really down. I don't know how I came to be telling Betty all of this, but I did. We were walking along, talking.

"I guess I had been doing some type of diatribe, because she stopped and just looked at me and said, 'Is this too big for your God? Can't your God take care of this?'

"Well, that shut me up pretty quick," he said. "It was like a slap in the face. Here was this person who didn't even believe in God, admonishing me for my lack of faith.

"That got my attention and helped me to quit looking at all the circumstances and to get back to what we know God had told us."

It did help me some to realize again that if we were fools, at least we were fools together. And, I also saw that his frustration was just as great as mine; so my chastising him for everything was certainly not going to change anything; and it was something that Satan could use to divide us.

I ceased my berating LeRoy quickly after that.

"Shouldn't we go see Mei Mei?" David asked the next day after our return.

"They told me not to go back for at least two weeks. I'm almost afraid what they'll do now if I do go back out there."

"What about Dad going?" David insisted. Marianne was right there agreeing with him, as if this were something that obviously needed to be done.

"She doesn't know anybody out there," David continued.

"She's lonely," Marianne added. "We need to take some of her toys and play with her."

"I don't know what we should do," LeRoy waffled. "They warned your mom to stay away. I don't know what that means for the rest of us."

"We can try," both children agreed.

On Tuesday, after our return to Nanchang on a Sunday, we decided to test the waters – to see if the authorities would agree for us to see Mei Mei at the orphanage. Dominick called from our apartment to talk to the school officials. Their response was, "Don't go out there. The officials at the orphanage will get mad again. It will cause more problems."

That only made me more depressed. I could not see any way out of this. I could not see how God was going to work this out. I was feeling more and more like I had abandoned Mei Mei and as though God was abandoning me.

My emotions were on edge. It felt like another dart had been thrown into my soul when we received this latest news.

When I placed Mei Mei in the orphanage, I believe I got a glimpse of what Abraham must have felt when he took

Isaac up the hill to be sacrificed. I had sacrificed Mei Mei to the system, and there had been no ram caught in the bushes for me. I was still looking for God to move and still seeing no movement.

We were still on the paper trail, but it was like a dog chasing rabbits. We would think we had something going only to see it disappear down another bureaucratic hole.

Tom came by a little later that afternoon. We told him what the school authorities had said. His response was to tell LeRoy to get his raincoat on and leave right away. His plan was to reach the orphanage before Director Qin left for the day. They rode quickly, not knowing what they would do if the director was not there. Actually they did not have a plan even if she was there, other than to ask her if LeRoy could see Mei Mei.

LeRoy waited in the lean-to that served as a bike-parking garage while Tom went in to see the director. In a very brief time Director Qin and Tom came out of the building together. They motioned for LeRoy to follow. The director took them directly to the building where Mei Mei was. Apparently our school officials had never even bothered to call the orphanage, because Director Qin seemed totally unconcerned that LeRoy wanted to see Mei Mei. She even said that we could visit Mei Mei all we wanted.

More lies. Our school had lied to us again. Where was the truth to be found in any of this? We could never determine if we were being told the truth about anything.

LeRoy said his heart was doing flip-flops as they were being taken toward Mei Mei. He was unsure how she would react toward him. She had last seen him in sunny Guangzhou. Now, after over four weeks, she would see him again. This time it would be in cold, damp Nanchang, and she was inside an orphanage. LeRoy later told me that he remembered very little of the orphanage as they walked toward Mei Mei, because his mind was so absorbed with what he would find when they came to Mei Mei.

She was asleep when they arrived, and there was a 16-year-old girl in the room. It was about five o'clock in the evening when they arrived. The girl woke Mei Mei. LeRoy said he was not sure if she recognized him. She had very little reaction to his appearance there.

They fed her her bottle and gave her a granola bar that we had brought back from Hong Kong. We were unsure how much nutrition she was getting at the orphanage.

They spent about an hour with her, just holding her and talking to her. LeRoy said she did smile once, but that she still did not really act as if she recognized him. He was baffled and a little hurt by this reaction.

They rode out of that part of town in the dark.

When they returned, I was anxious to know everything that he could tell me.

"How is she?" I asked as soon as they walked in the door.

"She's okay," LeRoy said as he was trying to take his wet shoes off. "She's okay" was not what I wanted to hear from him. It sounded more like his hedge words, as if he were telling me only partial truths.

He did fill me in and added, "Director Qin said that we can visit any time we want to."

"Does that mean me?" I asked.

"I guess so. I'm not sure. She was talking to Tom and me, but it sounded like it would be okay for all of us to visit.

"She also said that we should deal directly with her and no one else for the adoption. She said that the provincial officials have been doing all these things [making us jump through various hoops] because they don't want foreigners to know that Chinese abandon their babies."

I was happy to hear this news, but then I got angry again, this time at our school officials, who were supposed to be helping us.

Of course, David and Marianne were right in the middle of all this, and the first question from both of them was "When can we go see Mei Mei?"

So on Wednesday Marianne, David, LeRoy and Tom rode off on their bicycles in the cold rain – making the 45-minute bike trip to the orphanage. We determined that it was best that I remain behind. I honestly did not know what was best to do. I wanted to see her, to hold her, to assure her everything was going to be all right (of course I had no idea how things were going to be) and just be with her.

I watched my family ride off in the rain instead and sat down and to feel sorry for myself. Eventually I managed to get up out of that valley and started praying for them, that they would be allowed to see her, and that it would be positive for Mei Mei, for LeRoy, and for the kids.

They returned with their ponchos having kept most of the rain off, but they still looked as though they had been riding through a rainstorm when they walked in. They were cold, and they were wet, but they seemed to be in a good mood.

I made them sit down right away and tell me everything.

"She's okay," was LeRoy's answer again. I almost jumped him again, but Marianne quickly chipped in, "She didn't smile at us."

"She did later," David added.

"That's what I was going to say if you'd given me time," Marianne told him.

"Well, she really is okay except that they are still giving her injections."

"Still?" I questioned. "How many shots can someone so small absorb? If it's just a cold, how come she's still getting injections?

"Are they keeping her warm enough?" I continued with my questioning. They could never tell me everything I wanted to know about Mei Mei.

"She's in a dry place," LeRoy told me, "and that's good, but there are no warm places there. Everything is open. They don't have any heat anyway, so a closed door means nothing. She's layered up – she seems warm enough."

"She acted like she didn't know who we were at first," Marianne added.

"It did seem strange," LeRoy agreed. "She looked at us, but it was almost with a blank stare, like she had blanked us from her memory bank. I thought there would be more of a reaction when she saw David and Marianne."

"We played with her," David said, "and that's when she started acting like Mei Mei."

"Yes, at first it was like she had no comprehension of who we were," LeRoy agreed. "I picked her up and talked to her, and she mostly just ignored me. I didn't know what to make of it. Thankfully, after we played with her and held her and talked to her more, she seemed to be like her old self.

"I think they are really trying to take care of her. It appears that she is getting special treatment. From what Tom told us and what we could see, it appears that they have a 16-year-old girl who is assigned to take care of her."

My family thought all of this was a good report. I was still not so sure. Images of that orphanage, images of Mei Mei's reaching out to me, crying out to me, when I walked away and left her in that horrid place remained vivid in my mind.

There were many questions charging around in my mind. I so badly wanted to see her out of that orphanage, out of Nanchang and into the arms of people I knew would love her. But all we knew at this point was that we were all back in Nanchang, going on with our lives at the medical college, while Mei Mei was suffering through her life in a Chinese orphanage. If God was doing something, where was the evidence?

If God was moving, where was the proof?

Faith? Faith – there was nothing in the physical to show us God's faithfulness. All we knew was that Mei Mei had survived for two weeks in the orphanage. She was alive, even if she was still receiving injections for a cold. Yes, she apparently was receiving special care.

We tried to focus on the positives that we could see and to trust God for what we could not see.

We were walking that fine line once more and praying that we would not fall off on the fool's side again.

Chapter XVI

Orphanage Pilgrimages

W e continued to walk through life— washing clothes, cooking meals, staying involved with students and colleagues, teaching and enduring spring in Nanchang, when rain would fall for days, with only an occasional burst of sunshine. Such were our days as we left the winter months behind.

The above might also describe our attitude as we walked in a cloud of struggling faith and saw just an occasional burst of something positive.

As the spring semester became fully underway all the foreign Christians returned. They remained involved with Mei Mei – going out to the orphanage to see her when they could. Some of our Chinese Christian friends continued their daily pilgrimage to the orphanage. It was not a pleasant trip in the rain. Usually they would return wet, with mud splattered up the sides of their pants from riding through the mud puddles that dotted the streets in that area.

Once LeRoy had gone to the orphanage the first time, it became almost a daily ritual with him. David and Marianne would go with him fairly often, with Marianne riding on the back of LeRoy's bike. Usually Tom, Dominick, or another of our Chinese friends would accompany him.

LeRoy was letting Mei Mei know that we were nearby.

We were not sure what was going on in her mind, but we had to somehow let her know we were close.

However, after LeRoy appeared at the orphanage for five consecutive days, the officials at the orphanage decided that he was there too much.

They told him that it was not good for him to go there more than twice a week.

"Also," they said, "tell your friends that they should not come here any more."

They were speaking especially of our foreign friends. Foreigners showing up at the orphanage on a regular basis was apparently making them nervous. They had already received word from Beijing that stories about abuses in Chinese orphanages had been appearing in the Western press. They wanted to make sure that none carried a Nanchang dateline.

So, LeRoy was being told to "go away," but they had not limited him as much as they had me.

I had not gone to the orphanage to see Mei Mei since I walked away from her that last time. I was afraid. I was afraid to go to the orphanage because I did not want to see all the suffering babies. I was also very concerned about how Mei Mei would react. I was not sure what kind of reaction I would get from the authorities there, either. They had made it clear that they did not like for me to be there. And I did not know how I would react.

Others were continuing daily pilgrimages to the orphanage. I continued to wait, unsure of what to do about visiting.

We stayed in contact with John and Lynn and kept pushing the authorities in our area to do all they could to expedite the adoption process. But the paper trail continued to be elusive. We were seeing papers going places, but they never seemed to land on the right desk. We could never secure anything with official signatures. John and Lynn were having similar experiences in the US, but a lot of that had to do with our instructions passed on to them from authorities in Nanchang.

On Friday, March 6, after Mei Mei had been in the orphanage almost three weeks, LeRoy and Tom took all the paper work that we had to Director Qin. She discussed it with Tom and told him a few things that were lacking from the paper work that she wanted. What she required was a bit different from what we had been told by other officials, so we had John and Lynn send even more information. I cannot even remember what it was now since we had been chasing paper work for a long time with no results. Whenever they asked for more documents, we got them whatever they asked for, believing that at some point everything would be gathered together, and they would finally let Mei Mei be adopted.

On Monday, LeRoy and Tom rode out to see Director Qin again. She said that all the documents were then in order. She had everything that she needed, except for the fact that she had to have a paper from the Chinese embassy in Washington with the signature of the Chinese ambassador. Previously she had told us that an official paper from the Chinese consulate would be needed. She had now changed it from a consulate in San Francisco to the Chinese embassy in Washington, D.C. It really did not matter, because the consulate in San Francisco reported that they had lost some of the papers anyway. They were asking for new documents.

Tuesday, March 10. Lynn called us to report that they had all the papers in order on their side. They had documents for adoption in America, the necessary paper work for Mei Mei to immigrate to the US, plus everything that was needed in China. They had papers moving in all directions. They were dealing with two national governments while being told different procedures from different agencies. They had enlisted the help of Sen. Mark Hatfield {R-OR}. His office had helped considerably.

When I told Lynn that we were being told that everything would have to be approved by the embassy in Washington, with the signature of the Chinese ambassador, Lynn was flustered at first.

She took it all fairly calmly eventually, though, and said, "We'll see what we can find out about that right away."

She and John were taking the same attitude that we were taking: "You want us to jump through this hoop, we'll jump through this hoop. You want us to roll over and bark, we'll do it. We're going forward with this adoption process. We will not quit just because it looks impossible or because we receive ridiculous requests. We will not quit."

I had learned some years earlier that things did not always work the way I wanted them to in China. I also learned that when you are dealing with a government, nothing necessarily makes sense – no matter which government.

I also had my own axiom for China – "If it's logical, it's not China."

So we struggled on. We would not quit. It was of interest that this was also John and Lynn's attitude because they had not even met Mei Mei yet. They had not experienced the warmth of her smile or the joy of her life as we had. I believe that God had put a desire within them to take Mei Mei into their hearts.

I was sorely missing that smile and the joy of holding my little one. I had waited. I had struggled about visiting the orphanage. I did not want to cause any more problems that might slow the process. I was also concerned about seeing Mei Mei in those conditions. All the reports had been that she was doing well, but she was still in that orphanage, and I was not sure that I was ready to walk in there again.

The day arrived when I believed that God was showing me that I now needed to see her and that Mei Mei needed to see me.

It was almost as if hate were building in my heart and I

was guarding that hate, whereas God wanted to release me from it. I did not understand how seeing Mei Mei in the orphanage would do anything but reinforce my feelings, but I sensed that God wanted me to go.

We decided that I should go for my first visit on Sunday. It had been three weeks since I had last seen Mei Mei – close to a month since I last placed her in that orphanage.

We did not tell anyone that I was going. We got on our bikes – after a time of prayer – and started riding toward the orphanage. Our whole family was going. The orphanage officials had been accustomed to LeRoy, David, and Marianne appearing, so maybe I would go unnoticed by the officials.

As we rode toward the orphanage, I contemplated what reception I would receive from the authorities and from Mei Mei. How much does a baby know and understand? Would she recognize me? Would she remember that I was the one that had left her in that horrible place? Soon my questions would be answered; the gates of the orphanage came into view after we had passed through a small village. That area of Nanchang was very poor. The government usually places its orphanages in out-of-the-way places so that not even the local residents really know what they are like. I suppose their thinking was "out of sight – out of mind."

I had hoped to never ride through those gates again. In my daydreams, I had Mei Mei already adopted and in America before we even returned from Hong Kong. Actually, I had believed months ago that she would be in America by Christmas. I kept telling our children that was all I wanted for Christmas – for Mei Mei to be in the loving arms of the Bonifes!

LeRoy, David, and Marianne were a familiar sight coming toward the area where the babies were kept. Mei Mei and the 16-year-old girl slept in a room with 7 deaf boys. The only boys that we found in the orphanage were handicapped.

They were also the only ones older than infants. We never saw another older girl among the children. We think Xiao Hua (the 16-year-old girl) had been placed there when she was older. We never knew for sure since we refrained from asking polite questions lest they might think we were trying to find out information that was "none of our business."

The normal routine during our visit was to take Mei Mei outside for some fresh air to play with her and help her learn to walk. She had almost started walking before I put her in the orphanage. LeRoy had reported that she had taken about four steps on her own.

Mei Mei's face lit up when she saw David and Marianne, and she flashed her "Mazin' Maizer" smile. Then she seemed to notice me. She became a little solemn and sort of tilted her head. I was holding my breath. She then looked back to the children and gave them all her attention. I remained in the background, hovering nearby, and she occasionally looked my way with a puzzled expression. I even felt it was an accusing expression as well! I could just read her mind with her saying, "I know you; you're the one that put me in this place."

I so wanted to take her in my arms and hold her tight, but I did not want to frighten her. She was rejecting me. I could not blame her, but still I was hurt. I tried to keep tears from coming into my eyes. I was happy to see her, happy to see her enjoying David and Marianne, but I wanted to hold her. I wanted to feel her in my arms again, for her to know that I still loved her. I wanted to know that she still loved me.

Because I was unsure what I should do, I just waited, hoping that before we left that day, I would feel the comfort of Mei Mei in my arms. I am sure that I needed that more than she did. At last she seemed to become more accepting of me, and I was able to hold her. What joy it was to have her wrapped in my embrace again!

One reason that I had finally decided the time was right

for a visit was that I had been very concerned about LeRoy's report about a bad rash on her bottom. In my mind, I thought it was just diaper rash, and I had given LeRoy some cream to use to clear it up. I wanted to see for myself and be sure the young girl that was caring for Mei Mei knew what to do. Words could not adequately describe what her bottom looked like. I had never seen anything like what I saw that day. "Raw hamburger meat" was the best visual description I could think of at the time. It was red, blistered, cracked and bleeding a little in some places. It was hard for me to believe she was not screaming from pain. Another shock that day was to discover that *all* the babies' bottoms looked just like Mei Mei's! I cleaned her bottom as best I could and put some of the cream on the affected area.

Overall, it was a very good visit. I biked home feeling much better. As many already realize, facing our fears is necessary and usually is never as bad as we expect. I left determined to find out how to treat the rash. I could now do something to help Mei Mei, whereas before, I could only sit and wait for officials to sign papers.

The first person I called was Karen, an American teacher who was also a nurse. I described Mei Mei's condition and told her about the other babies. She said it sounded like ureic acid burn. The babies had just small strips of cloth placed between their legs. Those were changed only in the morning and the evening. The babies lay all day with the acid from their own urine burning into their tender skin. The little girls were always placed on their backs so the urine ran down and covered their buttocks.

Karen suggested a treatment of mild soap for cleansing and then a thick layer of petroleum jelly to provide a barrier between the skin and the urine and feces. Also, fresh air and sunlight on the affected area would aid the healing process, she said.

So on my next visit, I took Mei Mei outside and with the

help of an interpreter I was able to explain to Mei Mei's caretaker what I needed and what she would need to do to treat the skin condition. Thankfully, it was a sunny day and not too chilly for March. I stripped off her clothing from the waist down and lay her facedown across my lap. I had asked for a bowl with warm water. I gently bathed her bottom with a soft rag. Afterwards, I just held her in that position to "air dry" and let the sun beam down on her pitiful little bottom. An older worker rushed over and began to chastise me for not layering her up as soon as I had washed her. Most Chinese seem obsessed with a fear of being cold. I was always criticized for not dressing my own children warmly enough.

People in China would often describe the cold weather by saying how many layers they were wearing. If they were wearing only two layers, the weather was quite mild, and, if they were wearing five or six layers it was very cold.

I explained through the interpreter that this was part of the treatment to cure the rash on the baby's bottom. The worker was not satisfied with that explanation but at least she left us alone after that. She was probably muttering to herself about the crazy foreigners that were so barbaric.

Once Mei Mei's bottom was dried and "sunned," I put clean clothes on her and told Xiao Hua that she was to follow the same procedure daily. I was hopeful that soon the condition would be healed but I was afraid her little bottom would be scarred for life.

I refrained from going to the orphanage every day. For one thing, it would be almost physically impossible for me to do so. It was a very tiring ride to go out there – physically and emotionally. It had sapped LeRoy's strength when he was going daily while trying to maintain his regular schedule. It took 45-minutes by bike and bike was our only mode of transportation.

March 16 seemed like an appropriate day for my next

visit because we had decided to celebrate her birthday on that date. We were unsure of when she was born, or even how old she was. There had been a small note on red paper left in the cardboard box with her when I found her. It had a date on it. We supposed it to be her birth date, but it was done according to the lunar calendar, which would have made her about 1-½ years old when I picked her up from the street. The Chinese count you as one year old when you are born.

They celebrate the first birthday 100 days after the birth. It was often celebrated by having a banquet, with family and friends in attendance. It was an important celebration. More than likely, it was a carryover from older days when many babies did not survive that far. So if the baby survived 100 days, they marked that event with a celebration. Apparently that occasion made the child an official family member.

Thankfully there was no rain falling on us as we began our ride out to the orphanage. It was cloudy and a little cool, but there was no rain.

We were taking a small chocolate cake that I had baked. We had one candle on it that we planned to light. We also had a small stuffed dog that had "I love you" written on it.

We took her out in a small courtyard, sang "Happy Birthday" to her, watched as she stuffed chocolate cake in her mouth much like an American kid would do, and played with her for a long time. We helped her walk, and all of us cheered uproariously when she walked a few steps.

Before we left her behind that day, we gathered around her, held her, and prayed for her. Our prayers continued to be for her protection and for her to be adopted quickly. Her health was much improved, as she was no longer receiving injections. We were so thankful to know this part; it had seemed as though she had been receiving injections forever. Her posterior was still badly affected but was improving. I doctored her again while I was there that trip.

When we returned to our humble apartment on the

campus of Jiangxi Medical College, I caught myself humming as I prepared supper. I suddenly realized that joy had returned to me. There was a song in my heart again. It had not been there for some time, but it was definitely there now.

I was sure a big part of this new joy was being willing to release many things – especially my feelings toward the Chinese officials (with emphasis on those who had ordered me to put Mei Mei in the orphanage). I also believe that my Heavenly Father had shown me that He was indeed taking care of Mei Mei. He *had not* abandoned her. He *had not* abandoned me. If I could take my eyes off the circumstances and keep them on Him, I would be able to "stand, and see the salvation of the Lord" [Exodus 14:13]. I was feeling alive again. I could feel the depression lifting from me. I could read the promises that God had made to me and know that they would come true.

If I looked only at the circumstances, they still looked terrible; it looked like an impossible situation. But if I could keep focused on the Lord my God, I could "see" the victory won. He had put joy in my heart again. I thanked God for sustaining me through all this.

No, the circumstances had not changed. It did not mean that the paper work was zooming forward. To all outward appearances, nothing had changed. It had been a few days since we had last heard from John and Lynn. We were becoming concerned that this "surprise" of having to go through the Chinese embassy in Washington D.C. had caused more twists and turns in our plans.

Lynn called the next day. She was spending a lot of money – just on phone calls – in being faithful to keep us abreast of what was happening in the U.S. We continued to give them reports of what we knew in Nanchang.

We thought we might be at another serious crossroads when she called this time.

"We called the Chinese embassy in Washington," she reported.

"They told us that they have nothing to do with adoptions. They don't mess with such things is what they told us. We were told to deal with the Chinese consulate nearest us. That puts us back to San Francisco.

"That's really better."

LeRoy was talking to her, and he was telling her that this news was all fine, but when he hung up the phone, he was frowning. He did not say anything about it to Lynn over the phone, but we were concerned that the Chinese embassy people (and who knew if they knew what they were talking about?) were telling us something different from what the orphanage director was telling us. We wanted to do what Director Qin was telling us, because now everything was placed in her control. Everyone else who had been helping us (at least who were supposed to be helping us) had disappeared from the process. The only ones still involved at our school were Melissa and Betty. They were still doing translation work for us.

We did not like the idea of telling Director Qin that she was wrong about the D.C. embassy. We decided to say nothing; to just let it ride and see what happened. She should be happy if the papers came from America with all the proper documentation, and if she received her fee.

We were beginning to discern that the fee was really the big issue. Apparently all the talk about who was in charge, and who could do what, had to do with getting U. S. dollars.

Director Qin had informed us that Lynn would have to arrive with $3,000 US in cash. That money would have to be put in her hands before the adoption could be completed.

Lynn was concerned for two reasons: (1.) She did not want to carry $3,000 US in cash into China. (2.) She was unsure if she could trust any of the officials.

We thought the mistrust was well placed considering how

many times we had been lied to by a variety of officials in Nanchang. We had been learning that Jiangxi was considered to be one of the most corrupt provinces in China. Apparently the top leaders were pocketing most of the money while they let the city and province continue in decline.

Paramount Leader Deng Xiao Ping had been busy trying to modernize China, and Jiangxi Province was lagging far behind. We had heard rumors that Deng had stopped his train outside Nanchang and told all the top provincial leaders to meet with him there. According to the rumors, he had told them very clearly that if they did not quickly make improvements in Nanchang (the provincial capital) and in the province in general, they would no longer be in their leadership positions. It was still too early to determine if anything had actually changed.

John and Lynn continued to be unconcerned about the discrepancy between "Chinese embassy" and "Chinese consulate." They assumed that the official at the embassy in Washington, D.C. should have the final word in this regard. But they were concerned about the $3,000. It was going to cost Lynn somewhere over $1,000 to make the trip to Nanchang and return home. All the work they had already done, plus the many overseas phone calls, had their costs up to around $1,000 already. They were investing over $5,000 of their hard-earned dollars, and they had no guarantees. This was a first – an American adopting a baby from Nanchang. We did have the encouraging precedence of the Canadian adoptive parents. But still, this was Nanchang, and even the Chinese considered it a backwater place. In one of the popular U.S. guidebooks about China, they advise the reader early on, "Don't go there. It's not worth the trouble."

In addition, this was to be the first adoption from this province, if not from all of China, since Beijing had formalized the new adoption laws. The new national adoption law became effective January 1, 1992. We were unsure when anything would actually become official regarding Mei Mei's adoption because the provincial leaders were at a retreat conference to study the new law.

We had no clue that anything was moving forward. We had been expecting movement for months. We just "knew" that the process would leap forward after Mei Mei was in the orphanage. So much for expectations. We were learning more and more what it meant to walk with God step-by-step, day-by-day. It was not an easy school to be in. We wanted to graduate from that school immediately.

Chapter XVII

Decisions, Decisions

The time had come. We had to make a decision. The official documents had been signed, sealed, and delivered to John and Lynn. They had faxed copies of everything to us in Nanchang. We had delivered them, after translation, to Director Qin. She said that all the papers looked good.

Nothing else was going to happen until we put Lynn, and her original papers, and her $3,000 into the mix in Nanchang. There were still others who would have to approve the papers in Nanchang. Though Director Qin was directing the whole adoption process, the adoption would not be complete without official stamps from other offices in Nanchang. We also still had to have official approval from Beijing.

According to our knowledge, everything was set in the U.S. and Director Qin was happy. The last paper trail in the U.S. was to the Chinese consulate in San Francisco. We did not know anything about the offices involved in China outside Nanchang. We were again putting our trust in a Communist party member. We were putting our faith in the Communist government of China. We were trusting that the new adoption laws recently instituted would hold true and that the Nanchang officials would abide by them. But of course, our faith and our trust ultimately rested in the hands of the Living God. We were trusting that He would use the officials to rescue Mei Mei.

We were at a point of decision. Surprisingly, we seemed to make it with great ease. LeRoy picked up the phone and called Lynn.

"We believe that you should come to Nanchang." He said it calmly as if he knew what he was talking about. He was speaking with authority.

In fact, we did not know what we were talking about. We just knew that Lynn had to be in Nanchang for the next step to take place. However, we had no – absolutely no - assurances that her arriving in Nanchang would indeed change anything. The stalling might continue. Lynn might be stuck in Nanchang. Lynn was a schoolteacher. She was responsible to her students. She would leave John and Kristin behind in Portland. How long could she afford to be away from them? Each day spent in Nanchang would be more money spent on this process. How much money could she afford to waste just sitting in Nanchang?

We did not know the answers for any of these questions. We knew that we were asking Lynn to take a daring step. We were asking her to take this step with no assurances, yet LeRoy spoke about it with assurance. Perhaps something was beginning to build within us. Perhaps it was that something called "hope."

Lynn said that she would talk to John and get back to us. Within a few days she called.

"We have to get one more stamp from the U.S. government," she reported, "then my uncle is going to take all the official documents to the Chinese consulate in San Francisco. He is going to walk the papers through and stay there until he gets every official stamp he needs. He's not leaving until he has everything in hand."

"Well, how long will all this take?" LeRoy asked.

"We don't know for sure. If all goes according to plan,

we hopefully will have them back in a week."

"And, if everything doesn't go right?" LeRoy was not feeling very positive hearing this news. After all, just a few days before we thought that everything was ready on the U.S. side, when this new bump in the road appeared.

Oregon officials would not stamp California birth certificates, so John and Lynn had to send to California to have their birth certificates documented.

"It all looks good from here," was Lynn's response. "My uncle is a very patient man. He won't leave without having everything approved.

"We're going to call about my plane ticket," was how she concluded the conversation.

We sat down after talking to her.

"Well, what have we done now?" LeRoy asked.

"We've done all that we know to do at this point" was my quick response.

LeRoy was looking doubtful now that he knew Lynn was committed to coming to Nanchang.

One decision made. Was it the right decision? We had no way of knowing. If someone had been grading our decision-making over the past few months, we would definitely have received a failing grade. We had been seeking God during this time and desiring His leading, yet it seemed that every decision we made deserved a big fat 'F' – as in FAIL-URE. And now we were telling Lynn, "Come on over. Bring your 3,000 American dollars. Spend at least another $1,000 just getting over here and, and maybe, perhaps, they'll actually let you take this baby and fly out of here with her. Maybe."

Even though we could have been appropriately deemed "miserable failures" in our decision-making, we were both at peace about what we had just told Lynn. We both believed that she really was to take the steps to come to Nanchang.

We had another big decision we were trying to make during all this. We had to decide where we would be the next year. In China, the colleges and universities would sign only a one-year contract with an instructor. So, a decision was made each year and a new contract signed – or not signed as the case might be.

Shelly, our teammate who had been such a stalwart during this time, had made the decision not to return to Nanchang. She had spent 2 ½ years there – teaching at the medical college and being our teammate for two of those years. The latter accomplishment should have won her some kind of medal.

We were struggling with this decision. LeRoy and I were waffling so much that we were hoping our kids would break the tie. We took turns taking David, then Marianne, out to a special place where it would be just LeRoy and one of them, then just me with one of them. We were trying to get some response from them to see if God was showing them anything.

Last year, when we had to make this decision, I was ready to bail out and leave. I had done my time in Nanchang; I did not want another year. I was ready to go anywhere – anywhere except Nanchang. But I had been outvoted, so we stayed on and our family expanded by one Chinese baby.

Now, it was decision time again, and I was quite flustered about it among all the uncertainties with Mei Mei. It was no longer just me or just me and my family. We now had one member of our family who was not under our roof any more, not under our control any more. And judging by the way this adoption had *not* progressed so far, we were unsure when it would actually take place, if at all.

What if Lynn arrived and she was not allowed to adopt? What if she returned to Oregon empty-handed? What if she came and they told her "You can have any baby except Mei

Mei"? Once before, we had clearly been told, "Your friend can adopt; she can adopt any baby except that one" – meaning Mei Mei.

Could I walk out of Nanchang, move somewhere else, and leave Mei Mei behind? I could not see myself doing that. I had already been forced to leave her behind once. I could not imagine walking away from her and leaving her in that orphanage. That was beyond anything I could conceive of. I was determined to stay. I was determined to stay in China the rest of my life if that was what it took to assure that Mei Mei would be able to live.

If they would not allow John and Lynn to adopt her, then we would stay and keep bothering officials until they allowed us to adopt her. I would not leave her behind.

And yet it was decision time. We had to make a decision about where we would teach next year.

I decided to talk to Alice in the *waiban* office and see if she might be able to offer some guidance. Of course I was as Chinese as I could be and did my small talk before getting to the point.

"Alice, we are so thankful for your help with Mei Mei. You have been involved in this from the first, and we're thankful that you have helped us."

Some of this was a good "buttering job," but it was also true. I do believe that Alice was one of those who had truly wanted to help us; would have helped us more but her hands were tied. She was just a splinter on the power ladder.

Alice was an interesting person. During our first year in Nanchang, she had been an English teacher, so we had had some contact with her in the English Department. Her spoken English was good. That was not always true with English teachers in China – especially those teaching at medical colleges.

Though Chinese, she had grown up in Burma and had married a Chinese man also living in Burma.

In the late '50s and early '60s, Mao had issued an appeal for overseas Chinese to return to the "Motherland" and help build the "new society." As an idealistic young woman, Alice naively answered that call. A few years after her arrival, the Cultural Revolution, ten years of social and economic chaos, swept through the land. She had arrived just in time to experience one of China's most convulsive times. She was condemned because she was a foreigner (coming from Burma) and slandered because she was educated. It was amazing to us that she still remained in China. But she probably had no choice. It was not easy to get out of China. It was difficult to obtain a Chinese passport.

"Alice," I continued, "how many foreign teachers do they want here next year?"

"I'm not sure," she replied. "We are looking at two or three."

"What if we decided to stay another year?"

"I can't answer that now," Alice said. "No one has ever stayed longer than two years. Since you would be staying for three years, someone in the president's office would probably have to make that decision. We can't make that decision here."

Afterwards, when LeRoy and I discussed her response, we decided that she was probably telling us "no" about another year. Chinese rarely, if ever, tell you a direct "no." They are concerned that they will hurt your feelings, so they seldom tell anyone a true "no." They will go around it in a variety of ways, hoping that you get the idea without their actually having to tell you. Or they might send someone else to tell you "no" if you are not very good at taking hints.

We could see a multitude of reasons why they would not want us to return and they all had to do with a Chinese baby we called "The Amazing Mei Mei."

So we began to look at our options outside of Nanchang. We also prayed even harder for Mei Mei's adoption. I did not know what we were going to do, but I did know that I would not leave her sitting in that orphanage if there was anything I could do to prevent it.

We now believed we had clearly been shown a closed door for next year. We began searching for the door that God would open before us.

While we sought God's will for our future and continued to work toward Mei Mei's adoption, we were also continuing our daily lives with all the bumps, bruises and occasional joys that came our way.

One "bruising joy" was David's having the opportunity to have braces at minimal cost. It was a joy in that we were able to get him much-needed braces in Nanchang (of all places) at a cost at probably 1/10th of what it would have cost in America.

The bruising part of it was David's mouth. They had recently started doing orthodontic procedures in China, but the dentists were still fairly new to the procedures, and Chinese doctors and dentists were not known for their gentle ways.

Thankfully one member of our Bible study was an oral surgeon. He got us connected with an orthodontist. He was probably gentler to David than to the Chinese.

I ventured into the dental hospital to have a tooth filled one time. Our Chinese friend did it for me. One of his first statements was, "I won't hurt you." I think he meant it as a comfort, but it made me wonder why he had to assure me of the fact.

He had a needle nearby. That did not comfort me. I never liked to have Chinese needles injected into my skin. It was a common practice to reuse them.

But he did not reach for the needle; instead he reached for the drill – and he started drilling. Right before I heard that frightening whirring sound, he said, "Let me know if it starts to hurt."

I made sure that the arms of that chair were not going anywhere as they were firmly in my grip. My legs were so tense that I thought I was about to spring right out of the chair.

I became even tenser as he brought the whirring machine into my mouth. I tried not to flinch, because I wanted to keep my lips intact. He settled the drill into the affected tooth, and the "buzzing" sound filled my ears. Once I relaxed just a bit I actually let my bottom settle into the seat. I then noticed that I was feeling no pain.

He drilled away, stopped, drilled a bit more, and then proceeded to fill my tooth. I asked him about the needle.

"It's there just in case we need it," he responded.

"You mean if I told you it was hurting me, you would have stopped and given me Novocaine, is that right?"

"Yes, but it's small (meaning the cavity). No problem."

He was right. I did not need Novocaine. I was thankful.

Later I could give thanks for having taken this first step in dental care in China. It helped prepare me for what was to come. In less than a month I put myself in the hands of the same dentist. This time he did a root canal job for me. I was left with little choice with my tooth hurting so much. It was either pull it or do a root canal.

David endured more pain than he wanted as his braces were applied and then tightened regularly. Of course, braces are painful any time, but he often thought that the Chinese were practicing their torture methods on him. Actually, they were attempting to move the teeth faster than under most American methods.

At times we seemed to be moving from one adventure to the next in China. Teaching in China – especially in Nanchang – was also a great adventure because we never really knew what might happen next.

Nanchang was a wet city – especially in the spring. It could rain for weeks with only an occasional bright day. After many days of consecutive rain, LeRoy made the comment, "I expect it to start raining inside one of these days." His prophecy came to pass. Of course, in our previous apartment in Nanchang we had experienced a regular drip in our toilet room. It really was a "water closet," as the British call it. It was indeed a closet-size room with just a toilet inside. It might not have been so bad if it had been our toilet dripping – which is common in China – but in this case, it was Shelly's toilet, located directly above us, that was dripping. And it was dripping on our heads.

If one sat on the toilet in our "water closet," he would be dripped on from above. The pipes and wires in our apartment were not hidden away; they were all out in the open. Bare bulbs hanging from the ceiling served as our light source. So, in our water closet, the pipes from Shelly's toilet were above our heads. One of the pipes consistently dripped. We could never get them to repair it, but American ingenuity prevailed. We found that if we opened an umbrella in the water closet, it was just wide enough that we could wedge it against the walls, and the drops from above would hit the umbrella and roll harmlessly to the floor and down the drain. So, we used the toilet while shielded by an umbrella overhead.

Our indoor drip in the toilet was merely a daily occurrence, so that was not actually the fulfillment of LeRoy's prophecy. One day, after there had been a rather abrupt weather change, he walked into his classroom to find giant drops of water coming from the ceiling. Some type of tin roof reacted to the change in temperature and humidity by having enough moisture form indoors to let an occasional drop of water fall throughout the classroom. So there were "plip, plops" all over his class.

The blackboards were also affected. Whenever LeRoy put the chalk to the blackboard, a rivulet of water would run down the board. It became impossible to write on the blackboard under those conditions.

Of course there were times when we could not even get into our classrooms. Classrooms were always kept locked when they were not being used. There was one person who had the one key to the lock.

It was not unusual for teacher and students to be crowded around the classroom door, filling the halls, waiting for the person with the key to appear. At times, students would become so exasperated about the whole thing that they would break the lock if it was a small padlock. Of course, this event would mean a bigger, stronger lock the next time.

One student of mine was even more innovative. He climbed through the small transom window to enter the classroom and unlock the door. Some of my students were very dedicated to help in opening the door. Most just waited patiently.

There were also times when we could not get out of the classroom. I was locked in a classroom with all my students one time. Not only was there a padlock on the door, but also there was a collapsible metal grating across the end of the hall. Evidently the guard wanted to leave early for lunch that day, pulled the grating and locked it without even checking to see if the classrooms on that wing were occupied. Thankfully, we were able to shout to people in other areas of the building in order to let them know we were locked in.

They eventually found the man with the key. He grumbled a great deal about the whole affair, because they had awakened him from his afternoon nap to let my students and me out of the classroom.

Water could be a surprise in other ways also in that some mornings we would rise to find that our water had been turned off.

"Why is the water off?"

"They need to fix a pipe."

"How long will the water be off?"

"We don't know. It'll be back when they turn it on."

The Chinese always thought we were a bit weird because we were always asking "Why?" and because we always had to have some understanding of what was going on. We were still too much American. Americans always want to know "Why?" That question seldom bothers the Chinese.

"Why is the water off?" They could not fathom what difference it could make to us "why" the water was off. It was off – that was all; deal with it.

Perhaps they could understand our asking the "when?" question a little more easily. Nevertheless, they thought it absurd that we thought any of them would know when it would come back on.

Most people in the world just accept what is happening and go on with it.

The Chinese attitude was "The water is off – well, okay, it will be back on at some point. I'll do what I can do without water. It'll come back on sometime, and then I can do what I need to do with water."

We did learn to "deal with it" without bothering the Chinese too much in these matters. After all, they would often simply make up something as to why the water was off so that we would leave them alone. They also improved slightly in later years by notifying us when the water would be off. That was helpful. But usually, we had no prior warning, and we never did learn when the water would be turned back on.

It was the same way with the electricity. It would just go

off for no discernible reason. We quickly learned how to repair it if it was our fault and the electricity was only off in our apartment. Often such would be the case since we Americans tried to run too many electrical appliances on the Chinese low-wattage lines. So, our breaker would often be tripped. LeRoy would go out into the hall where the breaker was located. He would find the wire burned through. We always kept extra wire on hand. He would thread another wire between the power points, flip the switch, and we would continue on our merry way, except that we would turn off one of the electrical appliances this time.

We had one interesting weekend during March of that year when we were hit with the double whammy of having the electricity and water off at the same time. On Friday our water was off for a couple of hours. This did not bother us much because such was a common occurrence. On Saturday our water was back on, but the electricity was off all day. It did not come back on until dusk.

Sunday we awoke to find that the electricity was on, but the water was off again. The water remained off. We passed through Monday without any water. As the days passed with no water, you can imagine the problems with no water to flush the toilet, no water to boil for drinking, no water for anything. We needed water – just for drinking, if nothing else. We had drunk soft drinks in place of water, but that works only for a few days.

We became impatient – Americans are not known for their patience – and finally asked someone about the water.

"It will be on when it is on." In other words, "Don't bother me with these questions. How am I supposed to know this?"

But then we noticed people clustered around a pipe coming out of the ground in a field behind our apartment. We soon discovered that they were taking their buckets and getting water there. LeRoy lined up with the rest of them.

He did not bother to ask them stupid questions about this source of water. The questions were there, but he kept them to himself. Usually we accepted what the Chinese were doing as correct in similar situations. If the Chinese were drinking this water, then we could drink this water.

Of course we boiled the water before we drank it. But that was a daily chore even when we got water straight from our kitchen. We always had to boil water. For a family of four, it was a lot of water-boiling. We had to boil water for drinking and for cooking. We would never drink water that had not been boiled. Rarely would one hear of a Chinese drinking unboiled water.

And our trips to the orphanage continued. Mei Mei continued with her positive attitude; now she always greeted us with her "Mazin' Mazer" smile, bringing smiles to our own faces.

Tom came to us one morning to report that he had been out to see Mei Mei and that she had diarrhea. He said that it apparently was a rather bad case. He also told us that they had given her an injection. We found it hard to believe that that poor baby was receiving injections again. However, Tom called the orphanage the next day to check on her and found out that she was doing much better.

I determined to see for myself, so I made a quick trip out to enjoy her smile. She was indeed feeling better. Her rash was almost healed. She was generally doing well. God was watching over her and keeping her.

Now, we anxiously awaited the next step. We saw God answering our prayers in keeping Mei Mei safe. We were hopeful to see God move her safely, officially out of Nanchang and into the home of John and Lynn Bonife.

We had made all the decisions we could make. We waited to discover if we had made the correct decisions this time. In some situations the decisions were out of our hands, so we waited to see what God would do now. We continued to pray, to trust, and to proclaim His Word that this precious child was not an orphan, but a special creation of God with His wonderful special claim on her life.

We anticipated what God was about to do. We were anxious to see Him move.

I will contend with him who contends with you,
and I will save your children.

Isaiah 49:25

The Battle Rages On

The days drifted by. Time eased from one day into the next. We awaited word from Lynn that she was on her way.

We marked Mei Mei's anniversary of six weeks in the orphanage by playing with her inside in her dismal little room as the rain fell outside. Our spirits had been drooping as we continued to endure Nanchang's spring rains, while dreaming of the time when Mei Mei would be free of that horrid orphanage. Just the thought of going there took me a little lower emotionally that day. But, almost always Mei Mei greeted me with her "Mazin' Maizer" smile to lift me up. God was using the one who had suffered the most to brighten my outlook.

That six-week mark was the last day of March. I had expected her to have to suffer the orphanage for two weeks at the most. But still we awaited Lynn's call that she was on her way.

Of course, we had no assurances that once she arrived with all the papers bearing all the official stamps and with the $3,000 in hand, that Mei Mei would be loosed from that place.

On April 5 Lynn called to say that she would be in Hong Kong on April 10 (a Friday) and that she hoped to be in Nanchang that weekend. I wept when I heard the news. I wept with joy that the frustrations might finally be drawing to an end, and I wept with relief. And I wept with joy. The answer was finally coming.

Thankfully, LeRoy was the one who had received the call. I am afraid that I would have blubbered all over the phone.

But the Liar who had been fighting against us to destroy this child was not about to turn loose so easily. It became more and more obvious to us throughout this ordeal that Mei Mei was truly chosen of God, that she was special to Him. He was fighting for her. And He would eventually win the battle. We had been told more than once – through God's Scripture – that we were to wait. We were told to wait and that then we would see the salvation of the Lord. The Commander of the army of the Lord would fight for us. (Joshua 5:14)

Waiting had never been easy. We had tried things in our own power. But, finally, we were able to totally put Mei Mei into God's hands, and now He was going to lift her up.

But still the battle raged.

A few days prior to Lynn's call, the kids and Shelly and I rode out to see Mei Mei. She was not her joyful self even though she tried to smile at us. She had another cold, and she also had a fever. She was not feeling well. The staff gave her an injection while we were there. I almost reached out to stop them. I hated to see them coming at her with a needle when she had already suffered so much. It was all I could do to keep from slapping that needle away from her.

I had also wanted to slap a lot of faces during this whole ordeal. But again I stayed my hand, knowing I could not fight the battle in my own strength.

I also knew that I had to let them do what they thought was best, even if I did not agree with it. That sweet baby had been sick almost every day of the six weeks she had been in that orphanage. How I longed to sweep her into my arms and run with her from that horrid place!

Just a few days before Lynn was to board the plane for Hong Kong, LeRoy was at the orphanage. The vice-director, who was directly in charge of the babies, told him that Lynn should not come until April 20 because things were "still being worked out."

Tom was with him when this announcement was made. LeRoy discussed it with Tom. Director Qin is the one who had given us the go-ahead, not the vice-director. We decided to stay with her word. There was little we could do now anyway. Lynn had already purchased her ticket and would be on her way within a few days. We hoped that the vice-director was just talking with no authority to back him up.

Director Qin had returned to her hometown to attend her father's funeral. She was not due back at the orphanage until Monday, which would be after Lynn arrived in Nanchang. That was a concern as she had told us everything was okay and that Lynn could bring all her papers to Nanchang. And then another person, in charge while Director Qin was gone, told us something different.

We should have known it was just another of those many crooks in the road. We had faced them over and over again throughout this trial. Someone would tell us one thing only to have someone else tell us just the opposite. Still, it always stung when they did those things to us. Truth – it was out there somewhere among all the verbiage. Thankfully we knew the One who is the Truth. We were followers of the Truth. Jesus said that He was the Truth. As long as we kept our eyes on Jesus, we would be following the Truth.

On April 7 Mei Mei had been in the orphanage seven weeks.

Lynn was due in Hong Kong on April 10 and would be in Nanchang just a few days after that. We were expecting her to arrive on Monday at the latest after arriving in Hong Kong on Friday.

Anticipation was building that soon this would all be over. What a joy it would be for us to see Lynn arrive in Nanchang, bearing all the papers with all the official stamps and seals.

We were ready.

On Friday we went about our daily activities, but with an anticipatory air. We prayed for Lynn, knowing that she was on that long flight across the Big Pond (as LeRoy liked to call the Pacific Ocean); then she would land in Hong Kong and find that a whole day had passed while she was sitting on the airplane.

We did not expect to hear anything from her on Friday, but thought we might get a call from her on Saturday. No call. But of course it was Saturday when she arrived in Hong Kong – probably late Saturday.

We anticipated a call on Sunday. No call came. I was on pins and needles, just waiting to hear that Lynn had tickets and would arrive in Nanchang on Monday, or Tuesday at the latest. Or perhaps she would just appear in Nanchang on Monday. She may have been unable to contact us – that would not be unusual considering the phone system – and she may have decided to just fly to Nanchang and make it to our place as best she could.

We tried to go about our regular schedules, which included trips to the orphanage. Mei Mei was back to her smiling sweet self again, encouraging us greatly. I found that I could not walk through the days as I normally would. Anticipation was there in everything I did, in everything I thought.

My idea was that once we had Lynn in Nanchang, we were going to get Mei Mei out of the orphanage. We were going to have her back in our home. It would be just as before, and we would shower her with love. She would receive so much love that she would totally forget everything about the orphanage. I was determined to bestow more love on her than any baby had ever known.

We were deep into Monday, and still the phone lines from Hong Kong were silent. My anticipation was beginning to be replaced by anxiousness. I was concerned. Those thoughts of what could go wrong began to surface.

That afternoon we received word from Lynn via another American who had just arrived in Nanchang from Hong Kong. Lynn was actually staying in her apartment in Hong Kong, so she had all the news for us. We plied her with our questions, wanting to learn as much as we could.

Of course Lynn had to get a visa before she could enter China. That task would take a few days. It was normal procedure for this to be so. Somehow we had just assumed that Lynn would fly in one day, secure her visa, buy her ticket, and fly out the next day.

We should not have been so foolish to expect everything to happen so quickly.

There was another problem however. It had to do with the improving economic conditions in China. The airlines were totally booked. We found it a little difficult to believe that so many people would be flying to Nanchang. Nanchang was still lagging far behind in the economic resurgence taking place in the People's Republic of China. Of course, there were only a few flights a week from Hong Kong to Nanchang.

According to the messenger from Hong Kong, Lynn was to get her Chinese visa by Monday and she had a travel agent working on her ticket. The word was that she might appear in Nanchang on Tuesday.

And the Liar continued the battle. Tom had gone out to the orphanage on Monday to check with Director Qin after she returned from her home village. Tom's report was not good when he arrived at our apartment that afternoon.

"Now Director Qin is also saying that everything must wait until April 20."

We quickly pounced on him to find out why she would give us such news, whereas before she seemed ready for everything to go forward quickly. She had seemed to want the adoption to take place as rapidly as all the rest of us did.

He continued, "She said that the officials involved in adoptions here are presently in Beijing, learning about the new law. They get back April 14, and then they teach the people here.

"The law is official here on April 20."

A new bump in the road.

On Tuesday Lynn called from Hong Kong. She did not have very good news. She did have her Chinese visa stamped in her passport. That part was good news. However, it was also true, as we suspected that flights from Hong Kong were not easily attainable. It was the beginning of a long Easter holiday, and there was a major trade fair being held in Guangzhou – just a short flight or a 3-hour train ride from Hong Kong.

The Brits took a serious holiday over Easter. Their schools would be closed for two weeks as part of the Easter holiday. Since many of the schools in Hong Kong – including the universities – would be closed for such a long period, many people took vacations. So there was an increased amount of air traffic at the time. Lynn was unsure when she could get a ticket.

She was being told that Sunday would be the earliest she could procure a ticket. She did not want to wait a week in Hong Kong, where she was accomplishing nothing. She was just as anxious to be in Nanchang as we were anxious to welcome her. We never had imagined that Lynn would be stuck in Hong Kong.

Thankfully Lynn was an "old China hand" so she was not easily thwarted. If one door closed you started looking for a window to crawl through – just as I had learned from my student breaking into my classroom.

Lynn had taught in Yangzhou, a city near Nanjing, for one year. She had also worked in Hong Kong for a year. During that year she did a lot of traveling in and out and about China.

"I've been trying to call you," she said when we finally heard her voice on the phone. "I could never get through. The China phone system on the blink again?" she questioned understandingly.

"I can't get a ticket until Sunday," she told us.

We had little to say on the other end because we already knew all of this, and we did not want to convey our disappointment to her; we knew she was trying.

"I'm going to take the fast train to Guangzhou or take a bus to Shenzhen tomorrow. I'll fly standby if I have to."

"But, what if there are no flights available there?" I asked.

"I feel sure there will be flights. They fly to Nanchang more times a week from those airports. I'm sure I'll be able to get a flight out on the same day. I'm planning on being there tomorrow."

"We'll keep praying," I told her.

It was good to hear her so positive about flights to Nanchang, but it was impossible to know. Often the weather conditions would change all the flights. And it might not even be weather problems at your destination or your site of departure. We once waited at the Shenzhen airport for seven hours while the plane we were to take completed its trip to another destination and back before heading for our destination. The plane was flying from Shenzhen to Ningbo, then back to Shenzhen then to Nanchang. There was a rainstorm in Ningbo, so they had delayed that flight, which then delayed our flight.

And Lynn would be flying into Nanchang. Our weather was abysmal most of the time.

We prayed. She took the train to Guangzhou Wednesday.

We were feeling as though we were still right in the middle of the battle. We finally had Lynn in Asia with all the official documents and $3,000 in her hands, and yet she was struggling to get to Nanchang. It seemed like there were roadblocks and bumps and huge chasms in the road to rescuing our baby. Could we ever jump through all the hoops? Could we ever perform all the tricks the officials wanted? Would we ever see Mei Mei out of that orphanage and out of China?

Our answer to that remained "yes." It simply had to be. The life of a precious child was involved.

Wednesday came. We prayed for Lynn. We anxiously expected her arrival. But we had to continue teaching, seeing Mei Mei at the orphanage and continue everything else in our daily lives.

Our regular routine, which we hoped was about to be totally disrupted by Lynn's arrival, was already disrupted because some American teachers from other cities had arrived for a visit. Plus more of our Chinese friends than usual were in and out of the apartment, since they had learned Lynn was on her way. They were anxious to meet this woman who was making such a long trip to take Mei Mei back to America with her. Several wondered why an American would go to so much trouble and expense to adopt a girl.

Perhaps it was good that it was a busy time, keeping me busy, trying to play hostess to everyone. David and Marianne were always glad to see visitors appear, especially young American teachers. They were happy when the young singles who lived in our city dropped by, and even more excited when teachers from other cities would appear. Most of them treated David and Marianne like a younger brother and sister, which was usually a good thing.

The sun was setting on Wednesday, and still we had heard nothing from Lynn. "Now what?" was the question that kept zipping around my brain.

We went to bed that night not knowing what was going on.

We awoke Thursday morning hoping to see Lynn magically appear at our door before the day was done.

We went through our morning hearing no word from Lynn. We tried to stay busy, but it was difficult to keep ourselves focused on anything but the question, "What has happened to Lynn?"

Finally, that afternoon, Lynn called.

"I've been trying to call all day," she told us. "I never could get through until now."

"Where are you?" was my first question.

"I'm still in Guangzhou. But don't worry. Everything is okay."

"But when are you coming here?" I interrupted her to get to the most important point.

"I've got a ticket on the plane very early tomorrow morning. My flight arrives at 8:30."

"One of us will be there to meet you," I quickly assured her. She had never been to Nanchang. It was not exactly a tourist-friendly place. One of the guidebooks described it as "dull gray, nondescript; don't bother," so most tourists did not bother.

"That'll be great," she responded. "I'm sorry to be running later than I told you, but I think I've done some good here."

"Like what?" I asked. Later I thought I sounded almost accusatory, as if she should not be doing anything but getting to Nanchang, going straight to the orphanage, and removing Mei Mei from that place.

"I went to the consulate and talked to the same woman

you saw in February."

I frowned when I heard that, but only replied, "And?"

"Well, she wasn't much help, but she did tell me some things that we would need to do, so that part was helpful. However, she also discouraged me from even trying to adopt."

Lynn is a positive person and rarely would she speak negatively of someone, so I thought that more than likely the American government official in Guangzhou had called Lynn's intelligence into question for even thinking about adopting a Chinese baby. The woman had certainly made me feel like a member of the lower class when I was in her presence in February.

"I'll see you tomorrow," was her closing remark.

I cried when I hung up. Finally! Finally Lynn would be in Nanchang. Finally, the adoption process would begin in earnest when she arrived. I could barely wait. I cried, then I said, "Thank you Jesus," over and over again, and I smiled. I could finally actually visualize Mei Mei out of the orphanage. I could see the reality of it all coming to pass. I then smiled a bigger smile, and I almost shouted, "Thank God!"

Chapter XIX

Show Us the Fruit

During our two years in Nanchang we often wondered how many lives we had touched. We could count conversions on one hand. We thought that it seemed as though we were spinning our wheels, accomplishing little.

If we were being obedient to God in serving Him in Nanchang, why did we not see much movement of the Holy Spirit? Why were people only occasionally interested in the things of God? Why did it seem that it was always an uphill climb?

We were blessed with our small core group of Chinese believers, plus the Bible study that I had with two women. But we had continued these from the previous year. We felt privileged to be discipling people, but wondered at the lack of interest in others.

There were two people that God brought into our lives that second year who impacted us spiritually in a way that we had never experienced before.

Of course, that second year in Nanchang was wrapped around Mei Mei. Her life and what was or was not happening with her touched us in every way. She was the focus; but we had not forgotten Liu Hua Lan – the 16-year-old girl who was battling cancer.

It had been such a delight to see her born into the Kingdom. We rejoiced. And we were so thankful when we heard that the doctors had decided not to amputate her leg. We saw this development as a great victory in the battle for her life. We were there with her following a surgical procedure that the doctors hoped would help her. Her family brought her to our campus for us all to say goodbye as she was on her way home from the hospital. Her parents had managed to obtain a truck in which to take her home. They were bringing her by – in her body cast – to see us, but also to see Mei Mei. We had shared with her about Mei Mei and Hua Lan wanted to see her before leaving Nanchang. Hua Lan could not leave the truck, so we took the baby out to her. Hua Lan was all smiles because she was finally able to return home after being in the hospital for many weeks. Her parents were also beaming that day.

But, as all the turmoil with Mei Mei peaked in the spring, we learned that Liu Hua Lan had returned to the hospital in Nanchang, only to be sent home to Tang Gu County to die. The doctors reported that the cancer had spread.

In April, while we were in the middle of the Nanchang part of the adoption battle, Tom came by our home one day to tell us that Liu Hua Lan had died.

That news hit us hard. We had faced so many disappointments with Mei Mei, and now, as we were fighting hard toward victory with her, we received news of Liu Hua Lan's death. It felt like we had been dealt another blow and we could feel our "shield of faith" slipping again.

LeRoy especially felt the impact because he and Tom had led her into the Kingdom. He had also told her of God's healing power and had given her healing Scriptures to read.

He had been truly trusting and believing for God to heal her.

Tom was hurt by this news too. He was the one who had said, "Why don't we see miracles today?" He was the one who took us to meet her. He had believed for her salvation. He had believed for her healing.

In a later newsletter of ours LeRoy wrote:

> I question "Why?" and am still unsure of the answer, but I do believe that God planted a seed in Tang Gu County (Liu Hua Lan's home county). Her parents had told us that they knew of no Christians in that whole area. They themselves had never heard of Jesus. None of their friends had ever heard of Jesus. But that all changed through Liu Hua Lan.
>
> While still in the hospital, and shortly after her conversion, Hua Lan wrote a letter to her teacher that was read to her entire class at school. In that letter she wrote that she had opened her heart to Jesus and explained who He is. It was the first time the teacher or any of the students had heard of Jesus.
>
> When she returned to Tang Gu County in her body cast (following surgery), her friends came to see her. What they saw was a young girl with a radiant smile, a girl who should have been moaning and groaning. Every time I saw her in the hospital, she was proof of God's grace and His wonderful provision. Her friends, relatives and class-mates all saw that, too. I believe that God planted a seed in Tang Gu County through Liu Hua Lan, and from that one tiny seed, many beautiful flowers will bloom."

We know that she was one life saved. We hurt from the loss of her earthly life, but know someday we will dance on streets of gold with her.

We were anxiously awaiting Mei Mei's victory. The battle raged on.

Meanwhile God was moving in a way that we did not know. In China, we seldom knew what God was doing. We were thankful for the times that He showed us how He was using us in China. But often we remained ignorant of His actions. That was the case throughout this ordeal with Mei Mei.

Quietly, people were watching.

They were watching us. They were watching how we acted and how we reacted.

People who were involved with us in China – students or colleagues – knew that we were Christians. The government leaders and school officials told them very clearly. They told them that we believed in God, that we were followers of a Western religion. And then they warned them, "Do not talk to the foreigners about what they believe."

Young people are naturally curious. So, if they are told to avoid something, they are usually drawn to it. Such was the case of many of our students. They were curious about what we believed. And they were curious as to why we believed.

Prior to each academic year we were told – it was also written in our contract – that we could not teach religion. We did not want to teach religion. Religion had done nothing for us. Jesus had done everything for us.

We were always amazed how the Holy Spirit was already on the scene before we arrived at each place. We should not have been surprised, for we had people praying for us in America and we were trusting for God to open doors to give us opportunities to share about His great love.

It was interesting to tell a group of people that we believed in God and have that statement be greeted with laughter. We were never really sure what the laughter meant, but determined that it was more of a nervous laughter than anything else. They did not know how to respond to someone who told them that he believes in God. However, there was always someone who was curious enough to ask.

We encouraged our students to ask questions – a very unusual experience for Chinese students. The Chinese classroom is quite different from the Western classroom. The thinking is, "The teacher is the font of knowledge. The students are the empty vessels." The teacher will pour his knowledge into the students. They willingly receive all that the professor says, and on tests that follow, they will then tell him what he told them. We termed it "regurgitation."

During his introduction on the first day of class, LeRoy would tell the students, "Please ask me questions. It is very important to ask a question if you don't understand something. You can ask me any question. If I don't want to answer it, then I won't answer it." I also tried to encourage students to ask me questions.

Some of the older students began to enjoy asking questions, especially when they dealt with things about America.

At times we would be surprised as a question would come out of the blue; or we were surprised by the question itself.

I received one of those questions when I was giving an American culture lecture about Easter to more than 300 students. One of my favorite students – an 18-year-old boy – asked me about Ascension Day.

I responded by saying, "That's a good question." Then I told him about Jesus' ascending into the heavens. The same student raised his hand again. I was encouraged by his first question, so I quickly called on him again. His question this time was, "How did He do that?"

I think I might have slapped him if he were close enough! "How did he do that?"

I had never thought about such a thing. When you grow up in the church in America, this was simply something you knew about. It just happened that way; no questions asked.

Actually, I think I only stared at him for a minute, hoping my thoughts would come into focus. I finally told him, "Jesus was God on this earth. If you are God, you can do anything you want to do. He's not bound by the laws of nature."

That seemed to satisfy him at the moment. I could only imagine what went through their minds later. They had seen Superman movies, so I am sure they envisioned Jesus in His flowing cape shooting off into the middle of the universe somewhere.

We began to recognize in the early part of our Chinese life that we had to be careful using "Christianese," since the Chinese had no compass with which to navigate through spiritual waters. It was all brand new to them. They were a blank slate.

In one of LeRoy's first classes a man in the back of the room raised his hand to ask a question. He stood slowly and spoke very clearly. "Can you tell us about God?" LeRoy had been doing his regular English lecture. The class had nothing to do with the Bible, Christianity, or anything remotely related to anything Christian.

He continued with his question to be assured that LeRoy understood: "We know everything about Lenin and Stalin and Mao Ze Dong thought, but we know nothing of God. Can you tell us about God?"

That student opened the door, and LeRoy stepped into it. It was his first experience talking about God in a classroom in Communist China. His hand was a little shaky as he started writing on the board to explain to the class about a Living, Loving God. From all appearances, none of them had ever heard of anything he was sharing.

At one point during his explanation LeRoy realized that he had the whole plan of salvation written on the blackboard. The blackboard in a university classroom in the middle of the People's Republic of China was completely covered with words of God and words about God.

"Oops," was the first thought in LeRoy's head, when he realized what he had done. "Got carried away," was his second thought.

After the class ended (late, because LeRoy did not want to stop in the middle of answering this question), he was left alone in the classroom.

"Wow!" came to mind quickly. "What just happened here?" Then he looked at the blackboard again. The words "Bible," "Jesus," and "God loves you" were still there. He debated what he should do. Should he erase them? Perhaps he could leave them as they were. If they remained, there would be plenty of evidence to convict him of teaching "religion," a practice which is strictly forbidden in the teaching contract. He finally decided to leave the words of God and His love fully on display, and came home singing a song.

Over the years we realized that our students were hungry to ask questions about God. We just had to be ready to answer the questions. Often they would challenge us. And at times they would make snide remarks about our beliefs. Many times, during our years in China, we heard, "How can you believe in God? You come from the most technologically advanced country in the world. America is the wealthiest country in the world. You both have college degrees. How can you believe in God?"

They were stumped because they had been taught that such a belief was for poor, superstitious, ignorant people.

This was all good for us, since it made us look at what we believed and why we believed it. Mouthing our regular "spiritual phrases" that would readily be accepted in America would not work in China. China was a faith-builder for us in more ways than one.

God also built our faith as He slowly began to show us

how He was using Mei Mei's life to open the hearts of people around her.

God had knocked on the door of Melissa's heart as she watched us with Mei Mei. Melissa had grown up indoctrinated with the ideals of atheism – she had always been taught that there was no God. There had never been anything or anyone to dispute this teaching until our team arrived on the scene.

Melissa had been involved with Mei Mei from the beginning. She had come to our apartment to see the baby, and she had helped in the translation work. We had known Melissa the previous year. She would visit us occasionally then. She visited Shelly even more often.

Melissa knew something of the kind of people that we were; she knew that we were Christians.

She later told us that she saw our happy family and was drawn toward us because of the joy that she saw in all our lives. She also revealed to us later that she thought we were cheerful people because we never had any problems. Chinese tend to view Americans as a unique breed. They know that the United States is a powerful country. They know that we are a wealthy people. They know that "we have everything that we need." Most Americans may not realize this misconception, but compared to Chinese and the rest of the world, it is a true perception.

So, Melissa saw us as people who never had any difficulty. She failed to realize that just being an American in China was difficult. She saw our lifestyle compared to most Chinese and simply saw us as very blessed. Anyone who had no problems would be happy, she reasoned.

Mei Mei came into our lives. Melissa became more involved with us. As the months went by, she saw our love for this Chinese baby girl. She also witnessed all the difficulties we faced in the illness that almost took Mei Mei from us; and then the tribulations of putting her in the orphanage. Melissa was also one who knew how many times we had had doors slammed in our faces. She had seen me cry over this baby.

At one point during this ordeal Melissa said to me, "Now you know how we Chinese are treated every day."

She said very little to us, but she was watching. She told us later that she realized that we still had joy, even during difficult times. She said, "There was something in your lives that was different. Your attitude was different."

She began to open her heart to Shelly – telling her more of what she was thinking. Shelly told her about Jesus and what a difference He had made in our lives – that it was His joy within us that could sustain us and take us through difficulties.

Melissa had been struggling with some hard questions in her life because a friend of hers had drowned recently. That caused her to think about life and whether there was anything beyond life. It precipitated her asking about death, which led to Shelly's telling her about life in Jesus.

As Shelly shared more, Melissa recognized her need for a Savior, and on Palm Sunday she gave her life to the Lord Jesus.

Years later Melissa told us, "If it hadn't been for you, I don't know where I'd be today."

We shared very little with her verbally, but she was always watching us. We were surprised that this was the case, for there were many days when we became extremely frustrated and were not exhibiting the love of Jesus in any shape or form. Often we did not feel very spiritual, and we did not act very "Christian."

And Melissa was watching.

Melissa's story is worth a book in itself. The bottom line is that through miraculous means God converted her, took her from Nanchang, and put her in Wheaton College, a

Christian college in Illinois. After she graduated from Wheaton she started working with a mission agency that did radio broadcasting to the People's Republic of China. Now her parents listen to their daughter reading the Bible as they sit in their apartment in Nanchang.

When Melissa entered our lives, she was extremely timid. Her Chinese nickname was *Little Mouse*. She exemplified that moniker perfectly. But years later, she was being heard by millions of people across China. It is an amazing story of God's faithfulness – how He lifted her up as she submitted to Him. But, we knew very little of this as we battled on to save the life of one baby.

Chapter XX

*I will never leave you
nor forsake you.*

Hebrews 13:5

Baby in Our Hearts

F riday morning finally arrived. I was at the airport to watch Lynn's plane descend. It was no problem for me to get up and be at the airport early, since I had slept very little that night anyway.

I was more than ready for Lynn to be in Nanchang. We still had no assurances about the adoption. We did not know what would happen with Lynn's arrival. But we did know that nothing was going to take place until she placed all the official papers in the proper hands in Nanchang. The more quickly Lynn arrived, the sooner we could rescue Mei Mei from the orphanage.

My excitement almost overwhelmed Lynn as I threw my arms around her when she came walking off the plane. She was pretty excited to see me too; she needed someone there to escort her into the city. Traveling in China was never easy, even if it was a short distance. The bicycle was by far the best mode of transportation usually, but the airport was too far out of town to go by bicycle. It took about an hour by car.

Lynn was flying into Nanchang on Friday, April 17 – Good Friday. We considered it a very good Friday indeed.

I ushered Lynn into our apartment, where there was still more rejoicing over her arrival. LeRoy and I were definitely celebrating, but I sensed some hesitancy from Marianne and

David. It might have been because they had not seen Lynn for several years and thus thought they were not familiar enough with her to just be themselves. Or, I thought later, perhaps they saw her in a somewhat negative light. "This American woman is coming to take our baby away from us," might have been their thinking. "It's good that she's here to rescue Mei Mei from the orphanage, but it's not good that she's going to take Mei Mei away from us."

At the time, LeRoy and I did not struggle with such emotions. We were simply overjoyed that we could now begin the next step.

We called Tom as soon as the dust had settled from Lynn's arrival. He arrived at 11 a.m. and quickly made arrangements to transport Lynn out to the orphanage and start the papers moving.

LeRoy had been unable to go to the airport with me because he had a class that morning. Neither of us would be able to go to the orphanage with Lynn that afternoon because we were scheduled to do a culture lecture. Frankly, I did not want to go to the orphanage with Lynn anyway.

I was concerned about how Mei Mei would react to a new foreign face. Perhaps I also was struggling with the "letting go" even then. Yet, I did very much want Mei Mei to accept Lynn.

Lynn insisted on going to the orphanage as soon as possible. After all, she wanted to see, to hold, to meet, and get to know this baby in which she, John and Kristin were about to invest their lives. I doubt that anyone could have stopped her from going if he had hit her with a hammer. However, I was concerned about her reaction to the orphanage and the condition in which she would find Mei Mei. She had been sick so often. I did not want Lynn to walk through the sadness of that orphanage and also find Mei Mei sick. I was concerned what Lynn would think of us when she walked into the place where I had placed Mei Mei. When she saw the conditions of that orphanage would Lynn be angry with us? Would she try to take Mei Mei out of there right away? Would she change her mind about adopting Mei Mei at all?

Many thoughts raced around in my head. I was fearful of telling Lynn too much about the orphanage. We finally decided that we had few options in the matter. We let her go with only a few admonitions. After all, Tom was taking her there. We were praying that he would be wise and offer good counsel to any questions Lynn might pose. I had niggling thoughts that Tom might encourage Lynn to take Mei Mei from the orphanage and make a dash for freedom with her.

I had to put all those feelings aside and say once again, "Lord, you are fighting this battle. Please help me to let You do things Your way. Lynn loves You. Tom loves You. And we all love Mei Mei. Thy will be done."

We awaited Lynn's return from the orphanage with some trepidation. I had been able to roll my fears over onto God, but they still kept nibbling at my mind.

Lynn walked in our door, looked at me, and gently wiped her eyes. I waited, unsure of what she was going to say.

"She's so beautiful," she said as she lightly sniffed. "Thank you for rescuing her."

We hugged. I was relieved.

"She is so sweet. John and I began to love her as we looked at the pictures you sent, and as we prayed for her. But, to see her and to hold her… I could feel my love for her growing."

She wanted only to talk about Mei Mei. She sounded just like any other mother, bragging on her daughter. The more Lynn raved about Mei Mei, the better I felt. I was even beginning to glow a little as she thanked me again for my taking Mei Mei off the street and loving her.

There was very little, if any mention of the orphanage itself. My fears concerning her reaction to that horrid place had been misplaced.

I had been concerned prior to her trip there because Lynn had never been to a Chinese orphanage. I well remember my own first reaction to the place. It continued to sicken me every time we went there. I still could feel revulsion toward the institution welling up within me, even after my many trips. Also, at times I would still punish myself for having put Mei Mei in such a place.

It is still difficult for me to describe the orphanage in Nanchang. Countries such as China naturally try to hide the evidence of the more unsavory aspects of their land. Orphanages in China are a prime example.

They were almost always hidden away on the outskirts of a village, near a major city. They were old buildings and they were drab.

The Nanchang orphanage was definitely located on the wrong side of the river. There was a narrow road, filled with potholes, leading past the river bridge toward the orphanage. As we approached the premises we saw a brick wall completely surrounding the orphanage property. The wall was made with cinder blocks, topped with red brick to add an additional foot in height. Broken glass was embedded in the top of the wall. Garbage, trash, and other debris lay all along the outside wall. We would occasionally see a rat scurrying along among the garbage as we arrived on our bicycles.

China is made up of work units. All work units have a protective wall. The work unit is a community within a community. We were assigned to a work unit – Jiangxi Medical College. We had a north campus and a south campus. We entered through gates, with a guard stationed at the gate. Walls surrounded both campuses. If the guards did not recognize someone, they would stop them and ask for identification. Then the guards would ask, "What are you doing here?" We were never stopped. We were easily recognizable.

Inside the orphanage walls were the buildings housing the children and the few workers, plus there was a home for the elderly on the grounds as well. They were all two- and three-storied brick buildings. The inside walls were plastered and whitewashed, with a layer of green enamel painted halfway up the walls. The wooden floors, which had not seen varnish in years, had cracks between the boards, allowing insects to crawl through. The cold winds could also blow through those cracks and through those found in the window casements and other areas of the building.

The infants' room was filled with small wooden cribs painted turquoise, with two babies per crib. The room held about 30 cribs. All the babies lay on their backs and were covered with blankets. The little cloth strips between their legs were changed only once in the morning and once in the evening. The smell of urine and excrement was always present.

Three times a day, the babies would receive a bottle of milk. They did not hold the babies to feed them. A folded cloth was placed underneath the baby's chin. They used that to hold the bottle in place so the baby could drink. All the babies just lay there staring vacantly at the ceiling. They learned long ago that it was useless to cry, because no one would respond. No one would hold them. They were in a world unto themselves. The workers were there to meet the basic needs of the babies – nothing more. It was difficult to find fault with the workers. There were so very few of them trying to take care of so many children.

Older babies that could sit up were in a room with the same type cribs, but here there was only one child per bed. During the day, they were placed in a little wooden potty-chair and strapped in. A small metal bowl was placed under the hole in the chair. During feeding times, the chairs would be placed in a semi-circle. The attendant would have one bowl of rice gruel and one spoon. She would sit on a small stool in front of the children and give each a spoonful in turn. The same spoon went into each child's mouth. The mucus draining from one child's nose would end up on the spoon and be passed to the next child. It was the easiest and quickest method for the workers to feed the children.

Again, the minimum requirements for existence were met – nothing more.

The babies and little children did not know what it was to be held, cuddled and loved.

Actually, Mei Mei was being accorded special treatment. She was kept in the same makeshift wooden crib as the others, but she was in a room with older deaf boys. Xiao Hua, who was assigned to take care of her, gave Mei Mei more attention than the others received. She followed the only procedures she knew to care for a child, and she knew very little. She was also an orphan. She was older when she arrived at the orphanage due to a family break-up. She was the only older girl we ever saw in the orphanage. We did not understand why that was the case.

Since Mei Mei was toddling and in split-pants, Xiao Hua did what all Chinese did with children that age, she lifted her up and held her with her legs spread open and whistled. Mei Mei knew the cue. She wet on the hardwood floor. Then Xiao Hua would splash a little water over the urine on the floor – standard Chinese sanitation procedure.

During the winter, there was no heat in the orphanage, so the babies were covered with very thick blankets. The older children wore several layers of clothing. The windows were left open because the Chinese were firm believers in fresh air. It was as cold inside as outside, so it would not really have mattered whether the windows were open.

In summer, of course, there was no air-conditioning. The windows had no screens. They remained open, only wider than in the winter. Open windows would mean insects in any locale, but on the backside of Nanchang, with a small river nearby, there was an abundance of flies and mosquitoes. The flies especially liked the milk that was spilled on the babies as they tried to suck from their propped bottles. Also, the flies were drawn to the open sores on the babies.

There were only one to two attendants in each room to care for all the children. It was such a stark contrast to the six to eight attendants behind a small counter at a Chinese department store. China has far too many people and not enough jobs, but very few want to work in orphanages.

There were times that the whole governmental system angered me. From time to time I would walk into a department store downtown and feel the anger rising.

"How could they have 8 people behind a shoe counter, serving no one, while there are not a tenth of the workers needed at the orphanage?" At times I wanted to grab one of those department store workers who was busily sipping her tea and say, "Get out of here; go out to the orphanage where you're really needed." But people did not care about the orphans, and the government did not care about the orphans. No one cared.

At first I was very angry because the attendants did such a poor job of taking care of the children. But later, I realized they had an impossible task. They were to take care of children that no one wanted or cared about. Eventually, we were even told that each child was evaluated in regard to its health and possible chances of adoption. If the results were not favorable, that baby's milk would be watered down so that she would slowly starve to death. The "dying rooms" of China are true. I have been in them.

The only redeeming aspect of the orphanage was the outside area. The sidewalks were swept, and the area was landscaped to some extent. The hedges were used as drying racks and for airing bedding. Whenever it was a sunny day, blankets and clothing covered the hedges. It was the best drying facility they had.

A brand-new building was being constructed on the premises. A wealthy Hong Kong woman had donated money for the construction. It was a five-story building that was to house the administration and the elderly. There was no elevator, so the elderly would have to live on the ground floor. That meant that there were four floors for the administrative staff and their offices. The children would remain in the decrepit rooms in the old buildings, rooms that reeked of urine.

We were more anxious than ever to free Mei Mei from that place.

Saturday is a regular workday in China and we were ready to work. There had been some disturbing news from Director Qin yesterday. She told Tom and Lynn that there were problems between the social welfare offices and the Justice Department. Apparently more people wanted to get their hands on the American money. Another pothole in the road toward Mei Mei's adoption!

Lynn had already been in Asia one week, and we were just beginning the Nanchang paper chase with her. We prayed for swift approval at every point.

Shortly after the offices opened on Saturday, Lynn, Tom, and I met Director Qin at the Justice Department. We were blessed to have a friend there. His name was Qi Fong.

He greeted us warmly in Chinese. He was very pleasant, but was unable to do anything for us.

"His director will not be in until Monday," Tom translated. We were disappointed, but not disheartened. We wanted to see something move today, but Monday was only two days away. Then he told us what else the man had said: "It should take about a week."

We did not want to deal in weeks. We wanted to see a

victory every day.

Tom then translated for Director Qin: "She's going to take the documents to the police station to get Mei Mei's passport."

We were leaving the official documents in offices, handing them over to Chinese. These were not copies. These were the official documents with the official stamps. If they were lost, it would mean jumping through the hoops in the U.S. again. We continued to pray, and trust, and believe that God was watching over all the documents. We continued to believe that He would see us through.

After we walked out of the Justice Department building, Lynn and I got on a bus to take the hour's ride out to the Jiangxi Agriculture College. It, of course, was located out in the country. The regular weekly meeting of foreign Christians was being held at the Ag School that week.

Almost all of the foreign Christians attended these meetings. Chinese were not allowed. It would mean trouble for them and for us if they came. It was good for Lynn to have the chance to meet other people who had been involved in helping Mei Mei. They were all happy to see the beginning of the answer to their prayers.

Lynn had announced to us after her arrival that Mei Mei now had an American name. She and John had decided to call her Kali. We started trying to call her Kali. But, the other Nanchang foreign folks were still calling her Mei Mei, and she would always be "The Amazin' Maizer" to us.

The next day was Easter Sunday. It was a great day of celebration as we joined together to rejoice over Melissa's birth into the Kingdom of God. We had a party in Shelly's apartment. We did all the typical Easter things. Someone had sent an egg-dying kit. It was fun to see our Chinese friends dye Easter eggs. They were just as enthusiastic as children decorating eggs for the first time. The Chinese have a tradition of egg dyeing related to the birth of a son. When a son is born, the family boils eggs and dyes them red. They pass them out to family and friends just as some pass out cigars in the U.S. We also read Scripture and sang.

The sun was shining in Nanchang.

We had already incorporated Lynn into our family. She had moved into Marianne's little bedroom. Marianne was sleeping in with us. Our bed was actually two beds pushed together with a blanket across the space between the two mattresses. It was possibly larger than a king-size bed in America. But we all hoped this arrangement would not last long. All of us were willing to do whatever was necessary during the time Lynn was with us. Everyone's focus was getting Mei Mei out of the orphanage, and Lynn was the key player for our success.

By Monday morning we were all ready to charge into the fray, to start all those papers moving. We did not want to hear, "Wait." We did not want excuses. We did not want to hear, "The person with the authority is not here." We wanted and fully expected to see some action.

Lynn was already into her second week in Asia – even though she had been in Nanchang only three days. She could not continue to stay in Nanchang. Plus, we were all anxious to see Kali back in our home. On Tuesday, Mei Mei would have been in the orphanage nine weeks. Nine weeks! God had worked a miracle to sustain her during that time. But now was the time for her to escape from that place.

Lynn, Tom, and I hit the trail early Monday. We first went to the Justice Department. We met with a Ms. Cao. She gave us approval to begin the adoption process. That was Step One. We had to have approval from that department before we could even begin the process in Nanchang.

Ms. Cao called Director Qin to tell her that she needed

to go to the Nanchang Civil Administration offices. We were also told that final approval had to come from Beijing, but that Ms. Cao would call them to secure their permission. Tom translated to us that Ms. Cao said there was a possibility that Lynn could get Kali out of the orphanage in a week. She probably thought we would be overjoyed to hear this news. We were not. We could see no reason for Kali to remain in the orphanage. Director Qin knew that Lynn had all the needed papers. Lynn was in Nanchang as proof of her intention to adopt. She and John had gone to much trouble and expense to do everything required of them. It seemed obvious to us that she should be allowed to take Kali to our apartment while the process continued.

We did not want Kali to remain in that place even one more day – much less a whole week.

When Canadians had arrived in Nanchang to adopt, they went to a hotel. The day they arrived, people from the orphanage took their babies to them – special delivery – in their hotel rooms. They never even had to see that horrid orphanage.

We did not understand; we wanted them to release Kali. But, we kept our mouths shut. It was especially difficult for me; but I thought, after calling some of the officials "liars" – more than once – a few months ago, that it would be better for me to remain silent.

I had to continually remind myself that God had clearly shown us that this was His fight, and we were to let Him do it. LeRoy occasionally pointed this fact out to me when I started expressing my opinion about them on the ride home. My description usually began with "Those turkeys..."

I was amazed at how calm Lynn remained during all this. She was on the other side of the earth from her family, giving up her teaching salary, giving up her home life, crammed into a tiny apartment with our family. She was not comfortable as the rains returned, after they let her "enjoy"

Nanchang's spring sans rain for awhile. Yet, Lynn remained patient. She refused to let people fluster her. She was determined to ride this out. She had her mind set that the victory would be won and that, at some point, she would leave Nanchang, and Kali would go with her.

We returned home after a morning of office hopping. I was just beginning to return to a calm state Monday afternoon when Tom came to our apartment.

"I just talked to Director Qin," he told us after we sat him down and gave him a cup of tea. He merely let it sit there as he told us his news. It was not impolite to let the tea sit untouched. But it was considered impolite to not offer the tea.

"She called me and told me the civil administration – they said they have no forms."

"What?" we enquired, hoping that we were just not following his English well.

"The forms for Lynn to fill out for adoption – they don't have."

I think he was a little exasperated, so his English really was not correct at that moment, but we got the message.

"She's working on that," Tom said. He was telling us that Director Qin was trying to solve that problem. We failed to see how she could do so, but hoped that she could.

"We can call her tomorrow," Tom said, and then took a sip of his tea after he blew on it a bit to scatter the tea leaves.

Also on Monday, LeRoy taught his classes, David and Marianne continued their schoolwork at home, we said goodbye to two American friends from another city, and I went for my fourth in a series of visits to the dentist. He finished my root canal that day.

Just knowing it was completed made me feel better.

Our Tuesday was not a "feel better" day. Tuesday was a day when we had to once again remind ourselves that God was fighting this battle. We had absolutely no control over anything that was happening.

So many of our days in Nanchang had been full of frustrations – anger – hope – hopes dashed – hopes building – looking beyond – dreaming – some day, some time – disappointment – and then hope growing again. And, always we were clinging to the promises of God found in His Word and His whisperings to us in our hearts.

As I dreamed of the day when Kali would return to our home and pictured Lynn and her flying away from Nanchang, LeRoy told me the mental picture he carried.

"I want to see Kali, dressed in a beautiful, frilly dress that is new and clean. I envision her with those pretty little-girl shoes with white lace socks. I can't wait until the day when I see her dressed as a little girl should be dressed."

He was ready. I was ready. We were all ready. We so wanted the frustrations to end. We wanted to no longer be held by the chain with which Communist authorities had jerked us first one way then another.

We saw snippets of progress and begged God for that long-awaited full answer to our prayer – Kali in the home of John and Lynn.

That Tuesday, Lynn was anxious to spend time with Kali again. She wanted me to go with her. I was still hesitant to go. I was very concerned that Kali would reach out to me. It felt that it was important that Lynn and Kali begin to bond.

In February, when I placed Mei Mei in the orphanage, the officials tried to drive me away because they wanted to break the bond between Mei Mei and me. There had been a wrenching in my heart then, but Mei Mei still reached for me now. It was different, however, now it might have taken years for our relationship to be totally restored. It was as if she still held something in her heart – something against me.

But, she did indeed reach for me and smile at me

whenever I appeared at the orphanage.

I thought it most important that she reach for Lynn.

Still, Lynn insisted that I go with her.

Reluctantly, I agreed to go. We mounted our bikes and headed out. Lynn really did need someone with her. She had a back problem and should not have been riding on those bumpy back roads, but she was determined to visit Kali as often as possible. Our hopes had been smashed that the authorities would let Lynn have Kali with her once Lynn arrived in Nanchang. Yet, Lynn was determined to spend as much time as she could with Kali.

As we entered the compound, we parked our bikes in the covered shed and walked toward the building where Kali lived. Evidently Xiao Hua had seen us, because she came out to meet us holding Kali in her arms. The moment I had dreaded was now before me. Kali flashed her famous smile and reached out her little arms to Lynn. That was my first time to see them together, and I was thrilled to see the instant bonding. Kali seemed to inherently "know" that Lynn was her new mother. As Lynn held her, Kali gave me a big smile as well, and I snapped a photo that captured the moment. A huge burden was lifted off my shoulders that day. God reminded me again that He was in control and that I should put my fears aside.

After our time with Kali was up, Lynn asked to go in to the baby rooms. I had avoided the rooms housing the infants because I knew I could not look at those little bundles two-to-a-crib and not have a difficult time emotionally. Lynn was determined not only to go in, but to pray over each baby. Reluctantly, I followed her.

This became Lynn's pattern every time she visited the orphanage. She would first play with Kali. Sometimes she would bathe her or feed her. Other times she would only play with her, cuddle her, and talk with her. After her visit, she would head for the infant room to pray over the babies. I admired Lynn's determination to be a prayer warrior for those little ones. The sight of them was such heartbreak…all those little faces just staring at the ceiling all day long – staring, and waiting to die.

I wept just going in that room. It was all I could do to offer up a prayer to God for them. Lynn entered with a vengeance, lifting up each one before our Heavenly Father.

Another thing that amazed me was when I found out later that Lynn was praying for Kali's biological mother. She continued to do so over the years and still does so today, as far as I know.

I was happy to ride away from the orphanage, but I could not put the babies out of my mind. How I wanted Mei Mei out of there, if for no other reason, so I would never have to set foot in that ghastly place again.

More disturbing news came after Tom talked again to Director Qin. He gave us her report:

"The Civil Service people are on a business retreat to a mountain. They will get back on April 27."

I was ready to call everybody a bunch of liars again. I was very, very tired of being told one thing, then another. They had "jerked me around" about all I could take. But, thankfully, I was in my apartment when I received this news, and I could not lash out at any officials and call them "a bunch of liars" because none of the liars were present. Instead, I fumed inside and tried to turn it all over to God once again. That was very unsettling news for me after being in the dying rooms of the orphanage.

This word also seemed to unsettle Lynn. She had been such a stalwart of faith, remaining focused on her mission throughout this whole time until now.

We were *not* happy.

The good part of this recent news, however, was that Director Qin was now beginning to pursue the adoption like a bulldog. Whenever we encountered such obstacles, we thrashed about a while in anger, and then began praying once more – time and time again – giving it all to God yet another time. Director Qin had now become our partner in this endeavor. She went after it in the physical realm, while we fought the spiritual battle. We had done all that we could do in the natural dimension.

Director Qin called to the retreat site in order to get in touch with an official there, seeking to obtain some authorization to move the process along.

Kali had been in the orphanage for nine weeks as of Tuesday. "How long, oh Lord? How long?" I ached for the victory to be won.

Tuesday afternoon Qi Fong called Tom to report that we could get Mei Mei if and when Director Qin approved. We surmised that she was awaiting authorization from the Civil Service office.

Thursday afternoon Tom came stomping into our apartment. His displeasure was obvious. He was so upset that he could barely pull up the correct English words.

Tom was often displeased with the government. Unfortunately, it did not bother him to express it openly. Thus, the Public Security Bureau always followed him. It was surprising to us that he still walked the streets openly. We often had to try to keep him calm and his mouth shut.

It was true that during the adoption process, his whole manner had changed. He was decorum personified. He apparently wanted to make sure that this adoption was successful, and he wanted to prevent any delays.

Thus, he had never appeared upset at any time, especially since Lynn's arrival.

But now, he was upset. We were afraid of what he would tell us. We had been receiving less than good news as it was.

Wednesday – Qi Fong told us that all copies had to go to Beijing. Lynn needed to take all the official papers to his office on Thursday. Days were passing by, and still nothing significant had been accomplished. More papers going more places. The paper shuffle continued, when we thought we should have been far past this stage by that time.

But still we were confident that there was progress – that things were moving actually forward.

Thursday morning was another setback, however. Lynn and Tom took all the copies to Qi Fong's office as ordered. He would then send them to Beijing. We had to have Beijing's approval prior to any adoption.

Qi Fong informed them that the documents that had been translated into Chinese would have to now be typed, having been translated in longhand. This process would most likely take another day or two, he said.

Then Qi Fong informed them that both the orphanage and the civil administration office also had to redo all their documents before they could be sent to Beijing. They had had months to complete those documents, but now they would have to be done again. It was almost like starting over. Another circle; another chase; another delay.

No, Thursday morning was not a morning of good news, so when Tom came stomping into our apartment with steamy Chinese words coming forth, our imaginations went into overdrive.

"What, Tom?" I tried to get him to shift into English. "What happened?" I glanced at Lynn and saw that her mouth was drawn into a thin line, and worry was in her eyes.

"Director Qin," he said in English before charging off in Chinese again. He paused for breath and said, "She causes trouble now. I told her 'hurry' to do papers.

"She say, 'I busy; can't hurry.' One, two days — then she can work on papers.

"I said things to her."

I could imagine what he said to her. Tom was not a patient man. Yes, he had squelched his anger during all this time, but apparently this one more delay was too much.

Actually, I think we were relieved. I could see Lynn almost sigh with relief. Tom's tale was not good news, but it was not such bad news. It was just another in a long line of the delays that we had encountered over and over again.

Perhaps Director Qin had been instructed to slow up or she would get in trouble. We seldom knew the reasons and had finally learned that asking "Why?" seldom got us the truth.

Later that evening, when things had calmed a bit, Lynn and I sat down in our dimly lit living room and shared more of what each had been thinking. It was almost as if Tom's release of his angry feelings was a signal for us to let down our walls.

I finally told Lynn, "There are many nights when I still quietly cry during the night."

She looked at me and said, "Last night, I was crying. I thought I might have been so loud that everyone else heard me. I tried to be quiet, but I couldn't hold back any longer. I didn't want to tell you, but my back has been hurting more the last couple of days.

"I'm ready for this to be over with. And, there are times it seems that it will never end – that we'll just keep circling.

"I'm also ready to be home. I miss John. I miss my Kristin. I miss my home. Your family is great, and you've all been so wonderful, but I would love to leave here tomorrow and arrive the same day with Kali in Portland."

"I don't blame you," I responded. "Those delays! Often, we think we've made great progress, and then another delay appears. I think the victory is in sight, but then it slips away."

"I pray, and I know that God is going to do this," Lynn said. "I know that I'm going to leave here with Kali, but the almost daily turn of events is taking my breath. I can feel my strength draining, just going through this.

"It must have been so very difficult for you. I am so thankful for what you've done. I will leave here one day – soon! – with Kali."

She said all of this with such confidence that I smiled. I went to bed that night smiling. We did not know what the next day would bring, but my confidence in our Heavenly Father had been restored. He was fighting this battle for us, and we would see the victory.

Chapter XXI

Faith – Trust – Hope

Faith, hope, trust; we had bantered those words around during the year and at times felt like they had battered *us.* Sometimes, at night, when the apartment was quiet, we would lie in bed and talk about what had happened, what was happening, and what was to come. It was a peaceful time in some ways. Mei Mei was no longer in our room, demanding our attention.

When we could let God's peacefulness play over us, we could relax for a while and just enjoy His presence and the presence of each other.

We would talk quietly of faith, and trust, and hope, and our miserable failures.

"What does all of that really mean?" LeRoy asked me one night as we were letting sleep sink softly into our minds.

"What?" I asked, since I thought we were just discussing the day's events.

"You know, faith and trust and hope; what does it really mean?"

"Well, faith is the substance of things hoped for," I began quoting from Hebrews 11:1, when LeRoy cut me short.

"I know the verse. I can quote it too. But, what does that

really mean? We're talking about trusting God. We speak of having faith in Him and hoping in Him. But what choice do we have?"

"What?" was my reply again, as I completely failed to understand where he was going with all of this. I was beginning to be a little perturbed with him. For the most part, we had had a peaceful day – one of the few unhurried, unharried days of our Nanchang spring of 1992. And now he wanted to torpedo the closing hours of the day with a theological jam session. I did not particularly want to jam, but I yielded the floor. He obviously needed to talk about this.

He was still frustrated that I could not seem to get into the flow of the conversation. "What do you mean, what?" was his reply. That would not win him any debate points, but I let that go too. It was difficult for me to try to follow this conversation because it was rare for LeRoy to bring up anything remotely unsettling in the evening. He said his mind tended to dwell on such things if they were discussed late in the day and kept him awake. But here he was throwing out theological questions, and I was supposed to catch them.

So, I replied as casually as I could, "What are you talking about? I can't follow this."

"Perhaps that's the problem," he said quietly, as if that were supposed to help.

"I don't really know what I'm talking about. There's just been some things rumbling around in my brain over all this, and I don't know where it's going.

"I thought if I spit them out, maybe it would help."

"Okay, try giving me a little more of the in-depth version," I responded, "and see what happens."

"Well, we can quote the Scriptures about faith, hope, trust and perhaps I should chunk in love, even though that's not what I'm talking about. But without God's love, then is any of the rest of it possible? What is it really all about? What choices did we make in any of this?"

He had spit it out, all right. I was supposed to digest it and give wise counsel after that, I suppose, but I chose to remain quiet. Not something I do easily.

"Well, we had some choices, but look at what God has done in all this. I mean, we could have refused to become involved with Mei Mei. We could have gotten rid of her right away. We could have done that. But somehow, that did not seem an option. So, we had a choice, but it was almost like we didn't have a choice."

Now he was going in circles so fast I could feel myself getting dizzy. "What was that you just said?"

Repetition is good, I thought. Maybe he will say it in a way that can actually be mentally processed.

"What?" was his answer. If we had not been in the darkness of our bedroom, he would have seen me roll my eyes in exasperation.

"Go over that again," I responded like a sweet wife, "I really didn't follow what you said."

"It's almost like we're robots but we're not robots. After it was decided that Mei Mei would remain in our home, look at the other choices we made."

"We made the choices that we thought were best for her and for us and for everybody involved," I responded.

"Yes, but look at how stupid some of them look now. Look how many times we failed when we tried to go the way we decided," he continued.

I still had a hard time believing that we were having this conversation when we could be getting a restful sleep.

Other nights Mei Mei would rouse us from our slumber two, three, or four times during the night. How we longed then for a quiet, peaceful night. Now we *had* one, and LeRoy – the guy who usually did not want to discuss anything that I brought up at bedtime because he valued his sleep— was off and running tonight.

Of course, I really felt good that he did want to talk. And

our being able to spend uninterrupted time together had become a special treasure during all this. For months we had been exhausted by the time we went to bed, so we just went to bed. And during the day our lives were wrapped around so many other people. We had always been busy under normal conditions; but since the addition of Mei Mei into our lives, we were marching daily double time.

And China – China with over 1 billion people crammed mostly into China's eastern seaboard— was not known for peace and quiet anyway.

As LeRoy was continuing with his discourse, my mind was replaying some of the events of the past few months. Throughout the months that Mei Mei was in our home, she slept at the foot of our bed – the only space available – in a makeshift crib. Our routine – after we managed to get her in any sort of routine, was to get Mei Mei to sleep, finish whatever work needed doing that night, and quickly get into bed ourselves.

We greatly valued any hours of slumber we could get during those months of October through January.

On those evenings we would often collapse into bed after one final look at Mei Mei. Sometimes we would both stand over her looking at her in the dim light falling from the light in our living room, and we would smile. Then we would hurry into bed and pray for sleep to come quickly, also praying, "Lord, please, please, please let Mei Mei sleep through the night."

At times, before we would get to sleep, we would see a little hand appear over the side of that crib. Shortly, that cute little Chinese head would pop up. She usually looked right at us. Sometime she would be smiling when she came up. We were never sure if she was playing a game of "Gotcha" or if she was just happy to see us nearby.

Other times she came up crying, not happy over

something – and usually we could not find out what that something was until late in the night.

There were also times when we would have a good solid two, three or even four hours of sleep before she would be sitting up in her crib demanding attention.

"Why can't this baby sleep through the night?" was a lingering question. We never could seem to find the answer.

We did make some discoveries toward the answer, though, when the two ladies in my Bible study were over. Mei Mei was napping on our bed at the time. Of course, they wanted to see her. Everyone had to check on Mei Mei – Chinese, as well as foreign guests – whenever they came to our home.

Lynn – a middle school teacher – and Ingrid – a track coach – stepped from the door in our bedroom back into our living/dining area with a puzzled look on both their faces. "Why does she sleep on stomach?" Lynn asked. I thought there was something wrong, so got up and peered into our bedroom at the sleeping Mei Mei.

I failed to see anything unusual and thought that I must have misunderstood her. "What do you mean?" I asked.

"Her stomach. She sleeps on her stomach. Why? That's not a good thing," Ingrid spoke, while Lynn nodded her head in agreement.

I just looked at them for a moment. It was obvious to me that something was not registering in this conversation. I understood what was being said, but I could not comprehend the meaning.

"She sleeps on her stomach most of the time," I finally responded.

"That a bad thing," she pointed out again. "Bad for heart; can't breathe good," was Ingrid's explanation.

"Very bad for her," Lynn agreed.

I still just looked at them, not sure what to make of that information.

She continued, "Babies sleep on back." Then she smiled at me and dropped the conversation.

I brought the matter up when LeRoy appeared. He had been out getting beat up by the Chinese college guys on the concrete basketball court nearby. David had been there too.

LeRoy was usually in a good mood after getting slammed around on the courts. I never could understand that. He and David would tell of their exploits, assuming there were any to tell. Perhaps LeRoy's theory of a good sweat making you feel better was correct. It seemed to work for him. He theorized that sweating helped your body get rid of poisons floating around in it.

Of course, sometimes he *smelled* like poison after some of his basketball games.

"How did the Bible study go?" he asked.

"Oh, it was good. I always learn a lot just trying to answer their questions. They had an especially interesting observation today, though."

"Really, what was that?" LeRoy asked as he unlaced his tennis shoes.

"They said we're making a big mistake with Mei Mei," I told him.

"We already know we're making tons of mistakes. Has she discovered a new one? Or is this one somebody already pointed out to us?"

"She said that *all* Chinese babies sleep on their backs. She said it's bad for the heart and makes breathing difficult to sleep on the stomach."

After considering what they told us, we realized that Mei Mei had been in a Chinese home for the first few months of her life. So most likely, she had been sleeping on her back. Because most American mothers are taught to put infants on their stomachs, I had been following the way of my culture.

Since she was sleeping only bits at a time anyway, we

decided to try the Chinese way that night. Sure enough, she slept through the night for the first time since she came to our home. We realized that she had been waking herself up when she tried to flip over onto her back. We would rock her back to sleep and place her face down, where she would repeat the process and be awake on her back a few hours later. We had been causing the problem all along.

Not only were we mistake-prone; we were also slow learners when it came to nurturing a Chinese baby. Mei Mei had been trying to show us for months that she would be happy to sleep through the night if we would just put her in a comfortable position. All of this was after we had suffered through a couple of months of sleep deprivation.

I was still listening to LeRoy out of one corner of my brain, but I slowly raised up on my elbows and looked at the empty crib at the foot of our bed. How I longed for Mei Mei to be there again. She could wake me up all she wanted. I would not care. How could that crib sit there empty for so long? It practically cried out for Mei Mei to sleep there.

"What are you doing?" LeRoy questioned when he saw me staring at the empty crib.

"You got me to thinking more about Mei Mei and how much I miss her. I don't know what God's doing in this. My faith goes up and down. Sometime I get so angry that I don't trust anybody; but I still hope. I still hope, and I believe that somehow, some way, God will rescue Mei Mei."

"But, that's what I'm talking about," LeRoy continued. It was as if he had something he wanted to chew on, and it had to be chewed.

"God is doing this, and it doesn't much matter about our faith or trust or hope, even. What we've tried has failed. If God doesn't do this, it's not gonna get done.

"God has put us in a corner. *He* put us in this corner. We did not do it. Everything that we have done or tried to do with Mei Mei was another slap of paint on the floor that moved us ever closer to this corner.

God has put us here. So, we can talk about our faith in God and our trusting and hoping in Him; but we did not do this. It is almost like we had no choice. It's all about God's faithfulness and His trustworthiness – and that's all wrapped up in His love, and all we're left with is hope."

I was sure that this inner searching was good for LeRoy, but I did not want to do any inner searching, especially as it was nearing the midnight hour in Nanchang, China. I simply wanted to go to sleep and get some rest.

"I don't know about any of that," was my response. "I just know that I am believing God to move to rescue Mei Mei from that orphanage. I have faith in Him that He will take her to America. I trust that He will do it in His time. I continue to hope in His faithfulness to us and to her.

"Right now it's hard for me to theorize all this and try to figure it out. I don't really want to figure it out: I just want Mei Mei out."

"I agree completely," he replied, a little quieter now, "but it's interesting to me that apparently God has left us with no options. It's do it His way or get out of the way.

"The whole Christian life could maybe be summarized that way." LeRoy continued on for a while, but since he was only getting "Yeah's," and "Unn-uh's," and "Mmm's" from me, he also finally decided that it was time for sleep.

Of course, there were other times when I tried to put together all the "why's" and "wherefore's" myself as we talked out the situation together. But we never really reached an answer. We could only wait for God and do our best to follow where He was leading.

I had said prior to our going to China that if I led only one person to Jesus, I wanted it to be "The Billy Graham of China." That was before I knew how difficult it was even to interest most Chinese in the things of God. Could Mei Mei grow up to be "The Billy Graham of China"?

Chapter XXII

"Let Kali Go"

A nother week was slowly slipping by, with any progress toward Kali's escaping the orphanage moving at a snail's pace.

We were approaching Kali's tenth week imprisoned in that orphanage. Lynn was heading into her third week in Asia, completing her second week in Nanchang; and the spring rains had returned.

Lynn was battling on with an aching back, still determined to ride the bicycle over the muddy, potholed infested back streets that took her to the orphanage. She did not want to let one day go by when she failed to hold Kali. She continued to go into the dying room and pray for those babies.

The other foreign Christians in Nanchang had began a more steady parade to the orphanage themselves so that one or more of them would be out there at least twice a week. They went there to hold the babies, to feed them and do anything they could to help the workers. The babies were beginning to have arms wrapped around them. They were beginning to feel the warmth of love. Of course our friends always spent at least a little time with Kali.

The foreign Christian community decided that there was more they could do. Some of them were riding a couple of hours by bicycle to get to the orphanage. Yet they wanted to do more.

The Body of Christ in China was truly a beautiful picture of what it should be.

We were blessed with several young people, just out of college, and some older folks. The previous year we had several families with children. In 1991-92 it was more single people. Some of them were in their 40s. We were also of different denominations. I doubt I could tell you which denominations that most of them represented. We did not care. It did not matter. We were the Body of Christ and we needed each other. We needed that unity that Jesus had prayed for in John 17. What may have divided us in the U.S. was simply discarded as a waste of time and energy in Nanchang. We met together each Saturday to fellowship as brothers and sisters in Christ. We all looked forward to those weekly gatherings. It was a time of refreshing for us all. And like any good gathering of American Christians we would eat together following our service.

That group, from various parts of the US, with a sprinkling of Canadians, had also made Kali a part of their lives. They had become her aunts and uncles. All of them had photos of the baby. They expanded their involvement with Kali to reaching out to the children at the orphanage.

They were now ready to take a further step. They had contributed 1,000 yuan [approximately US$250] and they were ready to spend that money to help the babies.

Tom, Lynn and I met with a few others from our "church" and officials from the orphanage at a department store. We purchased items that the orphanage workers had never had available to them. We were hoping that our purchases would make work at the orphanage easier while providing mobility for the babies. We purchased 10 walkers [they had none] and 10 strollers [they had none]. We also bought 2 bicycles for the workers and a portable tape player so they could have music for the children.

It was a joy for us to see our friends investing so much time, energy and money in the orphanage. We were beginning to see some good emerging from Kali's confinement there.

But that did not lessen our desire for Kali to be free from that place.

Qi Fong had told us that we could get Kali from the orphanage whenever Director Qin approved. It was up to her. So far she had not approved and we did not understand why she wanted Kali to remain in the orphanage. We had no power to do anything. To be so completely powerless is a feeling of weakness. That frailty forced us to cling to God. And that was where we should be. That was right where He wanted us to be, clinging to All Power in the whole universe. Our power did not exist in this case. We had to wait on the All Powerful, All Loving God.

As we drew nearer to the end of the spring semester, with no tangible proof that Kali would leave Nanchang, or even escape from the orphanage, we still expected God's angels to swoop down and pull off the daring rescue.

We lived from day to day, clinging to God's Word and believing that somehow, some way He would liberate Kali.

As there was little progress during that time our days seemed to last for weeks. However, we still remained busy with regular activities.

Just our daily lives prior to the arrival of Kali were full to bursting at times. Then entered Kali, then came trips to the orphanage, then Lynn moved in with us. We continued our Bible studies. We continued our teaching at the college and instructing David and Marianne in their lessons. Foreigners continued to drop by and call to see if there had been any progress and just to visit. Our Chinese friends stopped in just to check on things.

We had bounced from great expectations to wearied frustrations throughout April. We crawled out of April, entering the bright hope of May with the rains falling and Kali still in the orphanage.

Friday— 24 April – All documents were express mailed to the Justice Department in Beijing. We would now wait to receive word from Beijing. If they said "No" it would be "No". We did not expect them to say "No". We expected to receive an affirmative – that the adoption had been approved in Beijing.

Since the papers had been sent by express mail we were looking at the very real possibility of having Kali back in our home by Monday. Ten weeks in the orphanage was surely long enough.

Once we received the word from Beijing we fully expected Kali to be in our home and then she and Lynn on the plane out of Nanchang just as quickly as we could obtain a ticket.

The 24th of April was party day as it was David's 16th birthday. It was also Angel's birthday; so we partied. We not only celebrated their birthdays but there was a feeling of exhilaration that we were near the top of the Adoption Mountain that we had been climbing for so long.

Monday was a quick reality check for all of us, but especially for me.

We had expected to hear from Beijing on Monday. Tom called Qi Fong at his office. He said it was too early. We were acting like Americans again, expecting things to happen when we wanted them to happen. We thought *express mail* meant that it would move quickly. We were possibly looking at two different definitions of *express mail*. We were also ready for Kali to be out of the orphanage.

I was hoping that Monday would be the day when she

would be allowed to return to our home. Perhaps I was reaching too far on that one.

I rode out to the orphanage alone that day, just to be with Kali for a while and to hold her; just the two of us together.

Xiao Hua was holding her when I arrived. I walked over to them and reached to take Kali. She turned away from me and held tightly to Xiao Hua. I reached out for her again and she buried her head in Xiao Hua's arm. It was if she did not even want to look at me.

The ache of rejection rose up within my heart. I had wanted her to bond with Lynn. I had to let her go, but I did not expect this. And it hurt. The hurt lodged deep within my being. There seemed to be no reason for this rejection. It was just there – another pain driven into my heart.

I only stayed a brief time, as I was afraid to let the hurt out in teardrops there. So, I cried as I rode away on my bicycle.

I had been hurt before during all this. It was another pain that I would have to endure. I decided to override the hurt by taking some action. I determined to go by the Public Security Bureau on my way home. I wanted to hear from them how soon we could have Kali's Chinese passport in hand. She was not going anywhere until she had a passport.

I was told that it would be seven to ten days before she would receive her passport. Another delay. Another disappointment. By the time I got home, after riding around Nanchang in the rain, I was feeling very low. I had reached my lowest point since before we knew that Lynn was on her way.

The delays, frustrations and rejection were taking their toll on me. I went to bed that night feeling sorry for myself and just generally feeling sorry. I was ready for some good news.

Tuesday – 28 April – Someone from the Justice Department called us in the morning to report that they had heard nothing from Beijing. That was not good news.

Tom was over later that afternoon. He called Ms. Cao about 5 p.m. She said that she had called Beijing at 4:30. They reported that they had just received our packet about 10 minutes prior to her call. *Express Mail?*

Ms. Cao had told them to hurry. It appeared that she was trying to help as much as she could. We were thankful for that.

Wednesday – 29 April – Lynn called the Justice Department. Same story— no word from Beijing. We had to have the "go" from Beijing. We were most anxious to hear that word. But, still we would have to wait for Kali's passport. It seemed like the waiting had gone on forever and it was now a regular part of our routine. We did not like this kind of routine.

As if to add insult to injury the electricity was off for 5 hours. Why? Why ask silly questions? It was just off.

We had decided to put Lynn to work while she was with us in Nanchang. LeRoy took her to his class to be interviewed. He had used this method of instruction before. He could have a day off and it would be good practice for the students to ask questions and listen to another American accent. Of course, Lynn, being from the Northwest, told us that she had the correct pronunciation of English words. She was insinuating that our Texas tones were less than perfect. She accused us of teaching our students to speak "Texan." She did have some proof as she knew LeRoy instructed his students to say, "Howdy, how y'all?" He said he was just offering some variety instead of the common "Hello."

The class provided Lynn an opportunity to share why she was in Nanchang. As she related the story of adopting Kali, she was able to then step over into sharing her faith. She told them that it was God's love that drove her and John to spend so much money and take so much time to adopt a Chinese girl.

Thursday – 30 April – Express mail was available but we were not receiving an express answer from Beijing and our frustration level was building. How long could we continue as if this were normal procedure in our lives? How long could Lynn continue living in Nanchang when her home was in Portland?

Tom was just as exasperated as we were with hearing nothing from Beijing. I was concerned that he might spew out some words toward the government that would land him in trouble. We knew that our phones were tapped, that our apartment was being watched.

Tom went down to the Justice Department in the morning and stayed there, demanding that they get an answer from Beijing.

Ms. Cao, who had been as kind and helpful as anyone in authority had been, was trying to receive an answer. She called the Justice office in Beijing in the morning. No one answered the phone. The Justice Department for all of China and there was no one to answer the phone.

Tom was still at Ms. Cao's office, demanding results. She called again in the afternoon. They still did not answer the phone. Actually she tried several times during the day and never got an answer.

Tom returned to our home late that afternoon to give us the report. He was not happy. When he was unhappy we had to try to restrain ourselves from showing our displeasure in his presence. We did not want him to get in trouble. But, we were also very disappointed. We had hoped that we might have Kali in our home by Monday; Tuesday at the latest. The workday had closed in Beijing on Thursday and still we had no answer.

Our week would not be classified as good. I had suffered through one of the worst Mondays I had ever had in Nanchang. And there had been some bad days in Nanchang. Tuesday, Wednesday and Thursday were not any brighter.

LeRoy and Marianne had both been battling colds. Lynn was fighting a cold as well as trying to ignore the pain in her back. We think the colds attacked us after our long ride in the rain on Saturday. We had about an hour ride to another school to have our church time together. We had ridden out there in the rain and it was raining when we returned. Not that that was anything unusual, but for some reason, it seemed to affect some of us. It was just one more thing that we were battling.

I was beginning to feel achy and feverish on Thursday. The news throughout the last week of April had been anything but good. I suppose it was made even worse because we were expecting good news; great news. We were looking for victory. Instead, we were getting slapped in the face with disappointment over and over again.

No good word on Thursday and tomorrow would be Friday, May 1. It would be the May 1st holiday – International Labor Day in China— and offices in Beijing and Nanchang would be closed. Now, it was beginning to look like we might not receive any official word until the following Monday.

Tom was over, joining us for supper. Shelly had decided to come down and join us also. Meals in our home were always a little comical anyway, but when we added more people it was bordering on the absurd. My kitchen was actually a tiny balcony off the bathroom. It was enclosed with windows that did not fit properly. A small shelf had been constructed to fit under the windows. My kitchen consisted of the shelf, a one-burner hotplate and a concrete-square sink with only a cold water tap. The kitchen was cold in the winter and extremely hot in the summer. Since the glass panes did not fit properly, the elements appeared inside as well as out. One winter morning, I entered my balcony kitchen to find everything covered with about an inch of snow.

Our living room was our dining room as well. At meal times, we would fold out a card table and pull stools around for everyone to sit. Entertaining extra people was always a challenge. By the time the food was placed on the table, there would be very little room for our small plates or bowls.

Still, we had enjoyed some precious times around that small table pitched in the middle of our living room. However, this was not one of them.

We were failing to enjoy our meal together because we were taking a hard look at the circumstances. It was a glum meal. During the middle of it we got a call. Someone who spoke no English was calling. LeRoy understood enough to get Tom on the phone.

We heard him repeating "*hao, hao*" and then "*keyi*" and followed that with "*dui, dui*" and concluded with a few more "*hen haos*". He was mainly listening and responding with "good" "yes" and "very good".

We were unsure who was on the other end or what they were saying but it sounded like good news because that was practically all that Tom was saying.

Tom turned away from the phone as he hung up and he faced us with the first smile we had seen on his face in at least a week. We were already beginning to smile. This looked like good news and we were ready for lots and lots and lots of good news.

"That was Ms. Cao," Tom said almost coyly as he slowly sat back down at the table and slurped some noodles into his mouth. I was going to be faithful to the ancient Chinese art of perfect patience, but could not restrain myself, so I blurted out, "What did she say?" I said it clearly and loudly.

He smiled and reported, "Ms. Cao called the director in Beijing at her home." I think Tom was smiling even more because he believed that his persistence of remaining in Ms. Cao's office and demanding results helped to bring about the phone call.

"She talked to the director. The director of the Justice Department in Beijing said that the adoption has been approved."

We sat there for a moment, stunned to finally be hearing this news. We had been grumbling in our noodles and God was working all the time. It took us a moment but we suddenly got into the rejoicing mode. We were all smiling those goofy smiles that indicate something tremendous just happened. It was so tremendous that we did not really know what to do, so we just smiled and said things like, "That's great; that's wonderful; Praise God; how great."

We repeated ourselves a lot.

When the reality hit, Lynn picked up the phone and asked to call the United States. She was unable to contact John so she called her parents to relay the news. They must have then passed on that news to John because he called within the hour.

The people at Beijing had been trying to work through 19 possible Canadian adoptions.

That is why they had been unable to give us an answer any sooner. Apparently the Canadian government had decided to stop adoptions from China for some reason. But there were 19 Canadians ready to adopt Chinese babies.

We thought all of Beijing and Nanchang should revolve around our situation. We tended to forget that they had a lot of other work to do. Thanks to the persistence of Ms. Cao we had received official word from Beijing.

As I was writing in my journal that night I wrote in very large letters **Official Word From Beijing "Let Kali Go." Thank you Jesus, Praise the King of Glory.**

After writing that I looked at what I had entered earlier that day. "We are so weary and do greatly desire to see Lynn and Kali flee from here and quickly get them on a plane to Oregon. Oh God, please make it happen now Almighty

God. Please free Mei Mei."

I went to bed with a smile on my face that night despite feeling like I was about to come down with a bad cold.

Chapter XXIII

*The snare is broken,
and we have escaped.*

Signed, Sealed – Delivered?

I awoke the next morning with an extremely sore throat. A bad sore throat in China is definitely not a good thing. The first thing they want to do is stick an IV into you. You never knew where that needle had been before. But there was another problem. It was a holiday.

We taught at a medical college. It was not very difficult to scare up a doctor. We called one who had been a faithful friend. But he had gone to Shanghai. His son, who was also a doctor, told us he would come over. He prescribed some traditional Chinese medicine and also applied acupressure to me.

We had always tried to avoid traditional Chinese medicine before. Chinese doctors would succeed in giving it to us at times. We would accept it graciously, smiling all the while, and then go pour it down the toilet after they left.

We had tried to force some traditional medicine on David and Marianne a few years earlier in order to stave off hepatitis, which our teammate had contracted. They learned well from their parents. They pretended to drink the putrid brown liquid concoction, but then poured it out their bedroom windows when we were not looking. When we found out about it, we were thankful once again that God was watching over us.

Dr. Tang Bao must have administered such medicine to foreigners before. He mixed the potion of roots, herbs, spiders, snakes, or whatever it was that he brought over. He poured boiling water over it. I stifled a gag. He smelled of it to make sure it was correct. I almost "lost it" then as some of the aroma wafted my direction. Then he handed it to me to drink. I quickly took a sip, hoping he would be satisfied with that. Thankfully, the smell was worse than the taste, so I held my breath and drank a little more. He was satisfied that I was going to drink the whole thing and quit watching me.

After he left, I thought that I was feeling better, but by that evening I was feeling even worse. My throat was so sore that I could barely rasp out a few words. Thankfully, Marianne, LeRoy and Lynn were feeling much better than they had been. David was not affected by whatever was assailing the rest of us. I had a double dose of the mystery bug.

Lynn was feeling fine and was so overjoyed by the approval from Beijing that she decided to ride out to the orphanage and tell Kali what had happened. Shelly, who also remained in good health, rode with her. Lynn reported that they had a really good time with Kali, even though she had a runny nose and was not feeling very good herself. Another cold probably meant more injections for her. I shuddered to think how many injections she had received and how many times they had used those needles before. God's protection was evident to us again and again.

We finally had official approval from Beijing. We had all the official papers with all the official stamps in all the official hands. Lynn was in Nanchang – and had been there for 14 days now. She had $3,000 with her, which she was willing to give to Director Qin at the orphanage.

We were expecting Kali's passport any day. Everything that needed to be done had been done. There was nothing left to do except to go to the orphanage and bring Kali home.

We were ready to celebrate. We were ready for her joyous homecoming.

She had been in that orphanage for almost 11 weeks. That was about the same length of time she had been in our home. How could this be? How could this have ever happened?

It was only through God's miraculous power that Kali had remained alive at that orphanage.

Friday was a holiday, so no one was working, and most Chinese were taking Saturday off too. To compensate for the holiday, everyone was ordered to work on Sunday. Classes were held on Sunday, and all government offices would be open on Sunday. That meant that Director Qin would be at the orphanage on Sunday. That was the day that we were making plans to break Kali out of the orphanage.

When Sunday arrived, I was still not feeling all that well, so LeRoy, Lynn and Tom got a car and headed to the orphanage for what we hoped would be the last time. We wanted to bring Kali home in style.

David and Marianne busied themselves getting ready to host the homecoming. I helped them some, but mainly directed. I had gone to the hospital on Saturday. The doctor there "dropped" a swab down my throat to take a culture. I almost choked and was surprised that I did not vomit right then. They had told me that my throat was "acute." I was unsure what they meant, but I did know that it hurt to swallow or talk. Chinese medicine, acupressure, gargling warm salt water – nothing had brought relief. I found out later that I had strep throat. One reason I had hoped to avoid going to the hospital was the intravenous drip. Sure enough, after he announced that my throat was "acute," out came the needles. Only, this time he was talking about a double dipper. I had a shot in my hip, and then he plugged me into the IV and told me to return that afternoon for another needle in my vein. I returned for two more days, morning and afternoon, to get more needles that were connected to an IV drip.

I was feeling somewhat better by Sunday morning, but not good enough to make the trip to the orphanage. I might as well have gone, for I was finding it impossible to wait for them to return. It was an exciting day!

I tried to rest, but I was too excited. I helped the kids get the apartment ready so that we could celebrate. David rode to a nearby store and found some balloons that he then blew up to add to the festivities. Marianne baked a cake under my supervision. I was ready to celebrate even if I still had a sore throat and fever.

Tom, Lynn, and LeRoy left for the orphanage as afternoon rest time was ending. I hoped that they would be able to get Kali and return home no later than 4 p.m. I had learned to try to temper my expectations, but I was certainly having a hard time awaiting their arrival.

Whenever I heard anything that sounded like a car nearby, I would look out the window. I had just resettled myself on the bed after looking out the window yet again when I heard the front door open. I jumped up and heard David and Marianne tearing around the corner to see who it was.

It was LeRoy. And he was alone. Kali was not in his arms. Tom and Lynn were not around either. I thought perhaps they were following him, so I took two steps over to the window and glanced down toward the alleyway. There was no car, no Tom or Lynn. I just saw a few Chinese casually walking by.

There was nothing casual about my question. "Where's Kali?" I asked abruptly, as LeRoy walked into the living area. I could already tell by the look on his face that this was not going to be good news. I could already feel myself sinking, realizing that heartbreak was about to slap me in the face again. I did not even want to hear the words that were about to come from LeRoy's mouth.

I took the few steps toward our bedroom and lay down on the bed. LeRoy, David and Marianne followed me in.

By this time, my question of "Where's Kali?" had reverberated from David and Marianne's mouths many times. LeRoy was still looking around at the three of us, bewildered.

"They wouldn't let us have her." He had finally managed to speak.

"Well, where are Tom and Lynn?" was my next question, hoping that they were still working on getting her and that they would soon arrive with Kali safely held in Lynn's arms.

"They went over to Qi Fong's office to see what he could do, if anything."

"What happened?" was all I could manage to get out, feeling more miserable by the minute.

"I don't really know what happened." LeRoy acted like he was still dazed by what he had encountered at the orphanage.

"We thought everything was set. We thought that everyone agreed that Kali could come home after Beijing said "Yes."

"Well, apparently we assumed too much – again." He sort of sighed when he said it, implying that we were being foolish once more. That was not the way I was feeling at the time. I was starting to become angry again as the sobs began to form in my soul.

I was sick and now I was angry and I was emotionally drained. I lay back on the pillow and allowed the teardrops to slip down the side of my face. I was trying to keep from totally falling apart.

"Director Qin got mad at us," LeRoy continued. He was still not actually looking at us as he related what had happened.

"We fully expected to leave with Kali today. But Director Qin acted like we were trying to kidnap her. When we walked out of her office, someone ran toward the gates, closed them and locked them: then they drove a car in front of the gates. I guess they thought we were going to take Kali and ram through the gates.

"It was so crazy. It was like we were walking through some Grade B gangster movie."

David and Marianne were looking at LeRoy as if he was making this all up. They were saying things like, "That's dumb" and "How could they do something like that?"

I mainly listened, trying to take it all in while attempting to discern what it meant toward our ever getting Kali out of that orphanage and onto a plane to America. I thought at the time that it probably had to do with who was going to get the $3,000. Prior to Beijing's approval, Director Qin had told us that we could take Kali home when Beijing approved. We assumed that is what she really meant. "Liars!" came to my thoughts almost immediately as LeRoy related the story. "Lies, lies, and more lies."

"We were lied to again," LeRoy said, as if reading my thoughts.

"Anyway, she got mad at us. We were trying to restrain ourselves from getting mad at her. Tom insisted that she call Qi Fong. She did. But he couldn't make her do anything.

"Now she's telling us that we can have Kali when all the fees are paid. Lynn insisted that Director Qin go along with them to Qi Fong's office so they could pay the fees owed there. She agreed. After they moved the car and unlocked the gates, we drove away from the orphanage, leaving Kali there.

"They dropped me at our front gate, and they've gone to Qi Fong's office to see what they can do. I think Lynn is becoming a ferocious bulldog. She was about to fume today. Of course Tom almost went over the top. Thankfully, he calmed down when the director said she'd go to Qi Fong's office with them."

I felt exhausted just listening to LeRoy relate the events of that afternoon. I could only imagine how Lynn felt today. I asked them all to let me rest. I shut the door to the bedroom after they walked out and tried to cry softly. I knew LeRoy would be back in there if he heard me crying, and I did not want to talk to anybody right then.

Would this ever end? Would the time ever come when we could say that the victory had been won? I remembered when I had put Kali in the orphanage to return to an empty apartment. I Am a Wounded Soldier was the song I heard that night. I was wondering just how many wounds I would have to endure before we could see the victory.

I could hear LeRoy talking to the kids in the next room. Their voices were getting angrier and angrier.

Lynn came home shortly before dinnertime. She seemed fairly calm by then. Tom was not with her.

"He went on home," she replied when LeRoy questioned her about Tom. "I think he's okay."

"How about you? How are you?" I asked.

"I'm all right. I was not all right this afternoon when Director Qin started acting so obstinate. Hopefully, this is just another one of those roadblocks we have to go around. Of course, we had a real roadblock at the orphanage this afternoon." She sort of laughed when she said that. That made us all relax a little, her laugh telling us that we were still on the road toward adoption.

"Did LeRoy tell you what they did there?" she asked.

We replied, "Yes," but she retold the story anyway. She added a little extra animation, so by then we had all passed from the angry stage and had returned to believing that God was going to do this.

We were all curious to know what happened at Qi Fong's office.

"I paid a fee there. It wasn't much, but that one is paid.

Director Qin saw the official paper, so she seemed satisfied with that. I tried to ask her about getting Kali after we paid the fee, but it was clear that she was not going to allow that to happen today.

"She then told me that Kali would have to have a physical tomorrow. She said that they would take her to the physical, and they made it clear that I was not supposed to be there. I guess they think I'll try to snatch her from the hospital.

"Such a strange day, but tomorrow looks good."

Lynn was back to her very positive self by nightfall.

That evening Dominick came over with a present for Kali. He expected her to be in our home. He wanted to join us in the celebration. His disappointment was obvious when he realized our hopes had been dashed again.

Our phones had been out all day and remained useless. Lynn needed to call John to tell him what had happened. He was expecting a phone call to let him know that Kali was safely in our home. Since our phones were not working, Lynn had to go to a hotel to call. Dominick escorted her there and back.

We were all feeling a little better by bedtime. My throat was even feeling better. We went to bed with hope in our hearts that tomorrow would be the day. Sunday had been a miserable failure, but God would still be present with the dawning of the sun on Monday. As long as we looked to Him, there would be hope. As long as we yielded "all things" to Him, there would be peace.

We went to bed on Sunday evening expecting great things the next day.

Sunday had started out as a beautiful late spring day in Nanchang. The sun was shining. Any day that the sun is shining in Nanchang is a good day. But Director Qin had clouded the day.

We awoke to another day of sunshine on Monday. We began that day with the fervent hope that it would be the day when Kali would leave that orphanage, and I would never walk into that place again.

Some of the orphanage workers took Kali to the children's hospital near us for her physical exam. Tom found out where she was and asked the doctor to stall on completing the physical. He then rode his bike over to our apartment. He and Lynn quickly rode over to the hospital so Lynn could be with Kali there. In less than an hour Kali arrived with her own entourage at our door.

Tom and Lynn were on bicycles. Kali was in a tricycle cart, which was very common throughout that area. An old man was pedaling the cart. Xiao Hua was sitting on a small folding stool in the cart, holding Kali.

When I saw the method of transportation anger welled up in me again. I was so upset that they would take Kali all the way to the hospital in a three-wheeled cart. They had cars at the orphanage. Director Qin rode around in a car. It had taken that old man well over an hour to pedal that cart to the hospital. It took the same returning. It was a warm day. Kali, who still had a cold, would end up being in that stinking cart for over three hours. I was furious that they would treat her that way. I had to release my fury, to somehow let it go so I could enjoy the short time that we were to have with Kali.

They all came into our apartment. Kali was home! But she could not stay. We were all consummately happy to see her in our home. She only looked around. She looked at all of us, and then looked around the living room. She seemed content and happy enough. Her nose was still dripping from her cold. Thankfully, I was feeling much better. I think, by then, that I must have been grinning like some kind of loon, at least that is the way Lynn, Shelly, David, Marianne and LeRoy all looked. Tom had the biggest smile of us all. Lynn was carrying Kali around the apartment, pointing out her crib and some of her toys that were still there. Nothing seemed to actually register as a remembrance with Kali.

The visit was over almost before it began, because they had to hurry back to the orphanage before Director Qin found out what was happening.

Xiao Hua got back in the cart, holding Kali, and they slowly rode away with the old man pedaling. We watched until they turned a corner at the end of our housing block, and then went back inside.

I think we all were pondering the possibility of Kali coming home to stay. Would it be today? Should we even attempt it? We were concerned that if we made Director Qin mad again, she might stall or even cancel everything. We had to be very careful, and we had to make sure we were listening to the Holy Spirit. We thought that it was a good sign that Lynn was able to be her in the hospital with no repercussions. It was good to have her in our home for just those few minutes.

After Kali left, we did an inventory of all of Director Qin's requirements. We went through a mental checklist. It appeared that everything was in order – that we had done everything she wanted. We also knew that Lynn was going to have to take the $3,000 with her to the orphanage and personally hand it over to Director Qin. It was all about money. Apparently Director Qin was concerned that if someone else received that money, she would not receive her cut. Or perhaps she was planning on keeping it all to herself. We were never really sure what kind of money game all the departments were playing.

Warnings had been issued from Beijing about "selling babies," because the Western media had been reporting exactly that. Here were the authorities in Nanchang fighting over the money, apparently unconcerned with what Beijing had ordered.

We were doing our best to exactly follow the instructions

given to us. We thought we had already been doing that. But we apparently missed a signal somewhere, for we surely erred on Sunday.

After praying about it and rechecking everything we knew, we decided to go to the orphanage again that afternoon. If we did not try, we could not bring Kali home. We prayed that we were in full compliance and that we had not missed some unspoken cultural message that they had been sending.

We asked Tom if he thought we were missing a cultural signal. He said if we gave Director Qin the money, then he thought we should be able to bring Kali home.

I was feeling better, so I decided to go. LeRoy had a class, so he was unable to go with us. Early afternoon, just after rest time, we asked the school for a car. They sent the Beijing jeep over to us. It was their newest and finest automobile. It was the same vehicle that we used when I had been forced to take Kali to the orphanage. I hoped that it was a good sign. Tom, Lynn, and I got in with the driver and headed for the orphanage. This was much better than riding a bike out there.

We went straight to Director Qin's office first. We did not want them to think we were trying to kidnap Kali or pull some kind of trick, so we did not go to see her first. Normally we would have gone directly to Kali just to make sure that she was still all right and to see her "Mazin' Mazer" smile.

Director Qin seemed amiable enough. She was not a woman who smiled easily. I had never seen one cross her face, but she had often scowled at me. However, this time her countenance seemed almost pleasant. I was counting this as another positive indication. After we sat down in her office and had sipped at our tea for a bit I realized that I had been practically holding my breath ever since we left our campus. Now I took a few deep breaths to steady myself. I wanted to be relaxed. I did not want to say anything that would in anyway jeopardize what we hoped to accomplish today. I certainly did not want to blurt out "Liars!" during the middle of this conversation. We were having that totally meaningless conversation that is always a prelude to business in China. We were also sipping our tea. The three of us were having a difficult time restraining ourselves from jumping straight into the subject at hand.

Director Qin shuffled through some of Lynn's papers as if looking at them for the first time. She said something to us as she was looking at the papers. Tom translated, "Everything looks in order."

I thought, "Well, of course they're in order. They've been in order for weeks, if not months, you turkey!" But I managed to keep my mouth shut and smile while continuing to sip my tea. Actually, the hot green tea felt good to my throat, which had been sore for so long.

Director Qin continued discussing various aspects about Kali's papers involved in the adoption. Tom continued translating. Lynn would nod her head occasionally and agree that everything was in order.

Finally it became clear that we were going to have to broach the subject of money. We knew that it was what she was circling around all the topics for. All that was needed now was to hand over the money. But for some unfathomable reason Director Qin expected us to mention money first.

Eventually, Lynn realized this fact and she finally mentioned the money.

"How much more do I owe for everything?" she said calmly.

Tom translated the conversation going both ways.

"You pay 100 US dollars extra," Tom translated.

I could see Lynn getting ready to say something, but she apparently thought better of it and let it go.

"The 100 US dollars extra is for special care. Mei Mei

got special care."

Well, we certainly could not disagree with that, but we did not expect to have to pay more money for this.

"So, how . . . um . . . uh . . . what's the total amount I'm supposed to pay?" Lynn asked with an additional question mark. She sounded as though she were wondering just how much higher this whole transaction would go.

I thought it was interesting that Tom was stressing American dollars; but I also knew enough Chinese to know that this was exactly what Director Qin was stressing. She apparently wanted to be absolutely sure that everything was done in American dollars.

"Money for adoption – 3,000 US dollars – the cash – so all is $3,100," Tom translated.

"I need to make sure that I get a receipt," Lynn emphasized. She was not going to just hand over $3,100 with nothing to show for it. It was a strange relationship we had with Director Qin. She seemed to have a split personality. At times she was cordial and helpful, apparently as determined as we were to see Kali adopted. Then, sometimes, she appeared obstinate – blocking the way, appearing to stop everything. Once again, it apparently all boiled down to who was going to receive the money.

Director Qin agreed to the receipt, took a paper out, and started writing the receipt.

Lynn told her then, "Be sure it says that I paid the $3,000 as an adoption fee."

Tom translated that, and she quit writing. It appeared she had changed personalities between the time she was looking down writing until she looked up at Lynn.

No, she would not put down that it was an adoption fee. "She will write it is a donation to the orphanage," Tom informed us.

"Donation?" Lynn replied in an incredulous tone. "What does she mean, 'donation'? I didn't fly over here and spend three weeks in this city to make a donation to this orphanage. I want her to write that I paid the money for the adoption."

I could not believe what I was watching. Here we almost had Kali in our grasp, preparing to head out a gate that would really be open this time, and Lynn was challenging this woman, who had the power to stop everything, over semantics.

Apparently Lynn had about reached her point of "enough is enough." Of course, there was the concern that if Lynn handed over the money as a "donation," they might accept it and tell her to leave without Kali. It sounded preposterous, but we had been lied to so many times before, we knew it was a possibility. If Lynn had a paper that said she had paid to adopt a baby, then she needed a baby to show for it.

Still, that whole scene playing out before me seemed surreal. Thoughts of the gate being barred and our returning to the apartment without Kali played across my mind. What was Lynn thinking? Give them anything. Sign anything. Take any receipt or no receipt. Just get Kali and leave this stinking place!

I was inching forward in my chair as Tom translated what Lynn said. I noticed the translation was short. Apparently he left out some of it. Translations can be a good thing at times.

Director Qin looked across at Lynn sternly and replied in a tone that was apparently intended to remind us that she was the boss, "No." I understood that part easily enough. Then Tom translated the rest. "It has to be donation. That's all."

Finally Lynn gave up. She dug around in her clothes and from somewhere produced the precious American dollars. I did not look at Director Qin's face during the transaction. I thought I might see greed popping out of every pore when she saw all those 100-dollar bills.

Lynn placed the bills – all 31 of them – on the desk.

Director Qin handed over the receipt. As Lynn accepted it, the director sort of smiled and reached for the money. She counted the money, smiled again, and stood up. That was the signal that the meeting was over.

We stood also. Now what? Director Qin remained quiet as she stood. We thought we might be missing some cultural signals again. We surely did not want to make a mistake now. Surely she would not expect us to leave and come back another time to get Kali. That would be too big a disappointment. I was sure that Lynn would not stand for it, but, again, we had no power.

We could only rest in God and His provision. I found that I was not resting at all. I was having trouble breathing again.

Smiling In Her Sleep

Yes, I was holding my breath again. We were at the defining moment. I was confident, but concerned. We had been lied to so many times by this woman who was safely tucking the US$100 bills in her desk, and by others. I looked at Lynn and Tom as we stood. I could see similar looks of concern on their faces. Actually, I think Tom had more of a determined look on his face. Lynn gave me a nervous smile.

Director Qin walked toward her office door. We were unsure if we were to follow, sit back down, or just keep on standing there, looking and feeling very awkward.

She opened her door, called out to someone down the hall, returned behind her desk, and sat down. She motioned for us to return to our seats.

Just as we were all sitting back down, still wondering what exactly was transpiring, one of the orphanage workers came through the door, holding Kali. Kali did not appear to be very happy.

Director Qin and the worker exchanged a few words. We had all stood up again. I noticed that Tom was beginning to smile as he listened to the conversation. Lynn and I remained oblivious to what was happening since I was unable to catch enough of the conversation, and Tom was not translating.

Then the worker put Kali into Lynn's arms, turned, and walked out the door.

Director Qin was starting to shuffle some papers on her desk and Tom was telling us, "We should go."

We gave Director Qin the obligatory "Thank you," hurried out the door and quickly got into the Beijing Jeep. We wanted to get out of the place with Kali as quickly as possible.

As we pulled away from the office building, I looked back hoping I would not see someone running out of the offices yelling at us. I checked the front gate to make sure there was no car blocking the path and that the gates were open. Within just seconds the driver had us through the gates, out of the orphanage, and onto the road toward our apartment.

I breathed again. Lynn was crying and holding very tightly to Kali. Tom, who was sitting up front, was looking back at us with a very large grin spread across his face.

We had just taken a huge, huge step and were so overcome with this victory that we were unable to speak. It was a very emotional moment for us all.

Three months previously I had forced myself to go to that orphanage and leave Kali there, not knowing if she would come out of that place alive. And now we had her in our arms, heading toward our apartment, where we would have a wonderful celebration of God's faithfulness.

Lynn finally stopped hugging Kali so tightly and sat her on her lap facing us, so that we could have a good look at her. Well, it was not a pretty sight. Kali was just as pretty as ever, but she was not flashing us her lovely "Mazin' Maizer" smile; furthermore, she was filthy and smelled of urine.

Actually, Kali looked a little bewildered. It was understandable. There was no way of knowing what was circling around in her mind. How could she possibly comprehend anything that had transpired during the brief months of her life? The school year of 1991-92 had certainly been difficult for me to comprehend. If I had made the decision retroactively, I would have never put myself into such a situation. I could never have imagined being so involved in the life of one small Chinese baby or just how much of my life that involvement would consume?

There had been incredible pain and heartbreak when disappointment built upon disappointment. Yet, as I gazed at Kali in her dirty clothes, and with dirt streaks on her face, I could finally begin to feel victory welling up within my soul. After having our hopes and dreams smashed to the ground so many times, we finally had a major victory. I was beginning to taste the ultimate victory of Kali in Oregon.

But the battle was not complete. We were still in the midst of it. While we had indeed won a significant victory, and God had shown us that He was definitely engaged in the battle, there were more battles ahead.

Kali was out of the orphanage, headed toward our home, but Kali and Lynn were still in Nanchang, the People's Republic of China, and we still remained powerless. Thankfully, our God remained all-powerful. Even in this victory, we knew that we still had to lean on Him, to let Jesus be Lord of this situation. For we had no power in ourselves. The ultimate victory belonged to our Heavenly Father.

When I had taken Kali to the orphanage, she was clean, dressed in clean clothes, and in good health. Over the months that she had remained there, we had taken several more clothing items for her, in addition to giving the orphanage more clothes and food for the other babies.

Kali was being sent home in one dirty, ragged outfit. It was the same outfit she had worn when I took her to the orphanage. Now that outfit was filthy and smelling of urine.

I thought of the morning I picked her up from the box on the sidewalk in October, with her tears making tracks down her checks; she had smelled of urine then also.

Just as I held her close to me that day, Lynn was now clinging to her as if to say that she would never let her out of her grasp again.

I became a little misty-eyed as I thought of all of these things on the ride home. But I was smiling through my tears.

We arrived just outside the doors to our apartment building. David and Marianne came quickly down the stairs. I saw anticipation on their faces, but some doubt was still there.

They had been unable to see who was in the jeep from our apartment window, and they still could not tell if Kali was with us or not.

David quickly opened my door. I could see the smile forming on his face when he saw Kali sitting in Lynn's lap. He reached for her like she belonged to him. I was trying to get out of the jeep as he was trying to pull Kali across me. Marianne's face lit up when she saw Kali, and she started hugging her, patting her, and kissing her. It appeared that David and Marianne were fighting over her. They totally ignored the dirt and the smell. They had grown as weary as the rest of us from going to that orphanage to play with her, then having to walk away and leave her there.

What a day of rejoicing when we actually walked into our apartment with Kali in our arms.

I was exhausted. I was overwhelmed with the emotion of this victory won. The fact that I was still sick took its toll. I had to retreat to the bedroom and try to rest for a while.

Lynn was determined to get Kali cleaned up just as quickly as she could. She put some water on to heat, preparing to bathe Kali in a small plastic tub that we had. David and Marianne were vying to be the first to bring out the

"Mazin' Mazer" smile. Kali was still bewildered and acting a little overwhelmed, plus she was not feeling quite well yet. Tom told us that they had given her another injection just that morning.

I heard David and Marianne laughing and knew that they had most likely finally coaxed a smile from Kali. They had been good at that ever since she had entered our lives. They did not want to fail to get a smile from her on her return to our home.

There was another commotion that sounded like more happiness spreading around. Then I heard LeRoy's voice. He had just returned from class to find the apartment full of rejoicing. In a bit, he looked in on me. I smiled a tired smile. His smile spread all the way across his face.

I just winked at him and said, "She's home."

He leaned over and kissed me – strep throat and all – and said, "Ain't it great?"

I smiled a little more. He shut the door and went out to play with Kali.

Lynn, LeRoy, and the kids scrambled around and found something for us to eat. Shelly was there to join in the celebration. I got up, still feeling like I had run a marathon and finished last. We gave thanks to God for His most excellent provision, for this victory won. We had to keep our praying short, because Kali was anxious to get to the food.

We had a very simple meal, typically Chinese – rice and whatever we could find to put over it. Kali tore into the food. Lynn was trying to feed her but was having a hard time keeping up. She finally put onto the bare table some rice with vegetables over it so that Kali could just scoop it straight from there to her mouth. We had no high chair, so she sat in Lynn's lap as she ate. We enjoyed watching her eat while we were eating.

In fact, we were enjoying everything that Kali was

doing. She looked much better after her bath. She smelled a whole lot better.

Marianne brought out the chocolate cake that she had prepared for yesterday's celebration. We had decided to save it for today. We placed that in front of Kali, and she started pushing cake into her mouth. We were finished eating while Kali was still pushing rice, vegetables, and cake into her mouth.

We finally realized that she was not going to stop. As long as there was food out there she was going to put that food into her mouth. We took her away from the table with her still reaching out for food. We had to move everything out of her sight, or she cried for more food. We realized that she had had a very meager diet at the orphanage.

We were all tired, but the excitement of Kali's homecoming kept us up, just reliving the victory of the day, all of us joyfully content that Kali was finally in our home.

We were also greeting new visitors to our home. Elaine Hartland and Heather Tardiff were flying in to Nanchang from Hong Kong that evening. LeRoy had hurried out to the airport after his class to greet them. They were two of the people who had been present when I was talking to LeRoy in Hong Kong about having to put Kali in the orphanage. They had been two of our top prayer warriors outside Nanchang. They were coming to lend moral support and to pray on site.

We were able to get them into a vacant apartment a few floors above us. They were overjoyed to hear the news that Kali was out of the orphanage. They were able to see her that night so that even more of us could give thanks to God for answered prayer.

It had been a great day of celebration but also a very tiring day. I think we were all nearing exhaustion when we went to bed. Kali went right to sleep. She had continued to act somewhat bewildered, as if her brain could not comprehend what was happening. She was among people that she had seen almost every day, but she was in a different place, and Xiao Hua was no longer around. Kali's nose was running from her cold, but she was not unhappy. She just seemed out of sorts – like things were just not right and she did not understand how to put everything together. She had flashed her "Mazin' Mazer" smile only a few times for us that day.

We awoke to rain falling on Tuesday. I was still not over the strep throat, my body continuing to feel the effects. I started coughing Monday, and that made my chest hurt.

Our Monday victory party had been great, but it was back to work on Tuesday, while we still awaited Kali's passport. Today we were told that we would need the "certificate of abandonment" to prove that neither Lynn nor I had bought Kali from someone off the street.

I could not understand why they would need such a document if she had been registered in the orphanage for three months. I was thankful that I had that document in hand; I had been told to find witnesses months ago. I had had no idea that I would need such proof at this point. So we were able to mark one more item off as done.

We were praying diligently that Kali's Chinese passport would be ready much sooner than expected.

Everything seemed to be going at a snail's pace. We wanted Lynn and Kali to get on a plane and leave Nanchang as quickly as possible. It was not time yet, since we did not have all the official papers from the Nanchang government in hand.

Qi Fong's office had to issue the official certificate of adoption. Okay, that was not a problem; as he had been in our corner all along. He then had to give the certificate to Ms. Cao (Justice Department) for her approval, and then it had to go back to Qi Fong. He would then send it to another office upstairs where it had to be typed in Chinese and English, back to Qi Fong for him to make sure that everything was correct, then back to Ms. Cao for her official stamp and signature.

It sounded like merry-go-round time again. Chinese do not usually busy themselves much doing anything. They had already told us that the typist had a great deal of work, so they may not have it done very quickly.

On Wednesday Dominick and Lynn were out on their bikes all over the city, hitting as many government offices as they could to try to accelerate the process. It was a long day of going from office to office and basically bothering people until they processed the papers.

They returned home late afternoon with all the papers signed. We had proof again that God was moving. What would have taken several days was done in one day. Everything was now official. Kali was officially John and Lynn's baby according to the Chinese government. All that was needed was a passport for Kali, with a visa stamped in the passport. The certificate of adoption was supposed to be taken to the police that afternoon. That was the final piece of paper needed to issue Kali's passport.

We totally abandoned any pretense of school for David and Marianne that day. I needed them to entertain and take care of Kali. They were more than happy to oblige. Kali was feeling better that day; the cold seemed to be almost completely gone. I was making marked improvement so I was able to spend some time enjoying her in our home that day.

Kali was still eating like there would be no food after that meal. As long as she saw food, she begged for it. We had to take her away from the table and put the food away or she would not stop eating. If the food was out of sight she was all right. If she saw it, she practically demanded that we give her more food.

Yesterday had been a most traumatic day. It was also busy. Word spread that Kali was home, and friends began to appear to see the miracle of God's handiwork.

That was true the next day, but not until in the evening. The morning and early afternoon were very peaceful. For most of that day it was just David, Marianne, and I enjoying Kali. And we certainly did enjoy her.

After we had pulled her away from the table at lunch, I rocked her to sleep. What a comfort to me. She seemed to enjoy it also. Tears slipped down my cheeks as I sat in that straight-backed chair and rocked back and forth, holding our "child of promise" and enjoying having her in my arms in our home.

After a while I lay her in the crib, which we had moved into Lynn's room. I laid her on her back this time and tiptoed out the door. I lay down to rest. David and Marianne were not resting. Every so often I could hear the bedroom door open, as they would look in on Kali. I tried to make them stay out so Kali could have a peaceful sleep, but they always had some good reason to go in. Marianne thought she needed to go in there to get something out of her room. Each time, David either said, "I have to check on Mei Mei" – we still called her that about half the time – or he said, "I had to get Marianne out of there."

They seemed to finally settle down, and I was about to doze when I noticed a flash from somewhere toward Kali's room. I quickly got up and took the three to four steps from my door to the bedroom door where Kali was sleeping. But David was in my way. He had one hand to his lips, signaling "Quiet" as he was coming out of the bedroom. He had a camera in his other hand. Then I realized what the flash had been. He had taken a picture of Kali while she was sleeping in her crib.

He pulled me back into my bedroom. He had a big grin

on his face and was laughing as he told me, "She was smiling in her sleep. I took a picture of her smiling in her sleep." He was quite thrilled with himself over this accomplishment. I actually doubted that he had a picture of her smiling while sleeping. However, after that roll of film was developed, sure enough, there was a picture of Kali in her crib, with her eyes closed and a smile spread across her face. She certainly looked contented.

That morning Lynn and LeRoy had gone to the police station to make sure they had the documents in hand for Kali's passport. They also wanted to urge them to hurry. Of course it was not a good idea to tell Chinese authorities to "Hurry." But they asked in a nice way as to when the officials thought the passport would be ready. We had already been told that it would take 7 to 10 days. Lynn and LeRoy went to the police station anyway and asked if it would be possible to pick up the passport that afternoon. They had just received the final paper late yesterday afternoon. Our reasoning was that it would not hurt to ask. And the last few days had seen things going at a miraculous pace.

They knew it was a nearly impossible request, but it looked as though God was at work in great ways now, and we had additional prayer warriors in the city. They were told that the boss was out of the office and that tomorrow morning would be the earliest we could expect to see the passport. We rejoiced at *that* news. We could only hope that the clerk knew what she was talking about.

They returned home early afternoon, very tired. Lynn was just settling in for some rest time herself when the phone rang. It was someone at the main police station, asking Lynn to return to their offices. She left immediately not knowing what they wanted. She hurried down there by herself.

Lynn returned about 3:30. She walked in the door sweating but smiling. She had a very large smile. When I looked up at her, she waved an official-looking document in the air.

"It's Kali's passport!" she laughed as she danced around our living room. Then she swooped over where I was holding Kali, picked her up out of my arms and danced around the room with her. "The visa is stamped in the passport!"

"That means she can leave China now – right?" I asked that question, already knowing that was what it meant. I just wanted to hear it said.

"Yes!" Lynn shouted. "Yes, yes. It's time to go home. Kali, we can go home."

It was a time for dancing and singing and shouting and rejoicing.

What usually took seven to ten days had occurred in one day. We knew then that God was responsible for it all.

Lynn had everything that she needed, and she had Kali.

Now what? The answer would be for Lynn and Kali to get out of Nanchang as quickly as possible. Dominick was with us that evening. He said that he would find out what he could about tickets for tomorrow. Finding tickets usually takes connections. Dominick did not promise us when he would be able to secure tickets. Usually you have to book them, then go to pick them up a few days later.

As the night wore on, our thoughts turned to the quickest way out of Nanchang. Lynn decided to at least pack and be ready. She had talked me into going with them. It did not take much talking. I quickly got some clothes together in a small suitcase.

What should we do?

The next morning found our family plus Lynn and Kali out on the streets of Nanchang before 7 a.m. It was time to leave Nanchang by whatever means possible.

We had no idea what God was going to do that day, but we had decided to take the steps of faith and give Him every opportunity to throw open the doors.

Chapter XXV

Left Behind

L eft behind, but not abandoned. Alone, but not lonely. I was sitting behind the large plate-glass windows of the restaurant at Hong Kong's Kai Tak International Airport, watching as each plane prepared for takeoff and alternately watching the newly arriving planes from all over the world. I was determined to stay at the airport until I saw the Cathay Pacific flight depart with my precious Mei Mei and her new mother aboard. There had been quite a few obstacles thrown up to prevent that departure, and I was going to watch that plane wing its way toward North America until it was only a speck in the beautiful May sky.

How different this day [May 14, 1992] was, compared to that February day when I stood on the Guangzhou dock watching the boat sail down the Pearl River carrying my husband and children away from Mei Mei and me. This time, there was only thankfulness to God for His provision and a special joy that Mei Mei was no longer an orphan. She was Kali Jane, the new daughter of John and Lynn Bonife and the new sister to Kristin.

As we took to the streets of Nanchang the morning after Lynn received Kali's passport, we had not known what would happen. We just knew that we had to try to leave Nanchang as quickly as possible. It had become obvious to us that God had very clearly put His finger on the process, and everything was moving at cyberspeed. We were struggling to keep pace with what He was doing. But we were laughing all the way as we raced on to victory.

On that Friday morning, we hailed a taxi and negotiated a reasonable price to be taken to the airport. We had told Dominick that we were going to try to fly standby. That did not compute. "What is standby?" he asked.

We explained. He sort of shrugged his shoulders, grinned at us, and said, "I never heard of this. We go to the airport and ask them. Maybe buy tickets there."

We went straight to the ticket counter when we arrived at the airport. They looked at Dominick as if to say, "You are acting as stupid as these foreigners are when you ask us such a thing."

But, my theory had always been, "It never hurts to ask," so we had Dominick asking.

The lady at the ticket booth was not smiling, but service providers in China in those days never smiled. They reasoned they had nothing to smile about, especially when they had to deal with foreigners who often asked stupid things like "Can we get on this plane leaving for Guangzhou in less than an hour without any tickets?" In those days you had to follow strict procedures to procure tickets. You could not book them too early and you could certainly not pick them up too late.

My other theory was "You never take 'no' for an answer." Chinese would almost always say "no" for their answer to such a question. Sometimes they would say "no" before they even heard the question.

Some years before, I had approached a counter in a department store in Wuhan, wanting to buy a sweater that I could see displayed on the shelf behind the attendant. The attendant was busily reading a newspaper. I thought that she had not noticed me approaching, but I guess I was wrong. I opened my mouth to ask to look at the sweater, but before any words came out, she answered my question. *"Meiyo,"* she responded to the question that had not been asked. *"Meiyo"* means "We don't have it, it's not here."

The attendant saw a foreigner approaching, decided that she did not want to have to deal with me and so told me quickly that she did not have whatever it was I wanted.

So, when the lady behind the counter at the airport now said, "No," we explained more of our situation. She seemed unimpressed. But we had not paid almost 100 yuan to a taxi driver to ride for an hour to get to the airport to simply turn around and retrace our steps. So, we remained and waited.

Again, I was reminded of our wait on the docks of Guangzhou, when I was left holding Mei Mei while my family left for Hong Kong.

The hour approached for the plane's departure. We could see people going out to the plane, walking onto it. Still, we were getting only a negative response.

It appeared that all the passengers had boarded the plane, and it was time for it to depart.

Dominick asked the attendant again. She then walked behind a wall that hid her from our view. We thought, "Well, that's it. She's walking away so she won't have to look at us." But about the time I had such reflections running through my head, she came back out front with someone who appeared to be her supervisor.

They took the money that Dominick had been holding out to them, gave us boarding passes, and told us to run to the plane.

"What about our luggage?" Lynn had a big suitcase, and I had another one that we had intended to check. They looked at us as if we were some kind of unique specimen of fools, said something to Dominick, and he said, "Hurry."

So we headed for the door — sprinted for the door. Well, anyway, it was the closest we could come to a sprint for a woman carrying a baby and me trying to carry along American-sized suitcases. We did get on that flight carrying a huge piece of luggage, a baby stroller, my small bag and one beautiful baby girl.

Dominick was stopped at the door. We stumbled our way across the tarmac to the plane.

The stewardess did finally help us get our luggage up the steps. The big suitcase would not fit in the overhead, so it was thrown into an empty seat in front of us. Before we could sit down and buckle up, the plane was backing out of the parking slot.

After we settled into our seats, the reality hit us. We were actually in the air, flying away from Nanchang. Flying away from the bureaucratic mess there, getting far far away from that orphanage. Leaving all those months of pain and sorrow behind.

I looked at Lynn. She looked at me. We both smiled.

Hot and steamy Guangzhou awaited us. We wondered what *interesting* incidents we would encounter there.

We had been told that all the procedures necessary for the U.S. immigration visa would take at least a week. We were hoping that the people at the U.S consulate in Guangzhou would be helpful, because we still had to complete certain procedures for Chinese approval. One thing our experiences had taught us in the past seven months was to try to do things the Chinese way. We had a letter of introduction from Dominick's mother, who had a former classmate at the Guangzhou hospital that did U.S. immigration physicals. We were told that the required tests took several days. We would need the official physical report, along with special photos of Kali with her right ear showing.

When our plane arrived in Guangzhou, we took a taxi across the city, and checked into a hotel located only a little over 100 yards from the American consulate.

We immediately mapped out our strategy. The physical for Kali would include blood work. We had been told that it would take close to a week to get the final physical release, since we would have to wait for the blood report.

This poor baby – who had been jabbed with so many needles over the past few months, who had just completed a physical, *with* blood work, in Nanchang before they ever let us take her home – was about to be subjected to yet another physical.

The next morning found us up and moving fast. Our first stop was the hospital. We entered with Kali, all her documents, our documents, and our letter from Dominick's mother. The letter was the first paper we presented when we found the friend of Dominick's mother.

Before that day was done; before the morning was even over, within an hour, in fact, we had all the documents in our hands, including the one indicating that her blood was perfectly normal, and we were headed for the American consulate. Never in all our time in China, both before the experience and after, have I known anything to compare with the speed of having this physical completed. They did not actually take any blood from her. They just wrote down the information we brought from the physical in Nanchang.

What was supposed to have taken a week had been completed within an hour. We now knew that God was working in a mighty way. Because ever since this whole process began, we had jumped through all kinds of government hoops only to find many more awaiting us, we were amazed to watch things race now. It seemed that once we left Nanchang, a mighty burden had been lifted. Even though we were still in China and still had documents to complete, it was as if every door opened instantly now, and every step we took was clearly directed by God.

We were on a whirlwind of completed tasks and loving every minute of it.

We hopped into a taxi and headed toward the photography studio that had been recommended by the U.S. Consulate for immigration photos. I was not sure how a photographer could make a squirming baby pose correctly in order to take a semi-profile picture showing the right ear, but even that was accomplished quickly. The U.S. government required that the right ear be in the photograph as part of the identification. Apparently an ear makes the identity clearer. We were not sure what purpose it served; we were happy to have the picture the way the U.S. Consulate wanted it.

What next? What else could we do today? We did not want to stop. But it was Saturday, and there was no one that we could see at the American consulate. We had done all that we could do for now.

We had seen God move mightily. We were ready to take on the world.

Instead, we went back to the hotel to rejoice in God's goodness and have some rest. All three of us really needed it.

The next day was Mother's Day. It was a great day for two particular American mothers. We decided to celebrate by going to the White Swan Hotel to have their buffet. It was a splurge, but we wanted to rejoice in God's goodness to us. The White Swan is a five-star hotel located on the Pearl River. It is just a short taxi ride away from the dock where I had waved goodbye to my family as they floated down the Pearl River to Hong Kong three very *long* months ago. If we could board a boat, we could float down that river to Hong Kong right now. But this time, we were doing things God's way and reveling in His provisions.

At the restaurant we sat by a window overlooking the Pearl River, thinking about being in Hong Kong in a few days. But today was a day of celebration so we ordered some of our favorite western food.

Kali was truly enjoying herself as she sat in a high chair in the nice restaurant of a western-style hotel. Her behavior had been close to impeccable throughout this trip so far. It was almost as if she sensed that she was on the verge of some fantastic adventure. Of course, she was still a baby (not yet one year old) and she acted like a baby. She also still had a voracious appetite. As we were enjoying our Mother's Day lunch, we decided to let Kali eat whatever she wanted. It was her celebration too. However, we soon discovered this decision to be a mistake. If there was food in reach or even in sight, she grabbed it and shoved it into her mouth. If there was food in sight she wanted it. We finally had to have the staff completely clear the table in order for her to be content to just sit in her high chair.

Lynn's appointment at the American Services Division of the U.S. Consulate in Guangzhou was for Monday morning. We had made reservations for the train on Tuesday. From what we understood, Lynn would turn in her application and official documents at the interview session on Monday and then return the next day for the immigration visa.

I went along to take care of Kali while Lynn was being interviewed. We thought the interview would be at a table with chairs in an office somewhere. Instead Lynn had to stand in a small cubicle facing the American services agent who was behind a glass partition. It reminded me of a visitor talking to a prisoner behind bulletproof glass. It was not very conducive to a friendly interview.

Nonetheless, the interview seemed to be progressing satisfactorily. I did notice that neither Lynn nor the U.S. government official was smiling. But, I thought, government officials seldom smile, so I thought very little about it.

I continued to entertain Kali. Not long into the session, Lynn called for me to come forward because the interviewer wanted to ask me a question. Naive is the only word that comes to mind. I could not imagine what she wanted to talk to me about. My name was not on any of the papers. At that point I was just a friend helping Lynn complete all the process.

The woman behind the glass did not smile at me as I approached her station. She did not even greet me; she did not offer any kind of polite beginning. She simply blurted out, "Can you honestly say you do not know the mother of this child?"

I looked confused and said, "I've known Lynn for several years." The woman looked stern, continuing to be one of the most impolite persons I have ever met. I was thankful she was assigned to the American Services divisions that dealt with U.S. citizens instead of dealing with Chinese citizens. I would hate for her to be the official "face" of America to the Chinese.

She gave me a look that clearly implied that I had to be one of the dumbest persons she had ever encountered. She repeated emphatically, "Can you honestly say you do not know the mother of this child?!"

Reality finally hit me. She was accusing me of buying the baby on the black market. I was shocked. To have gone through so much with the Chinese government officials and then to be accused of illegal activity by my own government's official. I could have screamed.

Everything had been a dream ride since we left Nanchang, until we encountered this American government representative. Was this going to be the place where our joy ride came to a screeching halt? Was our own government about to sidetrack everything?

Once I fully understood what she was asking and what

she was accusing me of, my brain finally started working. Now I was so thankful for the "proof of abandonment" document we were required to have before the adoption could proceed. Lynn and I dug through her stack of documents and pulled out the testimonies from individuals in Nanchang who had witnessed the "foreign woman picking up a female baby abandoned in a cardboard box on Bai Yi Lu on October 25, 1991."

I almost shook it in her face, but I was able to restrain myself. Lynn also remained remarkably calm. It was obviously the Holy Spirit walking her through this. I was extremely happy that this was all I had to do with this "official representative of the United States government in China."

I was seething, but Lynn continued to stay in control of the situation. The woman offered no apology for her accusation, and just glanced at the proffered document. She told Lynn to return that afternoon.

"What now?" Lynn asked the woman.

She gave a look that said Lynn must surely be another simpleton and said, "You can pick up the baby's immigration visa then."

I think a sense of wonder came over both our faces, but we maintained strict composure, at least till we got out of those offices.

We had a quick lunch, packed our suitcases, and checked out of the hotel early that Monday afternoon. The consulate was within walking distance, so Lynn trotted over there to pick up the documents. As soon as she returned, we hopped into a taxi and headed toward the east train station. I ran to the ticket windows. I had to pay a small fee to change our tickets for a train leaving that day. But we were heading for the border as fast as we could go and did not want anything to slow us down.

We had left in a taxi from downtown Nanchang early

Friday morning with no tickets to anywhere, hoping to get on a flight to Guangzhou, where we expected it would take at least a week to get everything accomplished.

Here it was only Monday afternoon and we were about to board a train in Guangzhou heading for the Hong Kong border. When God starts things moving, He kicks them into super overdrive.

Rejoicing? Yes, we were rejoicing all the way to Shenzhen. We stopped at the train station located right on the river where an immigration point separates Shenzhen and Hong Kong. Lynn was pushing Kali in her stroller, and I was lugging the suitcase and my small bag. Our first obstacle was a Chinese immigration official. We went to the Foreigners' section since Lynn and I were both U.S. passport holders. When they saw the baby, they wanted to see her travel documents. Lynn showed them Kali's Chinese passport and the folder with the U.S. Immigration documents and visa. It seemed to take forever before they were satisfied. I took a photo of Lynn holding both her passport and Kali's passport, with Kali smiling from her stroller.

As we were walking across the bridge, we stopped in the middle for another photo thinking the worst was over. Lynn was smiling with eyes full of tears. Kali was just smiling. I was busy trying to take the picture without getting run over by other people making their way between checkpoints.

At this point we were finally free of the bureaucracy of the People's Republic of China. We could feel ourselves relax, knowing that we had just crossed a line that would at last take us into places of freedom. Places, we thought, that would be rejoicing with us in the rescue of this child.

Then, what happened in the next few minutes and the upcoming days made me develop a very cynical attitude about all governments. A representative of the U.S. government had just accused me of stealing Kali from the streets of Nanchang. This experience had left me bewildered and upset enough with the American government. Now, another government was about to join the bureaucratic circus.

After I took the picture of Lynn and Kali on the bridge to freedom, we quickly made our way to the Hong Kong side and walked confidently up to the Hong Kong immigration checkpoint. Lynn again pulled out all the official documents necessary for Kali to enter Hong Kong.

"When do you plan to leave Hong Kong?" the officer asked.

Lynn replied, "I have an open return date on my airline ticket, but plan to make a reservation to leave in just a few days."

"Where is your ticket and the baby's proof of departure?" he asked next.

Lynn explained that for safety she had left her return ticket in the suitcase she had stored in Hong Kong.

That news brought a slight frown to his face, but it did not seem to be a big problem. Then, he asked about a ticket for Kali. Lynn explained that she was going to purchase that as soon as she was in Hong Kong.

The official then explained to Lynn that Chinese nationals (Kali) could not enter Hong Kong without a Hong Kong visa or proof of departure within two weeks.

We had never expected anything like what we were hearing from this Hong Kong immigration official. He was in Hong Kong. We were on the verge of entering Hong Kong, and it was beginning to look as if he were going to allow Lynn and me in but expected us to leave Kali behind. It seemed absurd that anyone would even consider such a thought.

That's why Lynn responded with, "What did you just say?" Neither one of us could believe it what we were hearing.

He repeated it in his most distinct English.

Lynn's rejoinder was short and sweet: "She's not trying to sneak into Hong Kong. She can't even walk yet."

We were both thinking that all of this was ludicrous. How could they think an infant would be able to overstay in Hong Kong! Lynn showed them Kali's U.S. immigration visa and explained that her daughter was on her way to becoming an U.S. citizen and was not planning to be an illegal alien in Hong Kong.

They asked us to leave the line and step into a small room nearby. We simply could not believe that this was happening after all we had been through and after the rush of everything falling into line over the weekend. Surely they would not stop us from taking Kali into Hong Kong. Yet that was exactly what they seemed to be planning.

Other officials were brought into the small room where we were detained, trying to figure out what to do. Thoughts of what had transpired in Guangzhou in February when we tried to walk Kali through Chinese immigration flashed across my mind. That too was a time when we had waited while officials conferred. Now, we were almost in Hong Kong, and we were once again waiting while officials conferred, only this time it was Hong Kong officials.

The officials spoke in Cantonese while Lynn and I could only look at each other in wonder. We were both on the verge of tears.

It seemed as if no one wanted to take the responsibility of allowing a mainland citizen into the territory without a visa or proof of departure. They finally allowed us to sit down. It eventually took almost four hours before they finally gave Lynn permission to take Kali those additional few steps that would see her into Hong Kong

Our emotions were drained. We were so weary. It seemed that we had been in the middle of this battle for so

322

long. And, just when we thought we had complete victory, we had been stunned again with the revelation that this sweet child was just paper work to many people. She was just another statistic. Well, she was much more than a statistic to me, my family, and the Bonife family, and we were going to fight on, no matter how many governments conspired against us.

We knew, especially after our time in Guangzhou, that God was on our side and that the victory *would* be won.

Lynn was so spent, emotionally and physically, that by the time we arrived at the apartment of Hong Kong friends later that day, she went to bed and remained there throughout the next day.

When she was feeling a little stronger the following day, she made reservations for her and Kali to fly out the day after that. Kali would not need a seat, but did need a ticket to board.

All of this went smoothly, and Lynn contacted John to tell him when to expect her the next day. John marshaled family and friends so that Kali would have a big welcome to the U.S.A. A Portland television station even planned to be there to record the event. A baby being adopted from Communist China was a newsworthy event at the time.

John, of course, was relieved and very happy to hear that his wife would finally be returning home and bringing their new daughter with her.

The next day was exciting for Lynn and me as well. Finally, the day had arrived when our precious Mei Mei would fly away to her home in Portland, Oregon. A home of love and tenderness, where God's love was evident. A place that she would come to know as her home. A place of comfort and security and joy. The very next day she would move into that home. A home prepared for her.

My emotions were bouncing all around inside of me. I was happy, rejoicing that the day had finally arrived; yet, I was sad to see her leave me; not knowing for sure when I would hold her in my arms again.

Still I was rejoicing as we approached the ticket counter at Kai Tak Airport.

Kali had been enjoying herself throughout this whole adventure. She was content and happy. She was eating everything she could get her hands on.

Lynn handed over her ticket.

"May I see your passports?" the check-in clerk at the Cathay Pacific Airlines desk asked.

Lynn gave her the two passports, one blue (Lynn's) and the other brown (Kali's).

The lady looked them over and said, "I'm sorry to inform you, but the baby cannot go on this flight because she does not have a Canadian visa."

"We're not going to Canada; we're going to Portland, Oregon," Lynn said confidently, with every assurance that this was a mere misunderstanding. "We just change planes in Vancouver."

"I am sorry, but you will go through Canadian immigration in Vancouver, and a Chinese national may not enter Canada without a visa." She spoke with an air of authority, quite sure that she knew what she was talking about. We were equally sure that she could not possibly know what she was talking about. Had the Canadian government now decided to join in this conspiracy of governments to thwart this little baby from reaching the home that awaited her?

Lynn was certainly not going to take this new announcement without a fight. She demanded to talk with a higher official.

A clerk who was listening in on the conversation leaned over and said, "Perhaps you could sign an affidavit promising to not leave the baby in Canada," she told Lynn. "Promise that you will take her to the U.S."

We could not imagine that we were now battling yet

another government. We had spent months sorting things out with the various governmental departments of the People's Republic of China, found ourselves almost turned away on the doorstep to Hong Kong, and now were learning that the Canadian government thought Lynn might try to sneak Kali into Canada and leave her there.

It was difficult for us to understand how these governments could invent such ideas.

Eventually, a Cathay official came over to us and tried to explain. "Most likely, the Canadian government will not pose a problem," he said. Well, that was good to hear. At least the Canadian government was not ganging up on us. "But," he continued, "it would be the airline's responsibility if they rejected the baby's entry. It would also be an expense to the airline to return the baby to Hong Kong."

When he said "return to the baby to Hong Kong," I thought Lynn's knees were going to give way.

After accepting the defeat and the delay, Lynn made reservations for the same flight the next day.

She called John to explain that his wife and baby daughter would not be on the planned flight. He then had to call friends and family to inform them that they would have to postpone the celebration one more day. Hopefully, it would be only one more day.

We gathered the luggage together and retreated to the apartment we had left with such exhilaration such a short time ago.

The next morning, I kept Kali while Lynn went to the Canadian consulate to obtain the necessary visa so that Lynn and Kali would be able to change planes in Vancouver. Canada now became the fourth government involved in this young child's life. The consulate staff was very nice and accommodating and the only government that did not charge a fee for their services, for which we were most thankful.

As it later turned out, Lynn and Kali went through both Canadian and U.S. customs in Vancouver. After they passed through Canadian customs, they walked about 100 feet to the U.S. customs officials. So Lynn needed the Canadian visa only for Kali to go to the next room! Governments work in strange and mysterious ways.

That afternoon in Hong Kong we returned to Kai Tak Airport with all the prescribed documents in hand. But we soon discovered there was one more obstacle to overcome. When they had checked for available seats for today's flight and made Lynn's new reservations, the clerk had failed to enter the request into the computer.

Oblivious to this fact, we had approached the counter with tickets, passports, Canadian visas, and all the Chinese documents legitimizing Kali's adoption. Lynn had called John to report, "We're on our way for sure."

John had called all the family and friends again. The television station was again to send a reporter and cameraman to cover the event.

Lynn presented her ticket to the clerk with the update in it, along with a stack of official documents.

The appropriate information was input into the appropriate computer, and the information returned that there were no such persons booked on that flight.

"I'm sorry, but you are not booked on this flight," the lady told Lynn. I am sure I would have seen the color draining from Lynn's face if I had not been in such shock myself.

I began to think we were in our own special version of The Twilight Zone.

The seat that was available yesterday, which Lynn could not use then because she had no Canadian visa for Kali, was not available today!

"Irate" would be the best word to explain Lynn's feelings. The airline had refused to accept responsibility for yesterday's fiasco and then failed to confirm the reservation for today.

Lynn was at a total loss for words. There comes a time when you have gone through so much that your brain says, "That's enough" and seems to have a difficult time coming up with the right words.

I stepped up and said, "I demand that you do something. We have done what you said. We were told yesterday that she was ticketed on today's flight. And now you tell us there is no seat available. You cannot do this." I was more than a little upset.

Their best offer was that Lynn and Kali could fly standby. They prepared some meal vouchers and said, "return later, and we'll see if a seat has come available."

We had little choice. It was their mistake, but we had no recourse. I'm sure we looked like two very beaten women as we moved away from the counter with our shoulders slumped in defeat.

We found a place to eat, and ordered some food. Kali continued to wolf down any food in her path. She was still like a steamroller when food was in front of her. She absolutely devoured it. However, Lynn and I were not enjoying our meal. When we gave thanks, we did thank our Heavenly Father that He was still in charge and asked Him to please open the way.

After the meal and a time of trying to lift each other up, we returned to the ticket counter.

"Yes, there is a seat available," the clerk told us, smiling in a most agreeable manner.

We returned her smile agreeably.

They handed a boarding pass over to Lynn and told her that she had even been given a bulkhead seat so that a bassinet could be anchored to the wall in front of her seat. Kali could sleep in it after the flight took off.

We both breathed a sigh of relief.

Before they went into the secure area for customs and immigration control I took a photo of Lynn with her luggage in a cart with Kali sitting in the cart's baby seat. Kali's last picture in Asia until she returns under her own power.

Tears? No, there were no tears now. First, I wanted to make sure they actually left, and I wanted to hear that they had arrived safely in Portland and had walked into that home prepared for Kali. I was so overjoyed that this day had finally arrived. There would be time enough for tears later.

Then is when I went up to the restaurant on the observation deck where one could watch planes arrive and depart. I would have to wait there for an hour or two, but after all that we had experienced, I wanted to see that plane take off with my own eyes.

I saw it pulling away from its parking spot on the tarmac and watched it head toward the runway, then lift into the sky, heading away from Hong Kong, toward a new life in the United States.

The Cathay Pacific flight to the Pacific Northwest was carrying the precious child that God had given me for a few months to nurture and love until she would "no longer be an orphan".

I was left behind in Hong Kong, but joyful at the miracle that flew away!

Epilogue

<u>Lynn's Journal</u>   May 11, 1992

NEW BEGINNINGS
   John and I have deeply appreciated the many prayers that have gone before us. The story of Kali isn't finished; it is a story of beginnings.
   After the border check in Mainland China, Jane, Kali and I walked across a bridge to LoWu, Hong Kong. That was it. Kali was leaving the country, the Communist country of her birth. She was leaving the very real potential of orphanage bondage. She was now headed to a country, a democratic country for a rebirth. Ahead for Kali lie all kinds of potential. Kali will learn how very much God loves her and wants her to trust His Son as her personal Lord and Savior. She will be given the opportunity to make that choice. {She did make that choice at four years of age.}
   Barbed wire separates China from free territory. Perhaps one day Kali will return to her birth land cutting through the barbed wire by proclaiming the Good News of Jesus.

LeRoy's Journal   July 12, 1992

Kali Jane Bonife dedicated to Jesus at Lents Conservative Baptist Church – Portland, OR

Glory to God in the Highest.

E-mail from Lynn   June 18, 2003

Dear Jane and LeRoy,
I will have Kali write you about her week being trained in child evangelism. At this stage in her life, she feels led to being a missionary. Just to hear her talk about the Lord, is something else.

E-mail from Kali   June 21, 2003

Hey Ramsey's
I just got back from camp on Friday. It was so neat to see God working through me and the life of others. Thousands (I think were reached) and hundreds were saved in that one week! I got to go on open air where we find kids and tell them the wordless book. Our missionary was Hudson Taylor and Mei Mei Lee. Mei Mei Lee is a missionary to Macau. My 5-day club alone raised $126.11 to buy wonder books. One kid gave his whole years savings. People started calling me Mei Mei at camp because word got around that I used to be called Mei Mei. I made many new friends. Our speaker was David York. He decided to be our CYIA pastor. He is good. Stay close to God. Tell Marianne and Tim hi and congratulations. Say hi

to David for me. Love you all.

Love,
Kali

P.S.

I would like to pray for you. Please email me some prayer requests.

Printed in the United States
20154LVS00002B/336